Ancient Africa and African Mythology

An Enthralling Guide to Empires, Civilizations, Myths, Fables, and Legends

© Copyright 2024 - All rights reserved.

The content contained within this book may not be reproduced, duplicated, or transmitted without direct written permission from the author or the publisher.

Under no circumstances will any blame or legal responsibility be held against the publisher, or author, for any damages, reparation, or monetary loss due to the information contained within this book, either directly or indirectly.

Legal Notice:

This book is copyright protected. It is only for personal use. You cannot amend, distribute, sell, use, quote, or paraphrase any part, or the content within this book, without the consent of the author or publisher.

Disclaimer Notice:

Please note the information contained within this document is for educational and entertainment purposes only. All effort has been executed to present accurate, up-to-date, reliable, and complete information. No warranties of any kind are declared or implied. Readers acknowledge that the author is not engaging in the rendering of legal, financial, medical, or professional advice. The content within this book has been derived from various sources. Please consult a licensed professional before attempting any techniques outlined in this book.

By reading this document, the reader agrees that under no circumstances is the author responsible for any losses, direct or indirect, that are incurred as a result of the use of the information contained within this document, including, but not limited to, errors, omissions, or inaccuracies.

Free limited time bonus

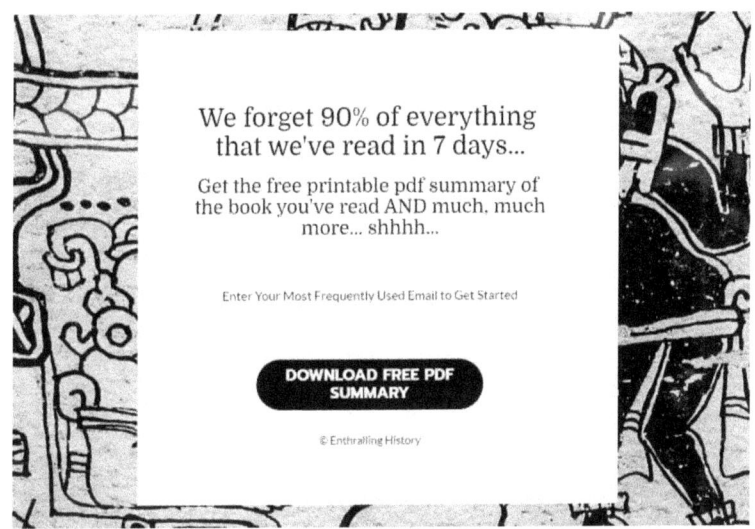

Stop for a moment. We have a free bonus set up for you. The problem is this: we forget 90% of everything that we read after 7 days. Crazy fact, right? Here's the solution: we've created a printable, 1-page pdf summary for this book that you're reading now. All you have to do to get your free pdf summary is to go to the following website:

https://livetolearn.lpages.co/enthrallinghistory/

Or, Scan the QR code!

Once you do, it will be intuitive. Enjoy, and thank you!

Table of Contents

PART 1: ANCIENT AFRICAN EMPIRES 1
   INTRODUCTION 2
   SECTION 1: HUMBLE BEGINNINGS 4
   CHAPTER 1: THE STONE AGE AND THE FIRST CIVILIZATIONS 5
   CHAPTER 2: THE AGE OF GREAT METALS: COPPER, BRONZE, AND IRON AGES 13
   SECTION 2: KINGDOMS AND CIVILIZATIONS 19
   CHAPTER 3: KUSH 20
   CHAPTER 4: AKSUM 27
   CHAPTER 5: PUNT: A FARAWAY LAND? 37
   SECTION 3: THE GREAT EMPIRES AND THEIR LEGACIES 45
   CHAPTER 6: ANCIENT EGYPT 46
   CHAPTER 7: KERMA 73
   CHAPTER 8: ANCIENT CARTHAGE 78
   CHAPTER 9: EMPIRE OF GHANA 92
   CHAPTER 10: SLAVERY IN ANCIENT AFRICA 99
   CONCLUSION 105
PART 2: ANCIENT CARTHAGE 111
   INTRODUCTION 112
   CHAPTER 1: THE PHOENICIANS 114
   CHAPTER 2: FOUNDATION MYTHS SURROUNDING CARTHAGE 119
   CHAPTER 3: SETTLEMENT AND THE BUILDING OF CARTHAGE 123
   CHAPTER 4: EXPANSION, INDEPENDENCE, AND EMPIRE STATUS .. 130

- CHAPTER 5: THE SICILIAN WARS 136
- CHAPTER 6: THE FIRST PUNIC WAR 145
- CHAPTER 7: HANNIBAL AD PORTAS ("HANNIBAL IS AT THE GATES!") 155
- CHAPTER 8: CARTHAGO DELENDA EST ("CARTHAGE MUST BE DESTROYED") 170
- CHAPTER 9: GOVERNMENT AND MILITARY 175
- CHAPTER 10: SOCIETY, ECONOMY, AND RELIGION 180
- CONCLUSION 187

PART 3: AFRICAN MYTHOLOGY 188
- INTRODUCTION 189
- CHAPTER 1: AFRICAN CREATION MYTHS 192
- CHAPTER 2: GODS AND GODDESSES I 200
- CHAPTER 3: GODS AND GODDESSES II 208
- CHAPTER 4: ANIMAL FABLES 214
- CHAPTER 5: TRICKSTER TALES 219
- CHAPTER 6: MONSTERS AND MYTHICAL BEASTS 232
- CHAPTER 7: HEROES IN AFRICAN MYTH 238
- CHAPTER 8: MYTHICAL AND LEGENDARY KINGS AND QUEENS 245
- CHAPTER 9: SHAMANIC STORIES 257
- CONCLUSION 262

HERE'S ANOTHER BOOK BY ENTHRALLING HISTORY THAT YOU MIGHT LIKE 265
FREE LIMITED TIME BONUS 266
BIBLIOGRAPHY 267

Part 1: Ancient African Empires

An Enthralling Guide to the Major Kingdoms and Civilizations of Africa

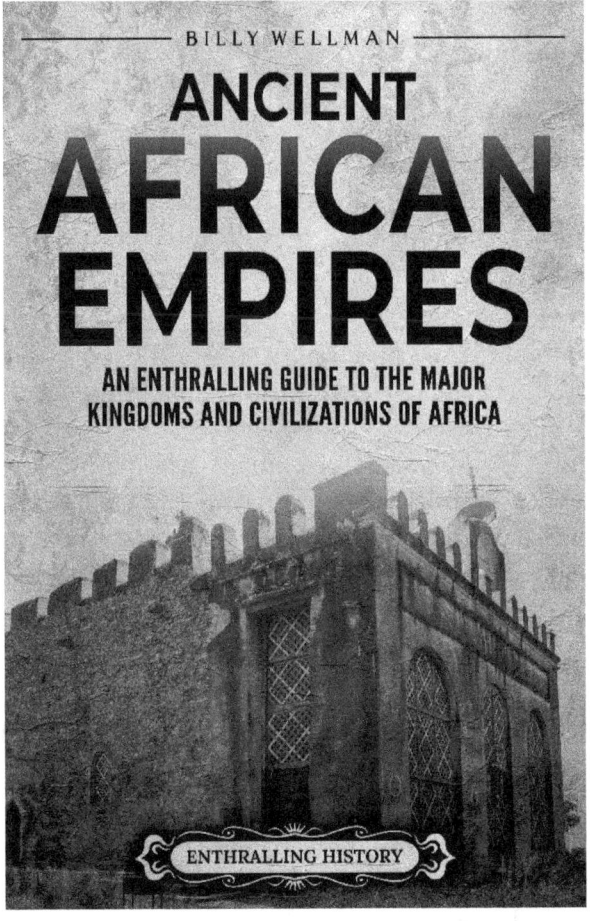

Introduction

Welcome to the captivating world of ancient African empires. Get ready to embark on a remarkable journey through time to explore the awe-inspiring stories of civilizations that once thrived on the African continent. This book will transport you to the heart of ancient Africa, where powerful empires rose and fell.

The contribution of African empires to world history and civilization is significant, but it remains largely unexplored. This book attempts to change this. We will unravel the enigmatic tales of some of the most illustrious empires in the annals of human civilization, focusing primarily on Egypt, Carthage, and Nubia. We will also investigate the fabled kingdoms of Kush, Aksum, and Punt.

Understanding the legacies of African history provides a profound insight into the roots of human civilization. These empires laid the foundations for cultural, technological, and societal advancements that continue to influence our world today. The diverse array of empires showcased here underscores the incredible diversity and dynamism that has always been a part of Africa.

The book has simplified the complex historical facts and events surrounding these ancient empires into easy-to-understand language. We know how mundane history books can be. They leave the reader feeling lost or confused. Our goal is to make you feel engaged with the past and eager to learn more.

Prepare to be captivated by the grandeur of pyramids, the brilliance of military strategists, the mystique of ancient rituals, and the resilience of civilizations that thrived in a land where history's echoes still resound today.

Section 1:
Humble Beginnings

Chapter 1: The Stone Age and the First Civilizations

Africa is called the Cradle of Humankind, as it is believed human life began there. The Stone Age was a time of learning and developing the customs, skills, and political organizations that evolved into sophisticated civilizations. Three distinct eras comprise what we refer to as the Stone Age and the beginning of modern human beings.

<u>The Paleolithic Era</u>

The Paleolithic era is the earliest period in human history. It spans from approximately 2.5 million years ago to around 10,000 BCE in Africa. During this time, human ancestors lived as hunter-gatherers, relying on the land's natural resources to survive. In Africa, the Paleolithic era was marked by the use of stone and rock tools, which were essential for hunting, cutting, and other crucial tasks for survival. These tools were primarily crafted from flint, chert, obsidian, and other locally available stones. Acheulean hand axes, a distinctive type of bifacial tool characterized by their teardrop shape, were commonly used during the Lower Paleolithic (the earliest part of the Paleolithic era). These hand axes were versatile tools used for cutting, chopping, and butchering.

Different views of an Acheulean hand ax.
Muséum de Toulouse, CC BY-SA 4.0 <https://creativecommons.org/licenses/by-sa/4.0>, via Wikimedia Commons; https://commons.wikimedia.org/wiki/File:Biface_Cintegabelle_MHNT_PRE_2009.0.201.1_V2.jpg

The Middle Paleolithic saw the emergence of more sophisticated tools, such as the Levallois technique, which allowed for the production of specialized flakes and blades. These innovations indicate an increased level of cognitive and technical skills among Paleolithic populations.

Paleolithic humans in Africa were primarily nomadic hunter-gatherers. They relied on hunting animals like antelope, buffalo, and wild boar, as well as gathering edible plants, fruits, and nuts. The discovery of fossilized animal bones with cut marks and stone tools at sites like Olduvai Gorge in Tanzania provides strong evidence of early hunting and butchering practices during the Paleolithic era.[1]

Mastery of fire was a significant milestone during the Paleolithic era. The ability to control and use fire provided people with warmth, protection, and the means to cook food, which profoundly impacted diet and survival. Archaeological sites like Wonderwerk Cave in South Africa have yielded evidence of early hearths and the use of fire, dating back over a million years.

Saharan Rock Art

Throughout the Paleolithic era, culture and technology gradually evolved. This evolution is marked by the development of new tool types,

---

[1] Kessing, F. M. (2024, January 9). Stone Age-African Tools, Artifacts, Culture. Retrieved from Britannca.com: https://www.britannica.com/event/Stone-Age/Africa.

increased social complexity, and potential regional variations. While less prevalent than in later periods, some evidence of artistic expression exists from the Paleolithic era in Africa. This includes rock art, engravings, and sculptures.

One of Africa's most intriguing aspects of the Paleolithic era is Saharan rock art. These ancient artworks provide a window into the lives and beliefs of early Africans. Found in various regions of the Sahara Desert, these rock paintings and engravings depict scenes of daily life, animals, and spiritual or ritualistic motifs. They offer valuable insights into ancient African communities' artistic and cultural expressions. The Blombos Cave in South Africa contains engraved pieces of ochre, suggesting early symbols or creative behavior.[2]

Wall art found in a cave in Chad.
David Stanley from Nanaimo, Canada, CC BY 2.0 <https://creativecommons.org/licenses/by/2.0>, via Wikimedia Commons; https://commons.wikimedia.org/wiki/File:Prehistoric_Rock_Paintings_at_Manda_Gu%C3%A9li_Cave_in_the_Ennedi_Mountains_-_northeastern_Chad_2015.jpg

As the climate and environment in Africa fluctuated over the Paleolithic era, humans had to adapt to changing conditions. This likely

---

[2] Museum, T. B. (2024, January 9). Rock art and the origins of art in Africa. Retrieved from Khanacademy.org: https://www.khanacademy.org/humanities/ap-art-history/global-prehistory-ap/paleolithic-mesolithic-neolithic-apah/a/apollo-11-stones.

played a role in shaping their tool-making techniques and resource exploitation strategies. During periods of climatic change, when large parts of Africa became drier, Paleolithic populations adapted by moving to more favorable regions and adjusting their subsistence strategies accordingly.[3]

The Mesolithic Era

The Mesolithic era in Africa, also known as the Middle Stone Age, was a transitional period that followed the Paleolithic era and preceded the Neolithic era. This era spanned from around 10,000 to 5000 BCE and witnessed significant changes in human societies and their ways of life. The Mesolithic era marked the shift from nomadic hunter-gatherer lifestyles to more settled and organized communities, setting the stage for the later emergence of agriculture and the Neolithic Revolution. While hunting and gathering remained important, Mesolithic communities began to establish more permanent camps and were not roaming constantly.

In the Mesolithic period, stone tools became more specialized and refined. While some of the tools continued to be made from stone, there was experimentation with other materials, such as bone and wood, leading to the development of new tool types. The creation of microliths, tiny and highly efficient stone blades, was a notable development. Microliths were used as components for composite tools, such as spears and arrows, indicating an advancement in hunting technology.

Art in the Mesolithic Era

Mesolithic African communities left behind evidence of cultural expression, although it was less elaborate than in later periods. This included the creation of small-scale art, such as carvings and engravings on bones, stone, and shells. The Apollo 11 Cave in Namibia dates to the Mesolithic period and contains some of the earliest known examples of portable art in Africa. These artifacts include engraved pieces of stone with geometric and abstract designs.[4]

---

[3] Smithsonian Institute. (2024, January 3). Climate Effects on Human Evolution. Retrieved from Humanorigons.si.edu: https://humanorigins.si.edu/research/climate-and-human-evolution/climate-effects-human-evolution.

[4] Cerise Myers, E. C. (2024, January 9). 5.2 Mesolithic Art. Retrieved from Libretexts.org: https://human.libretexts.org/Bookshelves/Art/Introduction_to_Art_History_I_%28Myers%29/05%3A_Art_of_the_Stone_Age/5.02%3A_Mesolithic_Art.

Societal Changes

The Mesolithic era in Africa coincided with climatic fluctuations, including the transition from the Last Glacial Maximum to a warmer and more stable climate. As a result, human populations had to adapt to changing environmental conditions. Populations began to adjust to regional environments and resource availability. This period saw a diversification in the types of foods consumed, including a greater reliance on marine resources in coastal regions. Coastal Mesolithic communities in areas like the South African coastline engaged in shellfish gathering and fishing, utilizing both marine and terrestrial resources for their sustenance.

The Mesolithic period witnessed innovations in social organization and technology. While not as complex as the societies of the Neolithic period, there was evidence of increased social cooperation and the development of more sophisticated tools. The emergence of fishing technology, including harpoons and fishnets, suggests a level of coordination and specialization within Mesolithic communities as they adapted to aquatic resources.[5]

Africa witnessed a lot of migration during the Mesolithic era. Major language groups, such as the Niger-Congo, started to be noticed as the Sahara became drier. The Bantu later spread into central, eastern, and southern Africa, displacing indigenous people like the Pygmies.

Societies were formed due to the development of tribal relations. The division of labor based on gender, with the men doing the hunting and fishing and women taking care of plant-based food, was typical.[6] Transition ceremonies from child to adult with established initiation rites happened. These ceremonies and trials passed on the working habits, oral traditions, and sacred knowledge from one generation to the next.[7]

The Mesolithic era in Africa represents a crucial phase in human history, bridging the gap between the Paleolithic hunter-gatherer lifestyle

---

[5] Kessing, F. M. (2024, January 9). Stone Age-African Tools, Artifacts, Culture. Retrieved from Britannca.com: https://www.britannica.com/event/Stone-Age/Africa.

[6] It must be noted that the division of labor was not set in stone. Times of need might call for women to aid in hunting or men to pick plants. Different tribal groups would have practiced different traditions as well. However, broadly speaking, men typically hunted while women gathered plants and other materials.

[7] S., A. (2015, December 21). Mesolithic Social Life and Art. Retrieved from Shorthistory.org: https://www.shorthistory.org/prehistory/mesolithic-social-life-and-art/.

and the agricultural revolution of the Neolithic period. It was a time of experimentation, adaptation, and the gradual development of technologies and social structures that paved the way for profound changes.

The Neolithic Era

The Neolithic era, often referred to as the Late Stone Age, was a transformative period in Africa that followed the Mesolithic era. The Neolithic period marked a significant shift in human societies, characterized by the widespread adoption of agriculture, animal domestication, and more settled, agricultural-based communities. The Neolithic era in Africa ranged from around 5000 to 2000 BCE, depending on the region.

Food Production

The most defining feature of the Neolithic era was the development of agriculture. African societies began cultivating crops and farming animals, providing a more reliable and abundant food supply. In the Nile Valley of Egypt, the cultivation of wheat and barley was practiced as early as 5000 BCE, transforming the region into a breadbasket and enabling population growth.

Consistent with the move to farming, the Neolithic period saw the domestication of animals for various purposes, including providing meat, milk, wool, and labor. This marked a crucial step in human history, leading to more complex and diversified economies. In North Africa, the domestication of cattle and sheep became prominent. The Saharan region saw the emergence of pastoral societies, which relied on herding domesticated animals for sustenance.

Settling Down

Neolithic communities established more permanent settlements, transitioning from the semi-nomadic lifestyle of their Mesolithic ancestors. These communities often built more substantial structures and engaged in rudimentary urban planning. The Nabta Playa archaeological site in the Nubian Desert reveals evidence of complex stone structures similar to Stonehenge, potentially serving as markers for astronomical events. These structures suggest a level of social organization and architectural planning.[8]

---

[8] Smith, P. (2015, September 16). Nabta Playa: The Oldest Man-Made Structure in the World. Retrieved from Historic Cornwell: https://www.historic-cornwall.org.uk/nabta-playa-the-oldest-man-made-structure-in-the-world/.

As African populations settled into permanent communities and worked to generate surplus food, Neolithic societies had the opportunity to engage in specialized crafts and develop more sophisticated tools and technologies. The use of pottery became widespread during this period. Neolithic Africans created pottery vessels for storage, cooking, and ceremonial purposes. Pottery enabled more efficient food processing and storage.[9]

Social Hierarchy and Society

As populations grew and communities became more settled, social hierarchies and organizational structures emerged. Leadership roles and divisions of labor became more defined. Small villages or clan settlements eventually evolved into city-states. Agriculture was the main driver of complex social structures in the Neolithic era.

Examples of substantial Neolithic settlements were found in Egypt's Western Desert. Sheikh el-Obeiyid has twenty-five circular and oval huts. Another significant archaeological find is Site 270 at Dakhla Oasis. Archaeologists uncovered two hundred circular and rectangular stone huts grouped in clusters that might have been social groups. These suggest evidence of community planning. Large communal buildings (some as long as twelve meters) might have served as centers of authority or for rituals.[10]

The Neolithic era in Africa laid the foundations for more complex and enduring societies on the continent. The shift from hunting and gathering to agriculture and animal husbandry was a revolutionary leap that led to population growth, technological innovations, and the rise of early civilizations.

In Summary

The Paleolithic, Mesolithic, and Neolithic periods are the underpinnings of early African civilizations. When we look at the Stone Age, from its use of stone tools that gradually developed into more

---

[9] Huysecom, E. (2024, January 9). Arguments for an Early Neolithic in Sub-Saharan Africa. Retrieved from Ounjougou.org: https://www.ounjougou.org/en/projects/mali/archaeology/arguments-for-an-early-neolithic-in-sub-saharan-africa/.

[10] Ancient Egypt Magazine. (2023, February 6). Neolithic Settlements of the Western Desert: Proto-villages of Stone Age Egypt. Retrieved from the-past.com: https://the-past.com/feature/neolithic-settlements-of-the-western-desert-proto-villages-of-stone-age-egypt/.

complex tools to the Saharan rock art that communicates the lives and aspirations of early folk to the transition from nomadic hunter-gatherer societies to settled agricultural communities, we can see the first steps in the evolution of later cultures.

These pivotal developments laid the groundwork for the rise of the first great African civilizations, setting the stage for a rich and enduring history.

Chapter 2: The Age of Great Metals: Copper, Bronze, and Iron Ages

In this chapter, we will delve into three major eras that shaped Africa's ancient past: the Copper Age, the Bronze Age, and the Iron Age. Each era represents a significant leap forward in the continent's cultural, economic, and technological landscape. To provide a comprehensive understanding, we will explore the key developments and innovations in each period and offer a timeline to illustrate the progression of events.

<u>The Copper Age in Africa (c. 4000 BCE-c. 2500 BCE)</u>

One of the most significant developments of the Copper Age was the discovery and utilization of copper for various purposes. Early African societies learned to extract copper ore from mines and develop smelting techniques to separate copper from its ore. This marked the inception of metallurgy in Africa.

While the exact timeline and specific details of the earliest copper metallurgy in Africa vary by region, it is clear that by around 4000 BCE, several African societies were already experimenting with copper working, marking the beginning of the Copper Age in the continent.

Evidence of early copper metallurgy comes from sites like Buhen in Egypt and various locations in the Agadez Region of Niger. These sites contain copper artifacts and remnants of copper mining and smelting activities. The copper used during this period was often relatively pure, known as native copper, which could be found in nugget form in certain geological formations.

Technological Advancements

Copper metallurgy brought about several significant technological advancements that had far-reaching impacts. For instance, early African metallurgists developed methods for heating copper ore to separate the metal from impurities, laying the groundwork for more sophisticated metallurgical processes in later ages.

Copper Age societies also began using copper to create a wide range of tools and weapons. Copper's malleability allowed for the production of more durable and practical tools than those made from stone, bone, or wood. Copper tools included knives, axes, chisels, and spearheads, which significantly improved agricultural practices, construction, and hunting.

As copper metallurgy advanced, specialized artisans who were skilled in working with copper emerged. These artisans played a pivotal role in producing intricate copper artifacts, such as jewelry and ornaments. This specialization contributed to developing a distinct artisan class within African societies.

Settled Communities

Copper tools allowed for more efficient farming practices, resulting in increased food production and population growth. This shift marked the beginning of more complex social structures and sedentary lifestyles.

Copper objects were used in rituals and ceremonies. Copper was used for sculptures in Africa, as evidenced by a life-sized statue of Pharoah Pepi I, who ruled in the Sixth Dynasty (c. 2325-2150 BCE).

Head of Pepi I's life-sized statue.
Jon Bodsworth, Copyrighted free use, via Wikimedia Commons;
https://commons.wikimedia.org/wiki/File:PepiI-CopperStatue-Cropped.png

Overall, the Copper Age in ancient Africa was a pivotal phase in the continent's history, marked by the emergence of metallurgy, technological innovation, economic growth through trade and interaction, and the beginnings of settled societies. These developments laid the foundation for future advancements in metalworking and the evolution of African civilizations.

Timeline of Key Events in the Copper Age

- 4000 BCE: Earliest evidence of copper working.
- 3500 BCE: Expansion of copper usage across different regions.
- 2500 BCE: Transition to the Bronze Age.

The Bronze Age in Africa (c. 2500 BCE–c. 1000 BCE)

The Bronze Age in ancient Africa, spanning from approximately 2500 to 1000 BCE, saw African societies make the transition from using primarily copper to using the alloy known as bronze, which is composed of copper and tin.

African societies discovered the art of alloying copper with tin, resulting in the creation of bronze. This alloy, characterized by its strength and durability, represented a significant advancement in metallurgical technology.

The adoption of bronze tools revolutionized agriculture during the Bronze Age. Bronze plows and hoes improved soil cultivation, making farming more efficient. Enhanced agricultural productivity led to surpluses, population growth, and the development of larger, more intricate societies. Introducing bronze for weaponry significantly improved defense capabilities and influenced military strategies. Bronze swords, spears, and armor became standard equipment, altering the dynamics of conflicts and power in the region.

Importance of Trade

Tin is a necessary ingredient for making bronze, and although there are tin deposits in central and southern Africa, there is no conclusive evidence there was an inner-African trade in tin during the Bronze Age. Egypt had tin reserves in the Eastern Desert, but these might only have been mined after 2000 BCE. Mesopotamia had tin deposits and might have shipped the metal as far west as Crete. Oxhide ingots, metal slabs that made it easier to transport copper or tin, might have been exported to Egypt in exchange for goods like ostrich egg shells. By way of Egypt, Africa became part of the eastern Mediterranean trade network, and trade stimulated the expansion of urban centers.[11]

Society and Art

The Bronze Age witnessed the emergence of more complex societies across the African continent. These urban hubs served as focal points for a myriad of advancements. Monumental architecture, such as the Karnak Temple Complex, demonstrated the power and affluence of kingdoms. Bronze transcended its utilitarian role and played a vital part in artistic expression and architectural innovation.[12]

Egypt had its glory years during the Bronze Age. Urban centers, such as Thebes, showcased the might of this nation, and art was created on a grand scale. Tombs give us a glimpse into the grandeur of the pharaohs. Egyptian gods were a significant artistic inspiration, although Egyptian art also often depicted pharaohs and animals. An essential artifact from the Egyptian Bronze Age is the Narmer Palette with its semi-nude figures.

The cultural and artistic flowering during the Bronze Age continues to inspire and influence Africa's history and cultural heritage. It stands as a testament to the adaptability and ingenuity of ancient African societies in shaping the course of their history and civilization.

Timeline of Key Events in the Bronze Age

- 2500 BCE: Advent of bronze metallurgy.
- 1800 BCE: Flourishing bronze trade networks.
- 1000 BCE: Transition to the Iron Age.

The Iron Age in Africa (c. 1000 BCE–c. 500 CE)

During the Iron Age, African societies experienced a profound transformation as they transitioned from the use of copper and bronze to iron. Iron was once thought to have originated in Egypt, but new evidence suggests that ironworking technology independently developed and predated Egypt in what is now Chad, the Central African Republic, and South Sudan and spread west along the Niger River to the Nok culture of

---

[11] Robert Maddin, T. S. (1977). Tin in the Ancient Near East: Old Questions and New Finds. Retrieved from Penn Museum: https://www.penn.museum/sites/expedition/tin-in-the-ancient-near-east/.

[12] College Sidekick.com. (2024, January 13). The Bronze Age. Retrieved from Collegesidekick.com: https://www.collegesidekick.com/study-guides/boundless-arthistory/the-bronze-age.

West Africa. Bantu migrations helped spread the technology.[13]

One of the defining features of the Iron Age in Africa was the mastery of iron metallurgy. Iron ore, abundant in western and southern Africa, became the primary source for crafting tools, weapons, and various other essential items.

Agriculture

The availability of iron tools revolutionized agriculture across Africa. Iron plows and hoes replaced their less durable predecessors, allowing farmers to till the soil even more efficiently than before. They could cultivate more significant areas of land, which boosted crop yields. This agricultural revolution profoundly impacted food production, leading to surpluses, population growth, and the emergence of more complex societies.

Military Advances

The durability and effectiveness of iron in weaponry transformed the nature of warfare in Africa. Iron swords, spears, and shields became standard equipment for armies, leading to more advanced military strategies and tactics. The ability to produce iron weapons in more significant quantities and with higher quality influenced the power dynamics of the time, often determining the rise and fall of kingdoms and empires.

Rise of Urban Centers and Trade

The Iron Age witnessed the growth of urban centers and the formation of complex societies. These urban hubs served as focal points for trade, administration, and cultural exchange. Advanced architectural structures characterized their development, including city walls, palaces, and ceremonial centers. This transformation led to the establishment of political hierarchies and state structures, resulting in the rise of influential African kingdoms and empires.

The increased production of iron tools, as well as agricultural surpluses, facilitated the growth of extensive trade networks. African goods, including iron tools, precious metals, and agricultural products, were traded within the continent and with neighboring regions. West

---

[13] Openstax.org. (2024, January 13). 9.2 The Emergence of Farming and the Bantu Migrations. Retrieved from Openstax.org: https://openstax.org/books/world-history-volume-1/pages/9-2-the-emergence-of-farming-and-the-bantu-migrations.

Africa significantly benefited from the mastery of iron metallurgy. Iron gave rise to the Kingdom of Ife and other important Nigerian kingdoms.[14]

Art during the Iron Age

Ironwork went beyond useful tools; it played a significant role in creative expression and architectural innovation. Iron artifacts, sculptures, and decorative elements adorned religious and ceremonial spaces, reflecting the diversity of artistic traditions and beliefs across various African societies.

Iron was used in West Africa for jewelry, art, and musical instruments. It had spiritual significance in many African cultures. These artistic creations showcased the richness of cultural expression and served as a testament to the creativity and craftsmanship of the era.

Iron artifacts were often used in religious ceremonies and rituals, as they were believed to possess mystical properties. Evidence of the ritual use of iron furnaces can be found in Tanzania and Rwanda.[15]

The Iron Age's legacy continues to influence Africa's history and cultural heritage. It paved the way for subsequent periods of innovation and progress on the continent.

Timeline of Key Events in the Iron Age

- 1000 BCE: Emergence of ironworking.
- 500 BCE: Rise of prominent African kingdoms.
- 500 CE: Transition to medieval African history.

In Summary

The Copper, Bronze, and Iron Ages in Africa represent a remarkable journey of innovation, cultural expression, and societal transformation. These eras not only mark technological milestones but also highlight the resilience and adaptability of African civilizations. Understanding the timelines and key developments in each age allows us to better appreciate these ancient African societies.

---

[14] Ross, E. G. (2002, October). The Age of Iron in West Africa. Retrieved from Metmuseum.org: https://www.metmuseum.org/toah/hd/iron/hd_iron.htm.

[15] Academic Accelerator. (2024, January 13). Archaeological Evidence for the Origins and Spread of Iron Production in Africa. Retrieved from Academic-accelerator.com: https://academic-accelerator.com/encyclopedia/iron-metallurgy-in-africa.

Section 2:
Kingdoms and Civilizations

Chapter 3: Kush

The Nile River has been the home of people for millennia. The enigmatic Kingdom of Kush was situated along the banks of the river. This ancient civilization, known for its rich history and significant influence, is a captivating subject of study for historians, archaeologists, and scholars. Its relationship with Egypt ebbed and flowed, causing interesting developments that, at one time, led to the conqueror becoming the conquered.

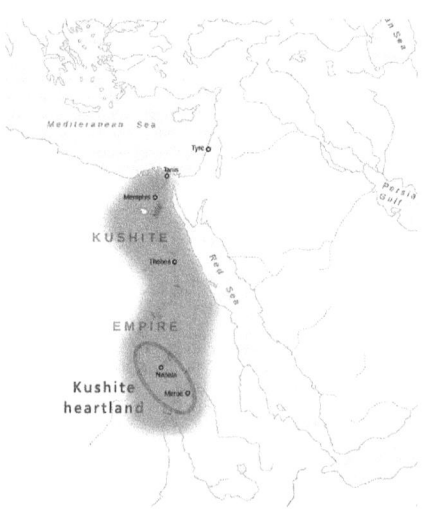

The Kingdom of Kush around 700 BCE.
Original map: Lommes Addition of Kushite heartland; Source: National Geographic 2019, CC BY-SA 4.0 <https://creativecommons.org/licenses/by-sa/4.0>, via Wikimedia Commons; https://commons.wikimedia.org/wiki/File:Kushite_heartland_and_Kushite_Empire_of_the_25th_dynasty_circa_700_BCE.jpg

The Location of Kush

Kush was an ancient African civilization that existed from around 1070 BCE to 350 CE. Its diverse economy played a significant role in the region's trade networks, making it economically crucial to Egypt and other neighboring civilizations.

Also known as Nubia, Kush flourished for millennia, encompassing modern-day Sudan and southern Egypt. Information about this civilization comes from a combination of archaeological discoveries, inscriptions, and references in the records of neighboring ancient civilizations.

Excavations in the Nile Valley have unearthed a wealth of material evidence, including architecture, pottery, jewelry, and burial sites. For instance, the ancient city of Kerma was a pivotal center of the Kush, and extensive archaeological findings there have provided invaluable insights into Kushite culture and history. The oldest known reference to Kush in ancient Egyptian texts dates back to around 2300 BCE. The Egyptians referred to Kush as "Kas" or "Kas-ti," and these references talked about the land south of Egypt and the interactions between the two regions.

The Economy of Kush

Kush was not an impoverished backwater. Like its northern neighbor, Egypt, it was a prosperous region that drew much of its wealth from the Nile. Agriculture was the backbone of the Kushite economy. The fertile Nile River valley provided an excellent environment for farming. Kushites cultivated crops like wheat, barley, sorghum, and various vegetables. They also engaged in pastoralism, raising cattle, goats, and sheep. The Nile's annual flooding ensured fertile soil for their agricultural activities.

The Nile supplied more than the water needed to grow crops. It was a major factor in the Kushites' commercial economy. Kush was strategically located along the Nile, making it a crucial trade hub. The Kingdom of Kush served as a bridge between Egypt to the north and sub-Saharan Africa to the south. Kush's geographical position at the crossroads of trade routes between Egypt and the African interior made it a commercial hub of significant importance. Some of the commodities that contributed to its commercial value included gold, ivory, and exotic goods.

Kush was known for its gold deposits, especially in the Nubian Desert and the Red Sea Hills. The Kingdom of Kush was a significant source of gold for Egypt and other Mediterranean civilizations. The Egyptian pharaohs were especially interested in maintaining good relations with Kush so they could enjoy a steady supply of this precious metal.

The Kingdom of Kush controlled the ivory trade, a highly sought-after valuable commodity by neighboring regions. Kush also facilitated the exchange of various exotic goods, such as rare woods, gemstones, and luxury items, which further enhanced its commercial significance.[16]

Kush controlled the upper reaches of the Nile River, which allowed it to regulate and tax trade that passed through its territory. Its control over the Nile also allowed it to impose tolls and tariffs on goods passing along the river.

Kushite Society

Like many ancient societies, Kush had a hierarchical social structure. The ruling class was at the top of the hierarchy, which included the monarchs (kings and queens) and the nobility. Beneath them were priests, administrators, and military leaders. The common people comprised most of the population, including farmers, artisans, and laborers. Since the Kushites engaged in the slave trade, it is likely their society had enslaved people in it as well.

Religion played a significant role in Kushite society. There was no formal Kushite religion, and the people practiced a blend of indigenous African religious beliefs and Egyptian-inspired religious traditions. The emphasis of their religion was for a person to be one with the natural world and live in harmony. They worshiped a pantheon of deities and often incorporated Egyptian gods and goddesses into their religious practices. Sebiumeker, lord of fertility and procreation, was a principal god. Temples and religious monuments, such as the Lion Temple at Naqa, were important centers.

The Kushite society spoke Kushitic, which was likely part of the Nilo-Saharan language family. However, the elite and educated class used a writing system heavily influenced by Egyptian hieroglyphics.[17]

Art and Architecture

Being strategically located at the crossroads of African and Mediterranean trade routes, Kushite society had extensive interactions

---

[16] Kemezis, K. (2009, November 22). Ancient Kush (2nd Millennium B.C. - 4th Century A.D.). Retrieved from Blackpast.org: https://www.blackpast.org/global-african-history/ancient-kush-2nd-millennium-b-c-4th-century-d/.

[17] Marc. (2022, October 14). The Kush Kingdom: A Major Power in the Ancient World. Retrieved from Ilovelanguages.com: https://www.ilovelanguages.com/the-kush-kingdom-a-major-power-in-the-ancient-world/.

with neighboring civilizations, including Egypt, the Mediterranean world, and other African societies. These interactions influenced their culture and art.

Kushite society had a rich artistic and cultural heritage. They developed an artistic style, often characterized by narrative wall paintings, egg-shell thin pottery, and bronze statues of deities and monarchs. The Kingdom of Kush is renowned for its distinctive, steep-sided pyramids, which were used as tombs for royalty and nobility. Notable examples exist at Meroë and Jebel Barkal.[18]

The economic ties between Egypt and Kush also led to cultural exchange. Egyptian art, technology, and religious beliefs influenced Kushite culture and vice versa—the exchange of ideas and practices enriched both civilizations.

Governance

The political structure of Kush evolved over the years. The region gradually transitioned from a series of independent city-states to a powerful kingdom. Kush rose on the ashes of an earlier civilization, Kerma, and would be the foundation for its successor state, Meroë. Each had its own rulers and centralized authority and were distinct phases of the development of Kush as a kingdom and a civilization.

Kush c. 1070-300 BCE

After the decline of the Kerma Kingdom (which has its own chapter later in this book), the Kingdom of Kush emerged in the Napata region, near modern-day Karima in Sudan. The Kushite Kingdom adopted elements of Egyptian culture and religion, including the worship of Egyptian deities. The rulers of Napata constructed pyramids similar to those of Egypt, symbolizing their status and influence. The most famous of these is the Pyramid of Taharqa. Kush eventually faced political challenges from the Assyrians and Persians and was succeeded by the Meroitic Kingdom.

Meroitic Kingdom (300 BCE-350 CE)

The Meroitic Kingdom was the most enduring period of Kushite civilization. It was centered in the city of Meroë, located near the modern

---

[18] Kemezis, K. (2009, November 22). Ancient Kush (2nd Millennium B.C. - 4th Century A.D.). Retrieved from Blackpast.org: https://www.blackpast.org/global-african-history/ancient-kush-2nd-millennium-b-c-4th-century-d/

town of Shendi in Sudan.

One of the most distinctive features of the Meroitic Kingdom was its own script, known as Meroitic writing, which remains only partially deciphered. Meroitic Cursive was used for record-keeping, and Meroitic Hieroglyphs was used for inscriptions on monuments and documents. The Meroitic Kingdom was known for its advanced ironworking industry, producing high-quality iron tools and weapons.

The Meroitic Kingdom declined, possibly due to a combination of factors, including invasions and internal rebellions. The Kingdom of Aksum eventually replaced it in the 4th century CE.

<u>The Egyptian Connection</u>

Kush's geographical location made it a strategic partner for Egypt. The two kingdoms often engaged in diplomacy, alliances, and trade agreements. Egypt relied on Kush for valuable resources and materials, like gold and incense, which were essential for religious and economic purposes. In return, Kush benefited from Egypt's military and political support, helping it maintain its independence and security.

The conquest of Kerma by the Egyptians was a setback, but it did not mean the Kushites would fade into history. They returned to prominence several centuries later. The rise of the Kingdom of Kush around 1070 BCE is often associated with the decline of the New Kingdom of Egypt and the disintegration of Egyptian control over its southern territories.

The New Kingdom of Egypt began to experience internal strife and external threats. Pharaohs became weaker, and Egypt was divided by power struggles and competing rulers. The Twentieth Dynasty of Egypt (c. 1186–1069 BCE) was marked by political instability and the decline of centralized authority, creating a power vacuum that allowed external forces to gain influence.

Egypt faced invasions by various foreign powers during this period. The Libyans' and Sea Peoples' invasions disrupted Egyptian rule and weakened central authority. The Libyans managed to establish themselves in the Nile Delta. Egypt was too busy fighting off attackers in the north to be concerned about what was happening in the south. Kush continued to control important trade routes that connected Egypt with the African interior, which allowed the Kushites to gain wealth and resources and further strengthen their position in the region.

Once Conquered, Now the Conquerors

Kushite rulers extended their influence into Upper Egypt, taking control of key cities and regions. Their presence and authority in Upper Egypt challenged the remnants of Egyptian rule and further established Kushite dominance in the area.

The Kingdom of Kush launched a series of military campaigns in Egypt. These campaigns were led by Kushite rulers who aimed to assert their authority over Egyptian territories. The Kushite rulers formed alliances with local Egyptian leaders who were dissatisfied with the existing political fragmentation. These local leaders saw the Kushite rulers as potential unifiers who could restore stability and central authority to Egypt.

The conquest of Egypt was finalized by Piye (also known as Piankhi) around 727 BCE, and he established Egypt's Twenty-fifth Dynasty. The Kushite rulers successfully consolidated their power in Egypt, with their authority extending as far north as the Nile Delta. They created a centralized administration and promoted political stability in the regions they controlled.[19]

The Twenty-fifth Dynasty

The Kushites' control of Egypt was made more accessible because of the past centuries of assimilation. Kushite pharaohs revered Egyptian gods and built temples for them, which helped them gain acceptance among the Egyptian population and legitimized their rule. The Kushite rulers also initiated various cultural and building projects during their rule in Egypt. They constructed pyramids, temples, and monuments, contributing to the region's architectural heritage. The new rulers of Egypt wore the double crown of earlier pharaohs.

---

[19] K. Krois. Hirst. (2019, May 12). The Kingdom of Kush: Sub-Saharan African Rulers of the Nile. Retrieved from Thoughtco.com: https://www.thoughtco.com/the-kingdom-of-kush-171464.

Statues of some of the late Twenty-fifth Dynasty pharaohs.
Matthias Gehricke, CC BY-SA 4.0 <https://creativecommons.org/licenses/by-sa/4.0>, via Wikimedia Commons; https://commons.wikimedia.org/wiki/File:Rulers_of_Kush,_Kerma_Museum.jpg

The Twenty-fifth Dynasty only survived for a short time. The Kushite control of Egypt lasted for several decades, with varying degrees of success. However, their rule eventually faced challenges from the Assyrians, who invaded Egypt in the late 7th century BCE. The Assyrians managed to defeat the Kushite rulers and effectively ended the Twenty-fifth Dynasty's control over Egypt. The Kushites withdrew to their homeland in Kush, and Egypt fell under the control of foreign powers.

Kush continued to be a regional power but grew weaker after the Roman occupation of Egypt. Kush collapsed in the 4th century CE.

In Summary

The Twenty-fifth Dynasty's control of Egypt represented a unique chapter in the history of both regions, demonstrating the fluidity of power in ancient Africa and the influence of neighboring kingdoms. The Kushites left a significant mark on Egyptian history and culture during their rule, and their legacy endures in the archaeological and historical record.

Chapter 4: Aksum

The Kingdom of Aksum, nestled in the northern regions of present-day Ethiopia and Eritrea, is a fascinating chapter in the annals of African history. Flourishing from around the 1st century BCE to the 7th century CE, Aksum is known for its multifaceted and rich civilization, which included the introduction of Christianity to the region and subsequent works of art and architecture.

<ins>Commercial Center</ins>

Aksum's economy was a powerhouse driven primarily by trade and agriculture, both of which played a pivotal role in the kingdom's rise and prosperity. Aksum's strategic location at the crossroads of significant trade routes made it an ideal hub for commerce. Its position along the Red Sea coast and its control over major ports, such as Adulis, allowed it to dominate maritime trade in the region. To the west, the kingdom had access to the Nile River, enabling inland trade connections with the African interior.

The Kingdom of Aksum at its greatest extent.
Aldan-2, CC BY-SA 4.0 <https://creativecommons.org/licenses/by-sa/4.0>, via Wikimedia Commons; https://commons.wikimedia.org/wiki/File:The_Kingdom_of_Aksum.png

The Red Sea was a vital corridor connecting Africa with the Arabian Peninsula, the Indian subcontinent, and the Mediterranean world. This geographical advantage turned Aksum into a bustling commercial center where goods from distant lands converged.

Aksum engaged in trade with diverse regions, forging economic ties with the Roman Empire, Persia, India, and the Arabian Peninsula. The kingdom's exports included ivory, gold, spices, obsidian, and exotic animals. Among its most prized exports was frankincense, a fragrant gum resin highly sought after in the ancient world. In exchange, Aksum imported luxury items such as textiles, ceramics, glassware, and precious metals. These trade relationships enriched the kingdom and allowed it to accumulate wealth and prestige on the global stage.

Aksum had its own currency system, with gold, silver, and bronze coins. These coins, known as Aksumite coins, served as a medium of exchange within the kingdom and facilitated international trade. The existence of Aksumite coins in various parts of the ancient world is a testament to the kingdom's extensive commercial networks.

Coins of King Ezana.
Classical Numismatic Group, Inc. http://www.cngcoins.com, CC BY-SA 3.0 <http://creativecommons.org/licenses/by-sa/3.0/>, via Wikimedia Commons; https://commons.wikimedia.org/wiki/File:AXUM._Ezanas._Circa_330-360.jpg

Agricultural Prowess

Agriculture was vital in ensuring the kingdom's food security and economic stability. Aksum's highlands and plateaus were blessed with fertile soils and favorable rainfall patterns conducive to agriculture. The region's agricultural productivity supported a variety of crops, including millet, barley, wheat, and teff.

The Aksumites were skilled practitioners of terrace farming. This technique involved constructing stepped agricultural platforms on hilly terrain. Terrace farming maximized agricultural output and mitigated soil erosion, ensuring long-term sustainability.[20]

---

[20] Eries.org. (2024, January 13). Kingdom of Aksum. Retrieved from Eriesd.org: https://www.eriesd.org/cms/lib/PA01001942/Centricity/Domain/1041/6.2%20The%20Kingdom%20of%20Aksum-1.pdf.

Infrastructure Achievements

Aksum's economic success was not solely reliant on favorable geography and agricultural practices. The kingdom's technological advancements and infrastructure were also crucial.

The Aksumites were pioneers in constructing dams and reservoirs to manage water resources. These structures were critical for irrigation, providing water for crops, and regulating seasonal flooding. The engineering feats of the Aksumites in harnessing and distributing water resources underscored their ability to adapt to the challenges posed by their environment.

Aksum is renowned for its impressive stone architecture, with obelisks, stelae, and monumental structures bearing witness to the kingdom's advanced stonework and engineering skills. The towering obelisks and stelae served various functions, from marking graves to commemorating rulers and their achievements. These monuments also showcased the kingdom's artistic prowess. Some examples of Aksum's impressive obelisks and stelae include the Obelisk of Axum, King Ezana's Stele, and the Great Stele of Axum.

The Obelisk of Axum.
Tesfawel, CC BY-SA 4.0 <https://creativecommons.org/licenses/by-sa/4.0>, via Wikimedia Commons; https://commons.wikimedia.org/wiki/File:Aksum_obelisk.jpg

Social Structure

Understanding Aksumite society is essential to grasp the kingdom's dynamics during its heyday. Aksumite society was hierarchical and characterized by distinct social classes. At the pinnacle stood the ruling elite, comprising the king and the nobility. Below them were freemen and peasants who toiled the land, ensuring the kingdom's agricultural productivity. Slavery was also a part of Aksumite society, with enslaved people primarily acquired through warfare and trade.

Aksum was governed by a monarchy, with the king as the central authority. The Aksumite king's lineage was believed to be traced back to the legendary Queen of Sheba and King Solomon, endowing the monarchy with a strong sense of legitimacy. The kingdom's political structure was centralized, with provinces and local rulers subject to the king's authority.

The Aksumite military was a formidable force, vital for safeguarding trade routes and protecting the kingdom. The kingdom's army included infantry, cavalry, and archers, and it was renowned for its use of war elephants, which provided a significant advantage in battle.

Religion of Aksum

Religion held a central place in Aksumite culture and society, with the kingdom making significant contributions to the early history of Christianity. Aksumites practiced a distinctive form of Christianity known as Ethiopian Orthodox Tewahedo Christianity. The term "Tewahedo" translates as "being made one." It reflects the church's commitment to Orthodox Christian doctrines and its emphasis on unity within the faith. This form of Christianity is still practiced in Ethiopia today.

This faith was pivotal in shaping the Aksumite identity and culture. In the 4th century CE, Christianity was officially adopted as the state religion, making Aksum one of the world's earliest Christian kingdoms.

Ethiopian Orthodox Tewahedo Christianity features distinctive liturgical practices, rituals, and traditions that set it apart from other Christian denominations. The church places significant importance on the Old Testament and emphasizes seven sacraments similar to those observed by the Roman Catholic Church.[21] These include the following:

---

[21] EOTC. (2024, January 13). Beliefs and Teachings of Ethiopian Orthodox Tewahedo Church. Retrieved from keraneyo-medhanealem.com: https://www.keraneyo-medhanealem.com/beliefs-

- Baptism
- Confirmation
- Holy Communion
- Ordination
- Holy matrimony
- Mystery of penance
- Unction of the sick.

The Ethiopian Orthodox Church maintains a hierarchical clergy structure, including priests, deacons, and bishops. At the apex of this hierarchy is the Ethiopian patriarch, known as the abuna. The abuna serves as the highest-ranking ecclesiastical authority in the Ethiopian Orthodox Church and plays a crucial role in guiding the spiritual life of the faithful.

Churches and monasteries are central features of religious life. Some of the most notable Aksumite churches are rock-hewn churches, such as the iconic rock-hewn churches of Lalibela. Monasticism also plays a vital role in Ethiopian orthodoxy, with monks and monastic communities preserving religious traditions and manuscripts.

One of the rock-hewn churches in Lalibela.
Bernard Gagnon, CC BY-SA 3.0 <https://creativecommons.org/licenses/by-sa/3.0>, via Wikimedia Commons; https://commons.wikimedia.org/wiki/File:Bete_Abba_Libanos.jpg

and-origins-7-sacraments-of.

The Ethiopian Orthodox Church continues to thrive and exerts a powerful influence in the modern era. The faith remains an integral part of Ethiopia and Eritrea's religious, cultural, and social life. It has contributed to preserving ancient Christian traditions, religious manuscripts, and a vibrant ecclesiastical heritage.

The History of Ancient Aksum

The history of ancient Aksum spanned several centuries, during which time the kingdom witnessed a succession of monarchs and underwent significant transformations. Before the official establishment of the Kingdom of Aksum, the region had a pre-Aksumite history marked by legendary figures and early rulers. This period, dating from approximately the 4th century BCE to the 1st century CE, contributed to the customs, governing patterns, and traditions that laid the foundation for what would later become Aksum.

As Aksum emerged as a significant regional power during the 1st century CE, the lineage of its rulers began to gain historical prominence. A mighty king in the history of Aksum was Ezana.[22]

Ezana and the Conversion

The 4th century CE is a watershed moment in Aksumite history, as this was the century when Christianity was officially adopted as the state religion. The early adoption of Christianity in Aksum holds immense historical significance. It predates the Christianization of other prominent regions in the world, including the Roman Empire, challenging Eurocentric narratives and emphasizing Africa's central role in the early history of Christianity.

This period witnessed the reign of King Ezana, a monarch whose legacy is intimately tied to the kingdom's religious transformation. Ezana's reign, which extended from 333 to 356 CE, was a turning point for Aksum. His most significant contribution was his conversion to Christianity, an event documented in inscriptions, including the renowned Stele of Ezana. It is a monumental obelisk bearing inscriptions in Ge'ez, the ancient Ethiopian script.

---

[22] Cartwright, M. (2019, March 21). Kingdom of Axum. Retrieved from Worldhistory.org: https://www.worldhistory.org/Kingdom_of_Axum/.

Stele of Ezana.
Sailko, CC BY 3.0 <https://creativecommons.org/licenses/by/3.0>, via Wikimedia Commons;
https://commons.wikimedia.org/wiki/File:Aksum,_stele_3_detta_di_re_ezana,_1%27unica_mai_cro
llata_04.jpg

The Kingdom's Golden Age

The centuries following Aksum's conversion to Christianity marked a golden age for the kingdom. It reached its zenith of power, conducted campaigns for territorial expansion, and created enduring cultural achievements.

King Kaleb (r. 514–542) stands out as one of the most influential rulers of this era. Under his leadership, Aksum expanded its territories into the Arabian Peninsula. His reign was marked by military campaigns and diplomatic achievements that solidified Aksum's status as a regional powerhouse.

The Decline and Fall of Aksum

The 7th century CE marked the beginning of Aksum's decline. Factors contributing to this decline included the rise of Islam, which disrupted Aksum's traditional trade routes, and internal conflicts within the kingdom. As the once-mighty kingdom faced mounting challenges, it began to recede from its prominent position in the region.

Environmental factors played a pivotal role in the decline of Aksum as well. One of the primary concerns was environmental degradation, including deforestation and soil erosion. The kingdom's ability to sustain its population and support its economy was severely hampered.

Aksum's prosperity was intricately linked to its role as a significant trading empire. However, the alteration of global trade routes, particularly the redirection of commerce away from the Red Sea, posed a significant threat to Aksum's economic stability. New maritime routes circumventing Aksum emerged, leading to decreased regional trade activity. As a result, Aksum began to lose its prominence as a trade hub, affecting its economic vitality.

The economic decline of Aksum was a multifaceted issue. Reduced agricultural output and a drop in trade revenue left Aksum in a precarious financial position. The kingdom struggled to maintain its infrastructure, support its military, and fund its administrative institutions. As Aksum's resources diminished, its ability to engage in large-scale architectural projects waned, reflecting its declining power and prestige.[23]

To assert that Islam harmed Aksum oversimplifies a nuanced historical narrative. The relationship between the Aksumite Kingdom and early Islam in the Horn of Africa is a complex aspect of history. It is crucial to consider the chronological context, the dynamics of religious transformation, economic factors, and competition.

While there were periods of peaceful coexistence and cooperation, there were also conflicts and tensions between the Aksumite Kingdom and early Muslim communities. These conflicts often arose due to territorial disputes, competition over trade routes, and religious differences. Some historians have noted clashes along the Red Sea coast as a result of these factors.

---

[23] Iniguez, N. (2020, February 28). The Rise, Decline, and Collapse of the Aksum Empire. Retrieved from Storymaps.arcgis.com:
https://storymaps.arcgis.com/stories/9b7b377398724be99a0d94dfa9f55550.

Political instability, including internal conflicts and disputes over succession, plagued Aksum during its later years. A lack of strong and cohesive leadership made it difficult for the kingdom to address its various challenges effectively. The absence of effective governance exacerbated the kingdom's vulnerabilities, leaving it ill-prepared to confront external threats and internal strife. While the exact chronology of events remains a subject of historical inquiry, it is clear that Aksum faced formidable challenges that tested its resilience.

<u>In Summary</u>

The history of the Kingdom of Aksum is a remarkable tale woven with the reigns of monarchs and the milestones they achieved. From its pre-Aksumite origins and the emergence of regional power to its conversion to Christianity and the golden age of expansion and cultural achievement, Aksum's history is a testament to the dynamism of African civilizations.

Chapter 5: Punt: A Faraway Land?

The Land of Punt, often referred to as the "Land of God," occupies a unique place in the annals of ancient history. This enigmatic land, known for its production and trade of valuable commodities such as gold, ebony, myrrh, and exotic animals, has captured the imagination of scholars, Egyptologists, historians, and many others for centuries. However, whether Punt was a real place or merely an El Dorado-like myth has been a subject of ongoing debate and intrigue.

We are going to investigate the arguments both for and against the existence of Punt, with a focus on evidence like archaeological findings, historical records, and stories and legends.

Archaeological Discoveries

Archaeological evidence forms a cornerstone in the argument for the existence of Punt. Ancient Egyptian hieroglyphs and inscriptions frequently mention Punt, its people, and their distinctive attire and features. These references underscore Punt's role in Egyptian culture and its enduring presence in historical records. Various discoveries provide tangible proof of Punt's existence and its historical interactions with ancient civilizations.

- The Palermo Stone is an inscription that provides clues that suggest there was a place called Punt. The Palermo Stone dates from Egypt's Old Kingdom period (c. 2500 BCE). It documents an expedition sent by Pharoah Sahure. The expedition fleet brought back a large cargo of myrrh, malachite, electrum, and wood (possibly ebony). The Palermo Stone is the first documented evidence that Punt existed. Unfortunately, it does not tell where Punt is located.

The Palermo Stone.
No restrictions;
https://commons.wikimedia.org/wiki/File:Abhandlungen_der_K%C3%B6niglich_Preussischen_Akademie_der_Wissenschaften_aus_dem_Jahre_(1902)_(16765759871).jpg

- The mortuary temple of Queen Hatshepsut at Deir el-Bahri, constructed during the 15th century BCE, contains intricate reliefs and inscriptions that offer a vivid account of the expedition to Punt during her reign. These inscriptions detail the exotic flora and fauna encountered during the journey, providing tangible evidence of Punt's biodiversity. The goods obtained from Punt, including myrrh, ebony, and incense trees, are depicted, reinforcing the reality of trade between Egypt and Punt. There is no indication on the temple walls where Punt can be found on a map, though.
- The temple complex at Medinet Habu, dating to the 12th century BCE and built during the reign of Pharaoh Ramesses III, is another significant archaeological source. Inscriptions and reliefs at this site corroborate the existence of Punt and the trade relationships between the two regions. A papyrus scroll describes the transport vessels bringing back goods from Punt. Still, there is no mention of the exact location of this land.
- Punt has left tantalizing linguistic evidence that adds depth to the debate surrounding its historical existence. While linguistic evidence alone may not definitively prove the existence of the Land of Punt, it serves as a critical piece of the puzzle in understanding the land's potential reality.

Hieroglyphs provide some of the best linguistic evidence. Punt is prominently featured in numerous Egyptian texts and inscriptions, particularly during the reign of Queen Hatshepsut. These inscriptions not only mention Punt but also describe the Puntites' customs and the valuable resources obtained from the land. The hieroglyphic texts often include distinctive symbols that signify Punt's location. Although they do not provide precise geographical coordinates, they are linguistic markers that link Punt to the rich tapestry of Egyptian records. The Somali language has similarities with ancient Egyptian vocabulary, suggesting a relationship between the Horn of Africa and the Land of the Pharaohs.[24]

The Words of the Bible

The biblical references to Punt contribute indirectly to the argument for its existence. The Old Testament mentions Ophir as a land associated

---

[24] Team, E. (2018, October 21). Kingdom of Punt: When Ancient Egypt Envied Somalia. Retrieved from Thinkafrica.net: https://thinkafrica.net/land-of-punt/.

with the trade of gold and other precious commodities, which aligns with the historical descriptions of Punt. The Old Testament includes the following verses that mention Ophir:

Genesis 10:29:

"And Ophir, and Havilah, and Jobab; all these were the sons of Joktan."

1 Kings 9:28:

"And they came to Ophir and fetched from thence gold, four hundred and twenty talents, and brought it to King Solomon."

1 Kings 10:11:

"And the navy also of Hiram, that brought gold from Ophir, brought in from Ophir great plenty of almug trees and precious stones."

1 Chronicles 29:4:

"Even three thousand talents of gold, of the gold of Ophir, and seven thousand talents of refined silver, to overlay the walls of the houses withal."

Job 22:24:

"Then shalt thou lay up gold as dust, and the gold of Ophir as the stones of the brooks."

1 Kings 9:26-28 gives ancient geographical context about Ophir's possible location. It might have been a land bordering on the Red Sea.

"King Solomon also built ships at Ezion Geber, which is near Elath in Edom, on the shore of the Red Sea. And Hiram sent his men—sailors who knew the sea—to serve in the fleet with Solomon's men. They sailed to Ophir and brought back 420 talents of gold, which they delivered to King Solomon."[25]

Whether Ophir and Punt are the same or if they were part of a broader trading network remains a subject of ongoing research and debate. As archaeological discoveries and linguistic studies advance, we may uncover more definitive evidence regarding the historical relationship between these enigmatic lands. The historical prominence of the Red Sea as a trade route has led some researchers to propose that Ophir and Punt could have been part of a broader trading network that extended across these regions.

---

[25] https://www.biblegateway.com/versions/New-International-Version-NIV-Bible/

The Queen's Expedition

The history of ancient Egypt is replete with remarkable pharaohs and monumental events. Still, few are as intriguing and enigmatic as Queen Hatshepsut and her expedition to Punt and the subsequent suppression of her legacy by her successor, Thutmose III. Queen Hatshepsut, one of Egypt's few female pharaohs, ascended to the throne during the Eighteenth Dynasty, approximately around 1479 BCE.

Queen Hatshepsut's reign was characterized by a keen desire to secure the prosperity and stability of Egypt. She recognized that access to valuable resources and strengthening trade relationships with other lands were essential. One of her most notable initiatives was the expedition to Punt.

The motivation behind this expedition was twofold. Firstly, Punt was renowned for its valuable resources, including myrrh, frankincense, ebony, and exotic animals. These commodities held immense value in the ancient world for their economic worth, use in religious rituals, and as symbols of power and prestige. Secondly, Queen Hatshepsut aimed to strengthen Egypt's diplomatic and trade ties with the Land of Punt, thereby enhancing her kingdom's economic and political influence in the region.

Queen Hatshepsut's expedition to Punt was documented in an artistic detail that has survived thousands of years. Her mortuary temple at Deir el-Bahri, located on the west bank of the Nile River, is adorned with vivid and intricate reliefs and inscriptions that depict facets of the Punt expedition.

The meticulousness of these records is a testament to the importance Queen Hatshepsut placed on documenting her accomplishments and the significance of her trade mission to Punt.

The inscriptions provide a treasure of information about the journey, including the exotic flora and fauna encountered, the unique customs and attire of the Puntites, and the goods obtained during the expedition.

The goods obtained from Punt during the expedition held immense value in ancient Egypt. Myrrh and frankincense, obtained from the resin of trees native to Punt, were essential in religious rituals and highly prized for their fragrance and symbolic significance. Ebony, another notable resource, was used to craft luxurious furniture and decorative items, further enhancing the pharaoh's prestige and the kingdom's material wealth.

The acquisition of exotic animals during the Punt expedition also contributed to Egypt's zoological diversity. Scenes from the reliefs at Deir el-Bahri depict the transportation of baboons, cheetahs, giraffes, and other animals to Egypt. These additions to the Egyptian royal menagerie were a testament to Queen Hatshepsut's success in Punt and a display of her power.

The inscriptions and reliefs at Deir el-Bahri depict scenes of exchange, gift-giving, and friendly interactions between the Egyptians and the people of Punt. These depictions emphasize the diplomatic nature of the mission and the desire to foster positive relations.

The Punt expedition allowed Egypt to secure valuable resources and establish itself as a dominant player in the Red Sea trade networks.[26]

The Suppression of Queen Hatshepsut's Legacy

Upon Queen Hatshepsut's death, her stepson Thutmose III assumed the throne. While Hatshepsut's reign was groundbreaking, her status as a female pharaoh raised complex issues of legitimacy. Thutmose III initiated a campaign to erase her legacy from the historical record.

Perhaps the most iconic example of Thutmose III's efforts to suppress Queen Hatshepsut's legacy can be seen at her mortuary temple at Deir el-Bahri. The walls of this temple, which had been adorned with vivid reliefs and inscriptions commemorating her reign and the Punt expedition, bear clear signs of deliberate defacement. Queen Hatshepsut's image was chiseled away. Her name was erased, and her accomplishments were obscured.

Despite Thutmose III's efforts, Queen Hatshepsut's legacy was not entirely obliterated. In modern times, Egyptologists and archaeologists have successfully reconstructed her history and accomplishments through meticulous research and deciphering ancient inscriptions. The expedition to Punt is one of the queen's most outstanding achievements, which a stone mason's chisel could not obliterate.

The Myth

The ongoing debate over the exact location of Punt has helped perpetuate its mythic allure. Punt's mythical aura was partly born from its immense wealth and the exotic nature of the goods it provided.

---

[26] Tyson, P. (2009, December 1). Where is Punt? Retrieved from PBS.org:
https://www.pbs.org/wgbh/nova/article/egypt-punt/.

In the ancient Egyptian mindset, Punt symbolized a distant and idealized source of wealth and luxury. Punt's portrayal as a foreign and exotic land, as seen in Egyptian inscriptions and reliefs, further solidified its mythical status. The people of Punt were often depicted with unique clothing and physical features, enhancing the image of an otherworldly realm. Gold, one of Punt's most coveted commodities, held a special place in the ancient world, signifying power, prestige, and divine favor. Punt's association with gold contributed to its mythical status.

The presence of linguistic and cultural influences between the peoples of the Red Sea and East African regions and the biblical narrative adds to the complexity of the debate. Exploring lesser-known indigenous accounts and oral traditions from these regions may provide insights into their historical connections with Ophir (Punt).

A Compelling Clue

Archaeology is an ongoing study of the past, and it frequently exposes evidence that has been buried for thousands of years. These uncovered facts can lead to amazing discoveries that will identify missing links. We may be closer to identifying the location of Punt thanks to the remains of a band of monkeys.

Nathaniel Dominy is an anthropologist at Dartmouth College studying isotopes of strontium and oxygen taken from mummified baboons of Egypt's New Kingdom era (c. 1550-1069 BCE). His research led him to discover that some of the animal remains were not Egyptian but came from the Horn of Africa region. This is an important discovery because the records show that Egyptians obtained baboons from Punt.

Gisela Kopp, an evolutionary biologist from the University of Konstanz, found evidence in another mummified baboon that the animal's point of origin might have been along the Red Sea coast. Both researchers believe that the baboons originated in the area of the seaport Adulis, which is in modern Eritrea.[27]

What does this mean? One possibility is that Adulis was the contact point between Egypt and Punt. Goods coming from the interior might have been traded on the port docks. It is also possible that there was no Kingdom of Punt. Instead, there could have been a city-state that had

---

[27] Mummified Baboons Point to the Direction of the Fabled Land of Punt. (2023, November 11). Retrieved from Ars Technical: https://arstechnica.com/science/2023/11/mummified-baboons-point-to-the-direction-of-the-fabled-land-of-punt/.

extensive trade relations with Egypt.

What is significant about this research is that it helps narrow down where Punt might have been. Baboons were revered in ancient Egyptian religion, and being able to purchase them would have been important to them. Obtaining these animals may have led to further trade, including the exotic commodities Egyptian expeditions brought home.[28]

In Summary

The evidence for and against Punt's existence presents a complex picture. Archaeological discoveries, including temple reliefs, inscriptions, and botanical remains, provide tangible proof of Punt's historical existence and its role in trade networks. Linguistic and cultural references reinforce the reality of Punt's presence in the ancient world. Ongoing archaeological research in the Red Sea and Horn of Africa regions continues to uncover new evidence that may shed light on the historical trade relationships and the locations of ancient civilizations, including Punt and possibly Ophir.

Punt represents a blend of historical reality and mythic elements that have grown around it over time, making it a subject of enduring fascination and exploration in ancient African history. Was it a real place on the map, or is Punt simply a legend of a fabulously wealthy country? Based on facts and stories, the best answer is that Punt is a little bit of both.

---

[28] Fitzgerald, S. (2023, November 21). Mummified Baboons in Egypt Point to a Long Lost Land. Retrieved from Atlas Obscura: https://www.atlasobscura.com/articles/mummified-baboons-punt.

Section 3: The Great Empires and Their Legacies

Chapter 6: Ancient Egypt

A book on ancient Africa has to include Egypt. It was the premier culture on the continent for centuries, and it still fascinates us to this day. People know quite a bit about the political and military history of the land of the pharaohs, and we will, of course, talk about it. However, we will also explore some lesser-known accomplishments that were just as significant.

Egypt's history is divided into four primary eras: the Old Kingdom, the Middle Kingdom, the New Kingdom, and the Ptolemaic era. We will discuss each one in sequence.

The Old Kingdom (c. 2686-2181 BCE)

The Old Kingdom represents a remarkable period in human history, especially in terms of its scientific achievements. This era, often called the Age of the Pyramids, was marked by significant advancements in various fields.

Science

- Astronomy and Mathematics:

    The Egyptians of the Old Kingdom developed a calendar based on their observations of the star Sirius and the annual flooding of the Nile. This lunar calendar was crucial for agricultural planning. Their understanding of geometry was essential for land surveying, especially after the Nile floods, and for the architectural planning of pyramids. Astronomical observations also played a significant role in religious practices. The movement of stars and celestial events were often interpreted as divine messages.[29]

- Engineering and Architecture:

The most outstanding scientific achievements of the Old Kingdom are undoubtedly the construction of the pyramids, especially the Great Pyramid of Giza. These structures are not just architectural marvels but also a testament to the Egyptians' advanced understanding of engineering principles. The pyramids demonstrate an advanced knowledge of engineering and mathematics.[30]

Those who believe in extraterrestrial beings are convinced the pyramids were built by aliens. There is, of course, no plausible evidence to support the assumption. The Egyptians gradually learned through trial and error how to construct these edifices (for instance, the Step Pyramid of Djoser, which was built earlier). The pyramids also demonstrate that Africa was not a primitive continent. The inhabitants were capable of astounding achievements.

The pyramids of Giza.
Ricardo Liberato, CC BY-SA 2.0 <https://creativecommons.org/licenses/by-sa/2.0>, via Wikimedia Commons; https://commons.wikimedia.org/wiki/File:All_Gizah_Pyramids-2.jpg

---

[29] Wendorg, M. (2023, April 23). Ancient Egyptian Technology and Inventions. Retrieved from Interesting Enginerring.com: https://interestingengineering.com/lists/ancient-egyptian-technology-and-inventions.

[30] Mark, J. J. (2016, November 9). Ancient Egyptian Science & Technology. Retrieved from World History Encyclopedia: https://www.worldhistory.org/article/967/ancient-egyptian-science-technology/.

- Medical Practices:

    The Egyptians had a basic understanding of anatomy, pharmacology, and possibly even surgical practices. The Edwin Smith Papyrus was written during the Middle Kingdom, but this work is considered a copy of much earlier texts. There is evidence of significant medical knowledge during the Old Kingdom.

    Egyptian medicine in the Old Kingdom included various herbs and other natural substances for treating ailments. There was also an understanding of surgical procedures, as evidenced by surgical instruments found at archaeological sites. Institutions known as "Houses of Life" had medical purposes and existed in the First Dynasty.

<u>Economics</u>

Advances in agriculture were crucial for maintaining a prosperous economy. The Egyptians developed sophisticated irrigation systems to control the flooding of the Nile, which allowed for consistent agricultural production. In addition to irrigation canals to manage the flow of the Nile's waters, the Egyptians invented a water wheel, the *shadoof*, to transfer water into a canal.

There was also an expansion in the variety of crops grown, including the introduction of new grains and fruits, which contributed to a more stable and varied food supply.

Egypt's agricultural economy enabled it to become a powerful economic force in the ancient world. The Old Kingdom saw the establishment of extensive trade networks, both within Egypt and with neighboring regions like Nubia, the Levant, and the Mediterranean. These trade networks helped in the acquisition of luxury goods and building materials not available locally. The ability to navigate the Nile and the seas opened Egypt up to a world of trade, cultural exchange, and military expeditions.[31]

---

[31] Historyskills.com. (2024, January 19). How Egypt Became the Greatest Superpower of the Ancient World. Retrieved from Hisoryskills.com: https://www.historyskills.com/classroom/ancient-history/egypt-ancient-superpower/.

Politics and Society

The Old Kingdom created a strong, centralized state governed by the pharaoh. The concept of the pharaoh as a god-king was solidified during this time. This notion reinforced the political structure, as the pharaoh's absolute authority was seen as divinely ordained. This period saw the development of an efficient bureaucracy that was essential for managing large-scale projects, tax collection, and administration.

The Old Kingdom had a social hierarchy with the pharaoh at the top, followed by nobles, priests, artisans, and farmers. The bottom rung of society was occupied by slaves. This hierarchy was integral to the functioning of society. If someone stepped out of their designed social role, the Egyptians believed it would bring disharmony to Egypt and cause chaos.[32]

This era significantly saw developments in Egyptian art, literature, and religious practices. The construction of pyramids and large tombs decorated with intricate art and hieroglyphs reflects the period's cultural richness. Writing was, without a doubt, the most significant educational innovation of the Old Kingdom. The Egyptian writing system included two thousand hieroglyphic symbols and an alphabet.[33]

Most Important Pharaohs

Several pharaohs played pivotal roles in shaping Egyptian history during the Old Kingdom. Their reigns were marked by significant accomplishments, particularly in architecture, administration, and religious practices. Here are some of the most prominent pharaohs from this period:

- Djoser (c. 2630-2611 BCE)

Djoser, the second pharaoh of the Third Dynasty, is best known for his step pyramid at Saqqara. This pyramid, designed by his vizier Imhotep, is considered one of the earliest large-scale cut-stone constructions. It marked a significant advancement from the traditional mastaba tombs and set the precedent for later pyramid construction.

---

[32] Mark, J. J. (2017, September 21). Social Structure in Ancient Egypt. Retrieved from History World Encyclopedia: https://www.worldhistory.org/article/1123/social-structure-in-ancient-egypt/.

[33] Lifepersona.com. (2024, January 19). The 9 Most Important Contributions of Egypt to Humanity. Retrieved from Lifepersona.com: https://www.lifepersona.com/the-9-most-important-contributions-of-egypt-to-humanity.

Step Pyramid of Djoser.
Charles J. Sharp, CC BY-SA 3.0 <https://creativecommons.org/licenses/by-sa/3.0>, via Wikimedia Commons; https://commons.wikimedia.org/wiki/File:Saqqara_pyramid_ver_2.jpg

- Sneferu (c. 2575-2551 BCE)

Sneferu, the founder of the Fourth Dynasty, was an incredibly prolific pyramid builder. He is credited with building three major pyramids: the Meidum Pyramid, the Bent Pyramid, and the Red Pyramid. These structures represent important stages in the evolution of pyramid construction, culminating in the Red Pyramid, Egypt's first successful attempt at a true smooth-sided pyramid.

- Khufu (c. 2589-2566 BCE)

Sneferu's successor, Khufu, is best known for the Great Pyramid of Giza, one of the Seven Wonders of the Ancient World. This colossal structure exemplifies the architectural skill and organizational ability of the Old Kingdom and remains a testament to the Egyptians' engineering prowess.

- Khafre (Chephren) (c. 2558-2532 BCE)

Khafre, Khufu's son, built the second-largest pyramid at Giza. He is also credited with the construction of the Sphinx, a monumental limestone statue with the body of a lion and a pharaoh's head, likely intended to be a likeness of Khafre himself.

- Menkaure (c. 2532–2503 BCE)

Menkaure, another son of Khufu, is known for constructing the third and smallest of the Giza pyramids. Although smaller, this pyramid is notable for its complex mortuary temple and exquisite craftsmanship.

- Pepi II (c. 2278–2184 BCE)

Pepi II, who ascended to the throne as a young boy, is believed to have reigned for ninety-four years, the longest of any Egyptian pharaoh. His reign eventually led to internal trouble in the government and the civil wars that marked the end of the Old Kingdom.

These pharaohs were instrumental in establishing many of the defining characteristics of ancient Egyptian civilization. The pyramids, in particular, stand as enduring symbols of the Old Kingdom's grandeur and the pharaohs' quest for immortality.

The Middle Kingdom (c. 2030–1650 BCE)

There was turmoil in Egypt after the Old Kingdom came to an end. However, Egypt was able to rebound from internal strife and enter into a period that was one of its greatest: the Middle Kingdom.

While the Middle Kingdom has often been overlooked by the achievements of the Old and New Kingdoms, it was a pivotal chapter in the ancient Egyptian narrative.

Mathematics

We should remember that the Middle Kingdom was built on breakthroughs that took place in the Old Kingdom, so many innovations were logical progressions of what came before. There is documentation from the Twelfth Dynasty that shows an interest in the use of fractions. Papyrus documents, such as the Moscow Mathematics Papyrus and the Egyptian Mathematical Leather Roll, date to the Middle Kingdom. Mathematical problem tests, including solutions, come from this Egyptian era as well. These suggest a practical approach to mathematics as opposed to a theoretical one. Fractions were essential for temple and pyramid construction and were used in the complex task of managing the nation's granaries and resources.

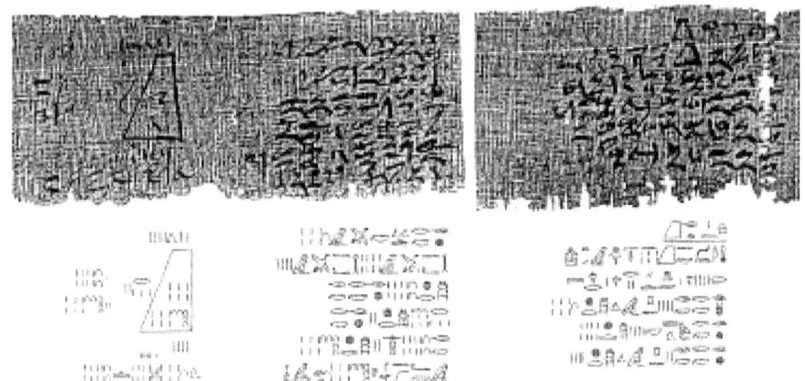

A mathematical problem in the Moscow Mathematics Papyrus.
https://commons.wikimedia.org/wiki/File:Moskou-papyrus.jpg

Architecture and Shipbuilding

The Middle Kingdom of Egypt was a time of political stability and cultural flourishing, which is vividly reflected in the era's architectural and maritime innovations.

Pyramids were still being built, although the building material gradually went from solid stone to mud brick with a limestone casing. The pyramids were no longer the burial chamber of choice by the end of the Twelfth Dynasty. Rock-cut tombs in the Valley of Kings and the Valley of Queens were used instead. What is interesting is the use of rudimentary urban planning in the construction of workers' villages near the burial construction sites.

Architecture became refined during the Twelfth Dynasty. The Karnak Temple Complex, especially the White Chapel, exemplified the new building styles.[34]

---

[34] Brewminate.com. (2019, April 17). The Art and Architecture of Middle Kingdom Egypt c. 2055-1650 BCE. Retrieved from brewminate.com: https://brewminate.com/the-art-and-architecture-of-middle-kingdom-egypt-c-2055-1650-bce/.

Pillars of the Great Hypostyle Hall at Karnak.
René Hourdry, CC BY-SA 4.0 <https://creativecommons.org/licenses/by-sa/4.0>, via Wikimedia Commons; https://commons.wikimedia.org/wiki/File:Temple_de_Louxor_68.jpg

The construction of large seaworthy vessels opened new possibilities for trade, military campaigns, and mining expeditions. These ships enabled the Egyptians to extend their influence and secure resources from distant lands, which was crucial for the kingdom's economy and position in the ancient world.

References such as the "Tale of the Shipwrecked Sailor" suggest the construction of large ships designed for long voyages, indicating an advanced understanding of shipbuilding. The design and function of these ships were likely tailored for specific purposes, reflecting a sophisticated knowledge of maritime engineering and the diverse needs of Egyptian society during this period.

While specific details on the materials and techniques are scarce, the Egyptians' tradition of shipbuilding and their access to quality timbers suggest a high level of craftsmanship. The use of cedar from Lebanon, known for its durability and strength, would have been pivotal in constructing sturdy and seaworthy vessels.

Society

The Middle Kingdom marked a transition toward a more centralized and efficient government compared to the Old Kingdom. A robust bureaucracy was developed, which was crucial in managing the country's resources, executing large-scale construction projects, and maintaining administrative order.

Additionally, this era is noted for legal reforms. The laws were more organized and codified than in the earlier periods, which helped maintain social order and justice. These reforms were essential in stabilizing a society that had experienced significant turmoil.

During the Middle Kingdom, there was a rise in the prominence and influence of the middle class, including artisans, scribes, and officials. This period is often characterized by a degree of social mobility, which contrasted to the more rigidly hierarchical structure of the Old Kingdom.

Arts and Culture

The Middle Kingdom is celebrated for its literary and artistic achievements. Literature from this period, including works like "The Tale of Sinuhe" and the "Instructions of Amenemhat," is renowned for its sophistication and depth. These works not only provide insight into the culture and societal values of the time but also reflect the intellectual and artistic endeavors of the Middle Kingdom.

Craftsmanship and industry also saw remarkable growth during this time. The period was known for its exquisite jewelry, pottery, and statues. These advancements were aesthetic and technological, reflecting a deeper understanding of materials and techniques. The skills and practices developed during this period laid the foundation for the artistic achievements of the later New Kingdom.

One of the most striking features of Middle Kingdom art was the shift toward realism. Unlike the idealized forms of the Old Kingdom, the art of this era depicted figures with more individualistic and realistic features. This change is evident in the portrayal of pharaohs, where their solemnity and individual characteristics are more pronounced, as seen in the sculptures of Senusret III. Block statues, a new form of sculpture, emerged during this period. These statues typically depicted a squatting figure with their knees drawn up to their chest and were often inscribed with autobiographical texts or hymns, adding a personal dimension to the art.

Statue of Senusret III located in the British Museum.
British Museum, CC BY-SA 3.0 <http://creativecommons.org/licenses/by-sa/3.0/>, via Wikimedia Commons; https://commons.wikimedia.org/wiki/File:StatueOfSesotrisIII-EA684-BritishMuseum-August19-08.jpg

Funerary art included items such as shabtis and scarabs. Shabtis were small figurines intended to serve the deceased in the afterlife, while scarabs were amulets believed to protect against dangers in the afterlife.

The Middle Kingdom also saw an increase in the representation and patronage of art by women. This is exemplified in the sculpture of a noblewoman from the Twelfth Dynasty, indicating a respected status for women in society and their active participation in the cultural domain.[35]

The art of the Middle Kingdom, with its shift toward realism, inclusion of diverse social classes, and incorporation of personal and symbolic

---

[35] Pressbooks.bccampus.ca. (2024, January 19). Middle Kingdom Art. Retrieved from Art and Visual Culture: Prehistory to Renaissance:
https://pressbooks.bccampus.ca/cavestocathedrals/chapter/middle-kingdom/.

elements, offers invaluable insights into the lives and beliefs of the ancient Egyptians during this transformative period. The legacy of Middle Kingdom art, therefore, lies not only in its aesthetic achievements but also in its reflection of a society in the midst of profound change.

Economics and Politics

The Middle Kingdom was a period of considerable economic expansion and prosperity. This era saw a significant increase in trade, both internally and with foreign lands. Trade routes were established and expanded with neighboring regions and possibly even with distant lands like the Aegean region and Mesopotamia. Exotic goods like gold, copper, lapis lazuli, and cedar wood, essential for temple and tomb constructions, were commonly traded items.

Trade routes extended to far-flung regions, enabling the exchange of goods like spices, perfumes, gold, and jewels. This trade took place over land and sea routes, thereby broadening Egypt's commercial reach. Markets in towns and villages became bustling centers of commerce, facilitating the exchange of goods and contributing to the diversification of the economy. Trade also introduced banking and money-lending services, often involving commodities like grain or salt.

The foundation of the Middle Kingdom's economy was its agricultural sector. Blessed with the fertile lands of the Nile Valley, the Egyptians cultivated crops like wheat, barley, and various vegetables. The Nile's annual flooding ensured rich, arable land, supporting a growing population and allowing surplus production.[36]

The construction of grand temples and monuments served religious and cultural purposes and stimulated the economy through the utilization of vast labor forces and resources. These projects provided employment for a large number of workers. The emphasis on preparing for the afterlife, manifested in elaborate burial practices and tomb constructions, further contributed to economic activities, especially in funerary goods and services industries.[37]

---

[36] Cassar, C. (2023, August 25). Exploring the Egyptian Middle Kingdom—A Historical Overview. Retrieved from Anthropologureview.org: https://anthropologyreview.org/history/ancient-egypt/exploring-the-egyptian-middle-kingdom-a-historical-overview/?expand_article=1.

[37] Cassar, C. (2023, August 25). Exploring the Egyptian Middle Kingdom—A Historical Overview. Retrieved from Anthropologureview.org: https://anthropologyreview.org/history/ancient-egypt/exploring-the-egyptian-middle-kingdom-a-historical-overview/?expand_article=1.

Military Expansion

The Middle Kingdom commenced with the reunification of Egypt under Mentuhotep II. He was a warrior pharaoh who reconsolidated the fragmented nation and initiated a series of military campaigns, particularly in the northwest Sinai region and Nubia.

War played a major role in Egypt's economic aspirations. Pharaohs like Amenemhat III launched successful campaigns against neighboring territories, increasing Egypt's wealth and power. Egypt's control over a more extensive territory allowed for greater economic stability and the accumulation of wealth. Establishing military fortresses, like the one in the region of Elephantine, was crucial in maintaining control over these acquired territories.[38]

The Mighty Pharaohs

The Middle Kingdom heralded a phase of political consolidation, cultural renaissance, and economic prosperity. The reigns of several pharaohs allowed this to happen.

- Mentuhotep II (c. 2061-2010 BCE)

    The Middle Kingdom started during the reign of Mentuhotep II. As we just mentioned, he was the pharaoh who reunified Egypt. After a prolonged period of disunity and chaos, Mentuhotep II defeated the rival Tenth Dynasty of Hierakonpolis, ending the First Intermediate Period. This reunification restored political stability and set the stage for a cultural and economic revival.

    Mentuhotep II was a patron of the arts and architecture. His mortuary complex in Deir el-Bahri, near Thebes, is a testament to the architectural innovations made under his reign. This complex, which predates the famous temple of Hatshepsut, showcases a unique architectural style that blended elements of traditional mastaba tombs with those of pyramidal structures, setting a precedent for future temples in Egypt.

- Amenemhat I (c. 1991-1962 BCE)

    The start of the Twelfth Dynasty under Amenemhat I marked the beginning of what is often considered the golden age of the

---

[38] Historyskills.com. (2024, January 19). What Was the Middle Kingdom of Ancient Egypt? Retrieved from Historyskills.com: https://www.historyskills.com/classroom/ancient-history/anc-middle-kingdom-reading/.

Middle Kingdom. One of Amenemhat's first actions as pharaoh was to move the capital from Thebes to a new city, Itjtawy, which is believed to be located near the pharaoh's burial site in Faiyum. This strategic relocation facilitated better control over the kingdom and symbolized a new era in Egyptian history.

Amenemhat I's reign was characterized by significant administrative and economic reforms. He initiated projects to increase agricultural productivity, particularly in the Faiyum region, which became a central agricultural hub under his rule. Moreover, his military campaigns to secure Egypt's northeastern borders were crucial in safeguarding the nation against potential Asiatic invasions, thereby ensuring the stability and security of his reign.

- Senusret I (c. 1971-1926 BCE)

Senusret I, also known as Sesostris I, was originally a co-regent with his father Amenemhat I and reigned from approximately 1971 to 1926 BCE. He expanded Egyptian influence into Nubia and the Near East through a series of successful military campaigns. These campaigns secured Egypt's borders and provided access to critical trade routes and resources, further bolstering the kingdom's economy.

Senusret I was a great patron of the arts. His reign saw a significant flourishing of artistic expression, with an emphasis on the construction of temples and shrines. The arts, particularly sculpture and relief work, saw remarkable advancements during his reign, characterized by a sense of realism and attention to detail not seen in previous eras. This cultural renaissance under Senusret I significantly contributed to the legacy of the Middle Kingdom as a period of heightened artistic and cultural activity.

- Amenemhat III (c. 1860-1814 BCE)

Amenemhat III's reign is often considered the zenith of the Middle Kingdom in terms of economic prosperity and architectural achievements. His reign is most notable for the extensive building projects he commissioned, particularly in the Faiyum Oasis. Here, he undertook an ambitious irrigation project that significantly expanded the region's agricultural output, transforming it into one of Egypt's most fertile areas.

His architectural legacy is marked by the construction of the Labyrinth, an enormous and complex temple complex near the Hawara pyramid. This building was renowned in the ancient world for its size and complexity, consisting of thousands of rooms and chambers that amazed visitors. Amenemhat III also constructed two significant pyramids at Hawara and Dahshur, which are notable for their innovative design and construction techniques.

The Black Pyramid at Dahshur.
Tekisch, CC BY-SA 3.0 <https://creativecommons.org/licenses/by-sa/3.0>, via Wikimedia Commons; https://commons.wikimedia.org/wiki/File:Black_Pyramid_of_Amenemhat_III.JPG

Amenemhat III's reign was also characterized by stability and prosperity, which fostered advancements in literature, arts, and statecraft. His economic policies and construction projects provided employment and stimulated the economy, while his patronage of the arts led to a flourishing of cultural life.

In Summary

The Middle Kingdom was a period of significant achievements in various domains. These achievements not only revitalized Egyptian civilization but also set the stage for the subsequent New Kingdom. The invasion of a Middle Eastern group known as the Hyksos ended this remarkable period.

The New Kingdom (c. 1570-1069 BCE)

The New Kingdom, lasting from around the 16th century BCE to the 11th century BCE, represents one of the most illustrious chapters in ancient Egyptian history. This period, encompassing the Eighteenth, Nineteenth, and Twentieth Dynasties, is often regarded as the height of Egypt's power and cultural richness.

Politics

Egypt had been occupied by outsiders, the Hyksos, who were finally expelled from Egypt by Ahmose I. The return of the pharaoh's throne to Egypt laid the foundation for the New Kingdom.

One of the most significant aspects of the New Kingdom was its vast territorial expansion, making it the most powerful Egyptian empire. The era saw Egypt reaching its greatest extent, with its boundaries extending as far as the Euphrates River and Nubia under the reign of Thutmose III. This expansion was not merely an exercise of power but also a strategic defense mechanism against potential invasions, as experienced during the Second Intermediate Period.

Egypt in the 15th century BCE.
ArdadN, Jeff Dahl, CC BY-SA 3.0 <https://creativecommons.org/licenses/by-sa/3.0>, via Wikimedia Commons; https://commons.wikimedia.org/wiki/File:Egypt_NK_edit.svg

Thutmose III, often dubbed the "Napoleon of Egypt," consolidated Egypt's dominance in the Near East. Under his reign, Egypt asserted its authority over Syria, reorganized the military bureaucracy, and attained unprecedented levels of power and influence. This military expansion and consolidation under Thutmose III laid the foundations for Egypt's sustained regional dominance. His annals, recorded on the walls of the Karnak temple, are a primary source of information about these military exploits.[39]

A wealth of archaeological findings and historical texts provide evidence of Egypt's imperial aspirations. For instance, temples from this era, like those at Karnak and Luxor, are adorned with inscriptions and reliefs that provide valuable information. For example, the Battle of Kadesh is famously depicted in the reliefs found in the temples of Ramesses II, offering insights into his military campaigns.

The Valley of the Kings and the Valley of the Queens also offer a wealth of information for scholars to investigate. Tombs of pharaohs and high officials contain inscriptions, paintings, and artifacts that shed light on Egypt's foreign relations and military might.

Papyrus scrolls were not just records of military glory. Diplomatic relations were necessary for the empire's stability. Amenhotep III's reign, for example, was characterized by his use of marriage alliances to maintain peace and extend influence. Documents like the Amarna letters, which are a collection of diplomatic correspondence, reveal the political and diplomatic landscape of the New Kingdom and its relations with neighboring powers.[40]

Architecture and Art

The New Kingdom is renowned for its architectural marvels and artistic achievements. This period witnessed the construction of monumental structures like the temples at Karnak and Luxor, the Valley of the Kings, and the mortuary temple of Hatshepsut at Deir el-Bahri. These architectural feats showcased the Egyptians' advanced engineering and artistic skills and reflected their religious and cultural values.

---

[39] Peter F. Dorman, M. S. (2024, January 19). Thutmose III. Retrieved from Britannica.com: https://www.britannica.com/biography/Thutmose-III/Adornment-of-Egypt.

[40] Scoville, P. (2015, November 6). Amarna Letters. Retrieved from Worldhistory.org: https://www.worldhistory.org/Amarna_Letters/.

Monumental temple complexes and elaborate tombs characterize the New Kingdom's architecture. Towering obelisks and colossal statues are testaments to the Egyptians' engineering prowess. New Kingdom pharaohs chose the Valley of the Kings as their final resting place, a shift reflecting both religious significance and concerns about tomb security. The valley was on the west bank of the Nile, where the sun set, so it had a symbolic relationship with death. The valley's isolation also offered better security from tomb robbers.

The temples of Karnak and Luxor are the best examples of New Kingdom architecture. These complexes, with their colossal columns, expansive hypostyle halls, and intricate reliefs, were not only places of worship but also centers of economic activity. The expansion of the Karnak Temple Complex, particularly under Amenhotep III and Ramesses II, showcases the period's architectural ambition and religious devotion. The temple of Hatshepsut at Deir el-Bahri exemplifies the New Kingdom's architectural ingenuity. With its terraced design and harmonious integration into the surrounding cliffs, Hatshepsut's temple remains a masterpiece of ancient architecture.[41]

The temple of Hatshepsut.
Diego Delso, CC BY-SA 4.0 <https://creativecommons.org/licenses/by-sa/4.0>, via Wikimedia Commons; https://commons.wikimedia.org/wiki/File:Templo_funerario_de_Hatshepsut,_Luxor,_Egipto,_2022-04-03,_DD_13.jpg

---

[41] Pbs.org. (2024, January 19). Art & Architecture. Retrieved from Pbs.org: https://www.pbs.org/empires/egypt/newkingdom/architecture.html.

The New Kingdom's architecture was imbued with deep symbolic and religious significance. Temples were often aligned with celestial bodies, reflecting the Egyptians' advanced understanding of astronomy and its integration into their religious and architectural concepts.

The grand building projects of the New Kingdom were not merely displays of religious and royal power but also significant drivers of the economy. They provided employment for many workers, artisans, and administrators and stimulated various sectors, such as agriculture, craft production, and transport. Politically, these architectural undertakings reinforced the pharaohs' divine status and legitimized their rule.[42]

Under Akhenaten, New Kingdom art experienced a significant shift, embracing what is known as the Amarna style. This period saw a move toward more naturalistic and less formal representations, especially in depictions of the royal family.

The New Kingdom also saw a proliferation of statues and sculptures ranging from colossal representations of pharaohs to smaller, more intimate statues of deities and individuals. These sculptures often display a high level of craftsmanship and realism. Items such as jewelry, pottery, and furniture found in tombs and archaeological sites are crucial in understanding the everyday artistic practices and aesthetic preferences of the New Kingdom. The skillful artistry seen in jewelry and decorative arts reflects a sophisticated understanding of materials and techniques.[43]

Economics

The New Kingdom witnessed economic prosperity fueled by wealth accumulated from military conquests, extensive trade networks, and efficient administrative systems. The Egyptians engaged in trade with their neighbors, exchanging gold, papyrus, linen, and grain for luxury items like incense, ivory, and exotic animals. This economic prosperity facilitated the construction of grand temples and tombs.

Control over trade routes and resources played a significant role in the New Kingdom's expansion. The wealth accumulated from these ventures

---

[42] Brewminate.com. (2019, April 19). The Art and Architecture of New Kingdom Egypt c. 1570-1069.BCE. Retrieved from brewmintate.com: https://brewminate.com/the-art-and-architecture-of-new-kingdom-egypt-c-1570-1069-bce/.

[43] Pressbooks.bccampus.ca. (2024, January 19). New Kingdom Art. Retrieved from pressbooks.bccampus.ca: https://pressbooks.bccampus.ca/cavestocathedrals/chapter/new-kingdom/.

funded military campaigns and building projects. Trade with regions like Punt, as depicted in the mortuary temple of Hatshepsut, is a testament to Egypt's economic outreach. The exchange of goods, ideas, and art during this period indicates a significant level of cultural interaction with other civilizations, such as the Nubians, Hittites, and Asiatic peoples.

Religious Upheaval

The New Kingdom was also a time of significant religious transformation. The most notable was the religious revolution under Akhenaten, who established monotheism centered around the worship of Aten, the sun disk. He moved the capital to Akhetaten (modern-day Amarna) and promoted Aten as the supreme deity, diminishing the traditional polytheistic belief system. Although this shift was short-lived, it had a profound impact on Egyptian religion.

The shift to monotheism, or more precisely monolatrism (the worship of one god without denying the existence of others), was unprecedented in Egyptian history. Akhenaten's religious reform involved the elevation of Aten and the systematic diminution of other gods, most notably Amun.

The religious reforms of Akhenaten had significant sociopolitical implications. By diminishing the role of other deities, Akhenaten sought to reduce the power and wealth of the priesthood. This move can be interpreted as an attempt to centralize religious and political authority under the pharaoh.

Following Akhenaten's death, there was a rapid restoration of the traditional polytheistic religious practices. His successor, Tutankhamun (the famous King Tut), played a pivotal role in this religious restoration. The capital was moved back to Thebes, and efforts were made to erase the changes, including the destruction or defacement of Akhenaten's monuments. This swift reversal highlights the deep-seated nature of traditional religious beliefs and practices in ancient Egyptian society.

Akhenaten's reign witnessed profound changes in artistic styles. Traditional rigid and formal artistic norms gave way to more naturalistic and relaxed forms, particularly in the portrayal of the royal family. This new art style, characterized by elongated faces and bodies, was a reflection of the broader religious and cultural shifts of the time.[44]

---

[44] Taronas, L. (2024, January 19). Akhenaten: The Mysteries of Religious Revolution. Retrieved from Arce.org: https://arce.org/resource/akhenaten-mysteries-religious-revolution/.

The Impactful Pharaohs

Some of Egypt's most legendary rulers graced the New Kingdom. Ahmose I, considered the founder of the Eighteenth Dynasty, successfully drove out the Hyksos invaders and unified Egypt. His successors, including Amenhotep I, Thutmose I, and Amenhotep III, continued to fortify and expand the empire.

A defining feature of this era was the remarkable reign of Queen Hatshepsut, one of the most influential and successful female monarchs in history. Hatshepsut, known for her effective administration and ambitious building projects, significantly contributed to Egypt's prosperity and architectural grandeur.

- Ahmose I (c. 1549-1524 BCE)

  The founder of the Eighteenth Dynasty, Ahmose I was the architect of the New Kingdom. His significance lies in his successful campaigns against the Hyksos, the foreign rulers who had occupied northern Egypt. By expelling them, Ahmose unified Egypt. His military achievements laid the groundwork for the prosperity and power that Egypt would enjoy in the centuries to come.

- Hatshepsut (c. 1479-1458 BCE)

  Hatshepsut, one of the few female pharaohs in ancient Egyptian history, was a figure of profound importance. Her reign was one of peace and economic growth. Hatshepsut is best known for her ambitious building projects, most notably the temple at Deir el-Bahri. Her successful trading expedition to Punt brought wealth and exotic goods and animals to Egypt, enhancing its cultural and economic status.

- Thutmose III (c. 1479-1425 BCE)

  Thutmose III, the stepson of Hatshepsut, emerged as one of the greatest pharaohs of the New Kingdom. His military campaigns expanded Egypt's borders to their furthest extent, extending Egyptian influence into Asia and Nubia. His reign was not just about conquest; he also significantly contributed to the arts and architecture in Egypt, commissioning numerous temples and monuments.

- Amenhotep III (c. 1386-1349 BCE)

    Amenhotep III's reign was marked by peace, prosperity, and artistic flourishing. Known for his diplomatic skills, he maintained Egypt's position through strategic marriages and alliances rather than military might. His architectural contributions are monumental, including significant additions to the Karnak Temple Complex and the construction of the Colossi of Memnon. His reign is often seen as the height of Egyptian artistic and cultural sophistication.

The Colossi of Memnon in 2015.

MusikAnimal, CC BY-SA 4.0 <https://creativecommons.org/licenses/by-sa/4.0>, via Wikimedia Commons; https://commons.wikimedia.org/wiki/File:Colossi_of_Memnon_May_2015_2.JPG

- Akhenaten (Amenhotep IV) (c. 1353-1336 BCE)

    Akhenaten, originally Amenhotep IV, is remembered for his religious revolution. He replaced Egypt's traditional polytheistic religion with the worship of a single god, Aten, and moved the capital to Akhetaten. His reign brought about a distinctive artistic style that emphasized realism. Although his religious reforms were controversial and largely reversed after his death, they represented a significant departure from traditional Egyptian culture and religion.

- King Tutankhamun (c. 1333-1323 BCE)

    The boy king of Egypt's reign saw the restoration of the old religious practices. Besides that, there is nothing really noteworthy about his reign besides his mysterious death at a young age. His tomb discovery was a major archaeological event because it was untouched by robbers. Before this discovery, we could only imagine how amazing the tombs of rulers were before they were robbed.

- Ramesses II (c. 1279-1213 BCE)

    Ramesses II, also known as Ramesses the Great, was one of the longest-reigning pharaohs of the New Kingdom. His reign was marked by architectural brilliance, military campaigns, and a large family that ensured a succession of rulers from his lineage. He is best known for the Battle of Kadesh against the Hittites, which led to the signing of the first recorded peace treaty in history. His building projects, including the construction of the magnificent Abu Simbel temples and the Ramesseum, his funerary temple, are among the most impressive in Egyptian history.

These pharaohs of the New Kingdom left an indelible mark on Egyptian history. Each ruler, in their unique way, contributed to the empire's prosperity and cultural richness. Their legacies have stood the test of time, from military conquests and religious reforms to architectural wonders and artistic achievements. Under their leadership, the New Kingdom witnessed the peak of Egyptian civilization.

The End of the New Kingdom

Despite its grandeur, the New Kingdom eventually succumbed to internal strife and external pressures, leading to its decline. The power struggle between the pharaohs and the high priests of Amun, coupled with the rise of regional rulers, weakened central authority. The New Kingdom's end marked the beginning of a period of fragmentation and foreign domination.

Nevertheless, the legacy of the New Kingdom is enduring. The architectural and artistic achievements of this period continue to captivate the world. Moreover, the New Kingdom's influence extended beyond its borders, impacting neighboring cultures and later civilizations.

The Ptolemaic Era (323-30 BCE)

Egypt's decline after the end of the New Kingdom included being conquered by outsiders, including the Kushites (who founded the Twenty-fifth Dynasty), the Assyrians, and the Persians. A significant change occurred in the 4th century BCE when Alexander the Great seized Egypt and ushered in the Ptolemaic era.

The Ptolemaic era stands out as a remarkable period in ancient history. It was a time marked by profound cultural, economic, political, and religious accomplishments, significantly shaping Egypt's historical narrative. Politically, the Ptolemaic era was characterized by relative stability and effective governance. The Ptolemies, adopting the title of pharaoh, skillfully integrated themselves into Egyptian society. By participating in Egyptian religious practices and respecting traditional customs, they gained acceptance and legitimacy among the Egyptian people. This approach to governance helped maintain internal stability and fostered a sense of unity within the kingdom.[45]

A remarkable aspect of the Ptolemaic era was the synthesis of Greek and Egyptian cultures. This fusion is evident in various forms of artistic expression, such as sculpture, where Greek hairstyles and features were combined with traditional Egyptian attributes. This cultural blend was not just a creative endeavor but also a strategic move to create a harmonious society, amalgamating the traditions of the Greek rulers with those of the Egyptian populace.

The Ptolemaic rulers were adept at expanding their territory and influence. Ptolemy II successfully grew the size of Egypt. These expansions were not military conquests and shrewd diplomatic maneuvers, such as establishing trade posts along the Red Sea and engaging in marriages for alliance-building. Such policies helped solidify Egypt's position in the region and enhanced its influence in the Mediterranean world.[46]

The Library of Alexandria

The Library of Alexandria was the premier accomplishment of the Ptolemaic era. This institution was not just a repository of books; it was also the epicenter of learning and intellectual activity in the ancient world. It was part of a scholarly complex known as the Mouseion that the Ptolemies constructed to advance knowledge and the study of ideas. Scholars from various disciplines gathered here, contributing to an unprecedented exchange of ideas and expertise. The library's

---

[45] New World Encyclopedia. (2024, January 19). Ptolemaic Dynasty. Retrieved from New World Encyclopedia: https://www.newworldencyclopedia.org/entry/Ptolemaic_dynasty.

[46] Wasson, D. L. (2016, September 29). Ptolemaic Dynasty. Retrieved from Worldhistory.org: https://www.worldhistory.org/Ptolemaic_Dynasty/.

comprehensive collection of manuscripts made it a beacon of scholarship and education.[47]

The library was built by Ptolemy II Philadelphus, who purchased the library's first books. Succeeding pharaohs continued buying manuscripts but devised a novel way of expanding the library's collection. Books were taken from ships entering the harbor of Alexandria and copied, with the originals then becoming the library's property.[48]

The Library of Alexandria's collection was staggering in volume and diversity. Estimates suggest it held over half a million scrolls, encompassing a vast array of subjects from epic poetry and drama to science and religion.

Scholars resided in Alexandria, enjoying royal patronage that allowed them to focus exclusively on their studies and teachings. Among them were Euclid, Herophilus, and Archimedes, whose works profoundly influenced subsequent generations.

The Library of Alexandria remains a subject of fascination and study, symbolizing the zenith of ancient scholarship and the tragic loss of cultural and intellectual heritage. In modern times, the revival of the Bibliotheca Alexandrina aims to recapture the spirit of its ancient namesake. Inaugurated in 2002, this modern library and cultural center in Alexandria seeks to rekindle the old library's legacy of learning and dialogue. This institution stands as a testament to the enduring allure of the Library of Alexandria and its lasting impact on the collective imagination of humankind.

Economy

Agriculture saw substantial advancements under Ptolemaic rule. The rulers implemented effective land reclamation and irrigation strategies, significantly increasing the cultivable land area. Introducing new crops, such as olives and superior wine-producing grapes, further diversified and enriched the agricultural sector. These innovations not only boosted the economy but also improved the quality of life for the Egyptian populace.[49]

---

[47] Haughton, B. (2011, February 1). What Happened to the Great Library at Alexandria? Retrieved from Worldhistory.org: https://www.worldhistory.org/article/207/what-happened-to-the-great-library-at-alexandria/.

[48] Mark, J. J. (2023, July 25). Library of Alexandria. Retrieved from Worldhistory.org: https://www.worldhistory.org/Library_of_Alexandria/.

[49] Ancientegptianfacts.com. (2024, January 19). Facts About Ancient Egyptians. Retrieved from

The Ptolemaic era marked a significant transition in Egypt's economy with the introduction of a minted currency system. This shift from a barter to a monetized economy facilitated trade and commerce domestically and internationally. The Ptolemies established Egypt as a pivotal trade corridor, linking the Mediterranean with Africa and the Indian Ocean. This enhanced Egypt's position as an economic powerhouse in the ancient world.[50]

The Harbor and the Pharos

The harbor of Alexandria was the epicenter of Ptolemaic Egypt's prosperity. As the busiest trading center in the Mediterranean, the harbor of Alexandria was instrumental in facilitating the growth and prosperity of Alexandria, making it the largest city of the ancient world at that time. The harbor's design and management were integral to its success as a commercial hub. Greek architects meticulously planned the city on a grid pattern, complete with wide main streets and framed by the significant Gates of the Sun and the Moon.[51]

Amidst Alexandria's architectural marvels, the Lighthouse of Alexandria, also known as the Pharos of Alexandria, stood as a testament to the city's advanced engineering and architectural capabilities. Constructed during the reigns of Ptolemy I and Ptolemy II, this monumental structure was one of the Seven Wonders of the Ancient World. Towering over one hundred meters tall, the Pharos was not just an impressive edifice but also a beacon of safety and guidance for sailors navigating the treacherous waters of the Mediterranean.

Its primary function was to guide ships safely into Alexandria's harbor. Historians believe that a fire, likely fueled by oil due to the scarcity of wood, was kept burning at the top of the tower to ensure visibility at night. This feature was groundbreaking for its time, and the Pharos soon became a model for lighthouses throughout the ancient world. The lighthouse's design possibly included a polished bronze mirror, reflecting the flame

---

Ancientegptianfacts.com: https://ancientegyptianfacts.com/ptolemaic-period-egypt.html.

[50] King, A. (2018, July 25). The Economy of Ptolemaic Egypt. Retrieved from Worldhistory.org: https://www.worldhistory.org/article/1256/the-economy-of-ptolemaic-egypt/.

[51] Bevan, E. (2024, January 19). Chapter IV: The People, the Cities, the Court. Retrieved from Penelope.uchicago.edu: https://penelope.uchicago.edu/Thayer/E/Gazetteer/Places/Africa/Egypt/_Texts/BEVHOP/4B*.html.

over greater distances and functioning as a sunlight reflector during the day.[52]

Prominent Pharaohs of Ptolemaic Egypt

- Ptolemy I Soter (323-282 BCE)

    Ptolemy I Soter, a general under Alexander the Great, assumed control of Egypt after Alexander's demise in 323 BCE and founded the Ptolemaic dynasty. His reign laid the foundations for the Hellenistic culture in Egypt. Ptolemy I's most notable achievement was the urban development of Alexandria, which would become a flourishing hub of commerce and Hellenistic culture. Under his rule, Alexandria emerged as a beacon of learning and culture, attracting scholars and artists from across the Mediterranean world.

- Ptolemy II Philadelphus (285-246 BCE)

    Ptolemy II Philadelphus, the son of Ptolemy I, is renowned for his cultural and economic contributions. He significantly expanded the Library of Alexandria, making it a symbol of scholarly excellence and a repository of vast knowledge. Under his reign, Alexandria witnessed unparalleled cultural growth, becoming the epitome of Hellenistic sophistication. Ptolemy II also focused on strengthening Egypt's economy. He established extensive trade networks and improved agricultural practices, ensuring prosperity and stability in the kingdom.

- Ptolemy III Euergetes (246-222 BCE)

    Ptolemy III Euergetes inherited a stable and prosperous kingdom. He is remembered for his military prowess and expansionist policies. His reign was marked by the successful Third Syrian War, which expanded Egypt's territorial boundaries. Ptolemy III's military campaigns were not only about land acquisition; they also served to secure trade routes and resources, bolstering Egypt's economic and strategic position in the region. His rule was also a period of cultural and economic flourishing, continuing the legacy of his predecessors in supporting the arts, sciences, and economic development.

---

[52] Cartwright, M. (2018, July 24). Lighthouse of Alexandria. Retrieved from Worldhistory.org: https://www.worldhistory.org/Lighthouse_of_Alexandria/.

- Cleopatra VII Philopator (51-30 BCE)

  Cleopatra VII, arguably the most famous of the Ptolemaic rulers, was a figure renowned for her intelligence, political savvy, and charisma. Her reign was marked by tumultuous events and strategic alliances with key Roman figures like Julius Caesar and Mark Antony. Cleopatra's primary goal was to preserve Egypt's independence amid the rising star of Rome. She undertook extensive efforts to revitalize Egypt's economy and restore its former glory. However, her reign culminated in tragedy with her defeat at the Battle of Actium and subsequent suicide, leading to the fall of the Ptolemaic dynasty and Egypt's annexation by Rome.

  Cleopatra's legacy is complex; she is remembered for her attempts to revive Egypt's fortunes and for her role in the dynasty's eventual downfall.

The Ptolemaic era ended with the death of Cleopatra and Egypt's absorption into the Roman Republic. Egypt would continue to be an economic power in the Mediterranean, but it would be a subjected nation. Egypt's glory days were over, at least for the moment.

The Ptolemaic dynasty was a time of intrigue, power, cultural fusion, and dramatic shifts in the political landscape of the ancient world. Egypt navigated an epoch that saw complex political scenarios and economic growth while nurturing a cultural environment that was unparalleled for its time. Ancient Egypt is an amazing saga in the history of humanity.

Chapter 7: Kerma

The Kingdom of Kerma was the earliest known centralized state in the Nile Valley south of Egypt. It was located at the site of the modern city of Kerma in northern Sudan. Kerma's society was characterized by a sophisticated culture with distinctive pottery, architecture, and a system of governance. Kerma was the middleman between Egypt and the African interior. The Kingdom of Kerma eventually succumbed to the expansion of the New Kingdom of Egypt under Thutmose I, and it was incorporated into the Egyptian empire.

<u>Interesting Political Structure</u>

A challenge scholars have with the Kerma civilization is that Kerma did not have a written alphabet, so what we know about this kingdom comes from Egyptian sources. This, of course, means Kerma's recorded history is biased in favor of the Egyptians. We do know that after Kerma absorbed the Sai Island Kingdom, the new state rivaled Egypt in size. The Kingdom of Kerma extended north to the First Cataract of the Nile River. We also know that Kerma was not a primitive assortment of tribes but had a social structure and governance that equaled Egypt.

Women had a role in ruling Kerma and would be co-rulers with their husbands or reign alone as sovereign queens. Provinces within the Kingdom of Kerma played a crucial role in its administrative machinery. Each province was managed by a governor known as a *pesto*, ensuring the smooth functioning of their respective provinces. They had a cadre of subordinates under them, indicating Kerma had a structured bureaucratic system.

These monarchs were not only political leaders but also held religious significance, predominantly worshiping Amun, a deity shared with Egyptian religious traditions. This centralized religious practice underlined the kingdom's governance and cultural identity.

The military strength of Kerma was a testament to its effective governance. Known as "the Land of the Bow," Kerma's soldiers were renowned for their archery skills. In addition, the Kermite warriors used spears, pikes, and khopesh swords. Their military might protected the kingdom from external threats and played a role in its expansionist policies.[53]

The social organization in Kerma, as evidenced by its burial practices, revealed a society where wealth and status extended beyond the ruling class. The cemeteries feature elaborate tombs for the ruling elite, prosperous merchants, and other affluent individuals, suggesting a nuanced social stratification within the kingdom.

Excavations at Kerma.
Lassi, CC BY-SA 4.0 <https://creativecommons.org/licenses/by-sa/4.0>, via Wikimedia Commons; https://commons.wikimedia.org/wiki/File:Kerma_city.JPG

---

[53] Team, E. (2018, November 3). The Kingdom of Kerma (2500-1500 BC). Retrieved from Thinkafrica.net: https://thinkafrica.net/the-kingdom-of-kerma-2500-1500-bc/.

The Economy of Kerma

The kingdom's strategic location on trade routes from central Africa to the Mediterranean allowed its economy to thrive. Kerma's rulers capitalized on their lucrative position by imposing taxes and tolls on trade caravans passing through their territory, contributing significantly to the kingdom's wealth.

Kerma's economy was bolstered by its rich natural resources, including gold, cattle, dairy products, ebony, ivory, and other valuable materials. Exploiting these resources under a centralized governance system facilitated economic prosperity, a key element in sustaining the kingdom's power and influence. Kerma excelled in industries such as metalworking and pottery.

Ancient Kerma bowl.
https://commons.wikimedia.org/wiki/File:Wallpaper_group-p1ng-4.jpg

A Deal with the Devil

Kerma's relationship with ancient Egypt was multifaceted, encompassing both cooperative and antagonistic elements. During the Middle Kerma Period(c. 1990-1725 BCE), which coincided with the Middle Kingdom of Egypt, there was Egyptian military activity in Lower

Nubia that suggests that Kerma was perceived as a significant threat to Egyptian interests. This era saw the construction of major Egyptian fortifications in the Middle Nile Valley, aimed at protecting the Upper Egyptian border against Kerma raids and securing valuable trade routes. The resources that Kerma possessed were highly coveted by Egypt, further fueling the rivalry.

Kerma ordinarily prospered when Egypt was in decline. The Hyksos' seizure of Lower Egypt gave Kerma a chance to gain a considerable regional advantage. The alliance between Kerma and the Hyksos during the Egyptian-Hyksos conflict is a fascinating example of ancient geopolitical maneuvering that influenced the relationships between states.[54]

The Hyksos were a group of Asiatic peoples who established themselves in Lower Egypt. The Second Intermediate Period of Egypt was a time of political fragmentation, and the Hyksos capitalized on Egypt's vulnerability by taking control of the northeastern Nile Delta and forming a significant military and political force in the region.

Previous Egyptian military actions likely influenced Kerma's decision to align with the Hyksos in the region. Kerma might have viewed an alliance with the Hyksos as a strategic move to counterbalance Egyptian power and protect its economic interests. A period of Egyptian internal weakness was an opportunity for Kerma to expand its power. This partnership allowed Kerma to extend its borders into Egypt and attack southern Egypt.

Caught between the Hyksos and Kerma, Egypt was helpless. However, this state of affairs did not last for long.[55]

Kerma's invasion and looting of Egyptian treasures was a humiliation Egypt would not forget. The Egyptian pharaohs of the Seventeenth Dynasty (c. 1580–1550 BCE) waged military campaigns against the Hyksos, who were being supported by Kermite mercenaries. Ahmose I, the founder of Egypt's Eighteenth Dynasty, defeated the Hyksos, ending their period of power. Kerma now became the target of Egyptian revenge.

After the Egyptians expelled the Hyksos, they launched punitive campaigns against Kerma, particularly during the reign of Pharaoh

---

[54] DeMola, P. (2013, March 14). Interrelations of Kerma and Pharaonic Egypt. Retrieved from World History Encyclopedia: https://www.worldhistory.org/article/487/interrelations-of-kerma-and-pharaonic-egypt/.

[55] Team, E. (2018, November 3). The Kingdom of Kerma (2500-1500 BC). Retrieved from Thinkafrica.net: https://thinkafrica.net/the-kingdom-of-kerma-2500-1500-bc/.

Thutmose I. The primary objectives of the Egyptian invasion were to neutralize the threat posed by Kerma, reassert Egyptian control over Nubia, and directly access the region's rich gold resources. Thutmose I's military campaign against Kerma was a calculated effort to remove a growing danger and to reclaim lost territories and resources.

Thutmose I pushed southward into Nubia. The Egyptian army, known for its chariots and archers, advanced toward Kerma's capital, overcoming its defenses. These campaigns culminated in a decisive Egyptian victory in 1504 BCE and the subsequent annexation of the Kingdom of Kerma into the Egyptian empire.

Egyptianization of Kerman

The conquest of Kerma had significant cultural and political consequences. The annexation led to the Egyptianization of the region, with Kerma's unique cultural identity increasingly influenced by Egyptian culture. This included adopting Egyptian religious practices, art forms, and administrative systems. Despite this cultural integration, there were continued instances of rebellion and resistance in the region, but these did not change the fate of the Nubian kingdom. Kerma became a significant province of the Egyptian empire economically, politically, and spiritually.[56]

In Summary

The Kingdom of Kerma stands out as a remarkable example of effective governance and sophisticated provincial administration in the ancient world. Its centralized political structure, efficient local governance, economic prosperity, military strength, and advanced urban planning collectively underscored a civilization that was both complex and progressive for its time.

---

[56] DeMola, P. (2013, March 14). Interrelations of Kerma and Pharaonic Egypt. Retrieved from World History Encyclopedia: https://www.worldhistory.org/article/487/interrelations-of-kerma-and-pharaonic-egypt/.

Chapter 8: Ancient Carthage

We often think of empires as vast expanses of land exploited for their natural resources that are forcibly extracted or cut from the ground. This image includes large occupational garrisons. However, some ancient empires did not consist of expansive provinces; instead, they had extensive coastal outposts. Those imperial nations relied on trade and did not always extend deep into the interior.

Carthage was an ancient empire whose holdings were based on commercial opportunity. Carthage was a maritime power that emphasized trade over other imperial concerns. It had nearly total control over the sea lanes in the western Mediterranean.

<ins>Roots in the Middle East</ins>

Virgil's *Aeneid* spins a tale of how Queen Dido founded Carthage. She supposedly laid out thin strips of ox hide in a semicircle around a hill with the sea forming one side. It is a delightful legend, but this story of the city's founding is pure fiction. The real story of Carthage began in what is now Lebanon; the main characters were the Phoenicians.

The Phoenicians established several colonies across the Mediterranean to facilitate their extensive trade network. Carthage, located on the coast of modern-day Tunisia, was one of these colonies. The city's Phoenician name, Qart Hadasht, meaning "New City," reflected its status as a new venture by these enterprising seafarers. Modern historians and archaeologists have examined both Carthaginian and external records and have largely settled on 814 BCE as the most probable date for Carthage's founding. This is based on a convergence of historical documents and archaeological data despite earlier foundation dates suggested by some ancient sources.

The strategic location of Carthage was crucial to its success. Positioned on the Tunisian coast, it controlled the passage between Sicily and the North African coast, making it an ideal spot for a thriving port and trading center. This advantageous position allowed Carthage to dominate maritime trade routes across the western Mediterranean.[57]

Initially a colony of Tyre, Carthage gradually asserted its independence, especially after Tyre fell to the Babylonians in 573 BCE. Carthage started to establish its colonies and expand its territory in Africa, marking the beginning of its transformation into a mighty empire.[58]

Ties to the Motherland

Carthage retained a strong Phoenician (Punic) identity despite its political independence. The Punic language, a dialect of Phoenician, was spoken in Carthage and remained in use for centuries after the city's fall. This retention of language and cultural practices illustrates the enduring influence of Phoenician culture in Carthage.

Government

Initially, Carthage likely operated under a monarchical system akin to other Phoenician city-states. The kings, while pivotal, did not exercise absolute power and worked alongside a council of advisors known as the Adirim, comprised of wealthy and influential members of society. This council played a crucial role in important state matters, including religion, administration, and military affairs. The Carthaginian senate (known as the *drm*) was a body of influential citizens who served for life,

A significant shift occurred in Carthaginian governance around 480 BCE after the death of King Hamilcar I. This period marked the gradual weakening of the monarchy and the rise of an oligarchic republic characterized by a complex administrative system, checks and balances, and public accountability.

---

[57] Hunt, P. (2024, January 22). Carthage. Retrieved from Britannica.com: https://www.britannica.com/place/Carthage-ancient-city-Tunisia.

[58] Dickinson College Commentaries. (2024, January 22). Carthage: Early History. Retrieved from dcc.dickoinson.edu: https://dcc.dickinson.edu/nepos-hannibal/carthage-early-history.

The Suffetes

At the top of the Carthaginian government were two suffetes, akin to modern-day presidents or prime ministers. They were annually elected by the city's wealthiest and most influential families. Contrary to the absolute monarchies of the time, the suffetes had limited terms and wielded judicial and executive powers. Their roles involved convening the supreme council, submitting issues to the popular assembly, and overseeing trials. This system indicated a plutocratic society where wealth played a crucial role in political participation.

Gerousia and the Magistrates of Five

Aristotle commented on Carthage's constitution and paid particular attention to the Gerousia, a council of elders. Comprising twenty-eight members chosen for life, this council advised magistrates and generals, oversaw justice administration, and served as an appellate court. Its members, selected from distinguished families, were typically over sixty years old, reflecting a system that revered experience and wisdom.

The Magistrates of Five, another essential body in Carthaginian politics, were responsible for justice and finances. Chosen for one-year terms, they played a significant role in the city's governance, particularly in selecting the Supreme Council of One Hundred. Over time, their influence waned, but their early role underscores the complexity of Carthaginian governance.

Aristotle believed Carthage's constitution was more oligarchic than aristocratic, as significant power was concentrated in the hands of a wealthy few. This oligarchy was maintained through a system that enriched sections of the populace, thereby stabilizing the state. The rulers, often wealthy individuals, were chosen not just for their merit but also for their financial status, reflecting a society where economic power translated into political influence.[59]

A distinctive feature of Carthaginian governance was its judicial board of 104 members, which examined the actions of military generals and other officials. This body, comprising lifelong senators, was tasked with assessing military commanders' performance and holding them accountable for the outcomes of their campaigns. A general who lost

---

[59] EDU, W. H. (2023, May 10). Aristotle's Analysis of the Carthaginian Constitution. Retrieved from Worldhistory.edu: https://worldhistoryedu.com/aristotles-analysis-of-the-carthaginian-constitution/.

could expect harsh consequences. Substantial fines might be imposed, and, in extreme cases, crucifixion could be the sentence. The range of penalties for failed campaigns underscores the stringent standards upheld by Carthage. Suicide was a means of avoiding execution.

The administrative structure of the Carthaginian Empire was marked by a degree of autonomy for regional governors, particularly in local governance, while retaining centralized control in military and foreign affairs. This balance of local autonomy and central oversight was crucial for managing Carthage's expansive territories, which spanned parts of North Africa, the Iberian Peninsula, and various Mediterranean islands. While enjoying a measure of self-rule, these regions were obligated to pay tribute and provide military support to Carthage.[60]

Society

Carthage had a popular assembly known as the 'm (ham), which was responsible for voting on issues proposed by the suffetes and senate and for electing officials, including the suffetes, chief priest, treasurer, and military commanders.

Carthaginian citizenship was male-dominated. Women, slaves, and foreigners were not allowed to participate in government. One's social and political life in Carthage was primarily determined by one's status as a citizen, artisan, foreigner, or slave. Artisans, less skilled workers, women, and slaves formed a significant portion of the city's population and contributed to its economic prosperity.[61]

The religious landscape of Carthage, rooted in Phoenician polytheism, significantly influenced its cultural and political life. The empire's artisans and traders dealt in a wide array of commodities, including spices, textiles, and slaves, demonstrating Carthage's economic diversity and its pivotal role in ancient trade networks.[62]

---

[60] Cartwright, M. (2016, June 16). Carthaginian Society. Retrieved from Worldhistory.org: https://www.worldhistory.org/article/908/carthaginian-society/.

[61] Cartwright, M. (2016, June 16). Carthaginian Society. Retrieved from Worldhistory.org: https://www.worldhistory.org/article/908/carthaginian-society/.

[62] LibreTexts. (2024, January 22). 4.2 Ancient Carthage. Retrieved from Libretexts.org: https://human.libretexts.org/Courses/Lumen_Learning/Book%3A_Early_World_Civilizations_(Lumen)/Ch._03_Early_Civilizations_of_Africa_and_the_Andes/04.2%3A_Ancient_Carthage.

The Economy

Economically, Carthage was a powerhouse. Carthage's economy was predominantly driven by its extensive trade network, which spanned from the western Mediterranean to the shores of North Africa and beyond. The city-state's strategic location near the narrow sea passage between Sicily and North Africa placed it at the crossroads of vital maritime routes, facilitating the flow of goods in the Mediterranean. Carthage's harbors buzzed with ships loaded with a variety of goods, highlighting the city's central role in Mediterranean commerce.

A modern illustration of what Carthage once looked like.
damian entwistle, CC BY-SA 2.0 <https://creativecommons.org/licenses/by-sa/2.0>, via Wikimedia Commons;
https://commons.wikimedia.org/wiki/File:Carthage_National_Museum_representation_of_city.jpg

The spirit of exploration was evident in Carthaginian society, as exemplified by navigators like Hanno and Himilco. Their voyages extended Carthage's influence and opened new trade routes. Hanno's exploration along the African coast and Himilco's ventures along the northwestern shores of Europe were not just about discovery but also about establishing new trade connections and colonies.[63]

Carthage was renowned for its diverse trade, dealing in precious metals like gold, silver, tin, and copper alongside everyday commodities like

---

[63] Staff, E. (2021, October 31). Carthaginian Trade: Trade Routes of Ancient Carthage. Retrieved from Carthagemagazine.com: https://carthagemagazine.com/carthaginian-trade-routes-of-ancient-carthage/.

animal skins, wool, and ivory. A significant and darker aspect of their trade was in slaves. The city was also known for its craftsmanship, producing and exporting art, textiles, weapons, and a range of manufactured goods. The Carthaginian navy, a powerful force in the Mediterranean, protected these trade interests and aggressively maintained control over critical maritime routes.[64]

Carthaginian Military

The Carthaginian Empire, known for its formidable presence in the ancient Mediterranean world, presents a picture of military might and sophisticated governance. Following substantial losses in the Sicilian Wars during the 5th and 4th centuries BCE, Carthage resorted to an extraordinary military strategy: the extensive use of mercenary forces.

This pivot was necessitated by the need to replenish their depleted ranks. Carthaginian recruiters scoured the Mediterranean, drawing soldiers from diverse regions, including Gaul, Iberia, Libya, and Greece.

A distinct feature of the Carthaginian military was its use of war elephants and chariots. These elephants, often armored, were deployed to disrupt enemy formations. Despite their formidable presence on the battlefield, their effectiveness was tempered by their unpredictability and the enemy's adaptation strategies. Chariots, used until the 3rd century BCE, were primarily operational in North Africa and southern Spain, highlighting Carthage's adaptation of its military tactics to different terrains.

A blend of heavy infantry formations akin to the Greek phalanx and agile cavalry and skirmishers characterized Carthaginian military strategies. However, the effectiveness of these forces hinged significantly on the commander's ability to galvanize such a varied contingent into a unified, formidable force.[65]

---

[64] Cartwright, M. (2016, June 17). Carthaginian Trade. Retrieved from Worldhistory.org: https://www.worldhistory.org/article/911/carthaginian-trade/.

[65] Cartwright, M. (2916, January 8). Carthaginian Army. Retrieved from Worldhistory.org: https://www.worldhistory.org/Carthaginian_Army/.

The Punic Wars
First Punic War (264-241 BCE)

The western Mediterranean just before the start of the First Punic War.
Harrias, CC BY-SA 4.0 <https://creativecommons.org/licenses/by-sa/4.0>, via Wikimedia Commons; https://commons.wikimedia.org/wiki/File:First_Punic_War_264_BC_v3.png

Carthage was the uncontested power in the western Mediterranean for centuries, but by 300 BCE, that status was beginning to change. The Roman Republic had grown from a small cluster of settlements to become the primary power in the Italian Peninsula. And it was expanding. It would not be long before Carthage and Rome would lock horns.

The First Punic War, a significant and lengthy conflict fought between Rome and Carthage, offers a fascinating study of the interplay of military innovation, economic resources, and strategic diplomacy. Fought primarily for the control of Sicily, the war reshaped the power dynamics in the Mediterranean and laid the groundwork for future Roman expansion.

The Conflict's Origins

The genesis of the First Punic War can be traced to the complicated geopolitical situation in Sicily. The island was a melting pot of cultures and various powers. The Greeks, Carthaginians, and native Sicilian tribes often fought for supremacy. Sicily's strategic location in the center of the Mediterranean made it a valuable naval base and commercial asset. The immediate cause of the war was a conflict involving Messana, a city in Sicily.

The Mamertines, mercenaries of Italian origin, had seized control of the city and faced opposition from King Hieron II of Syracuse. Their appeal for help turned into a diplomatic crisis when both Rome and Carthage responded, thus setting the stage for a broader conflict.[66]

The naval engagements defined the war. Rome went from being a land power to having one of the most powerful navies in the ancient world. Carthage had a long-standing tradition of seafaring and thus had a powerful navy. Rome initially could not stand up to its maritime enemy. However, the Romans demonstrated exceptional adaptability and resourcefulness and embarked on a rapid naval buildup.

They introduced the corvus, a boarding bridge that allowed them to leverage their superior infantry tactics at sea. This innovation was pivotal in their first significant naval victory at the Battle of Mylae in 260 BCE and later at the major Battle of Ecnomus in 256 BCE. While not decisively ending Carthaginian naval dominance, these victories showcased Roman tenacity and ingenuity.

Rome was not the only military innovator. Carthage enlisted the Spartan captain Xanthippus to reorganize its army. Embracing the Macedonian model of combined arms, Xanthippus restructured the army to maximize the effectiveness of its diverse elements, including its cavalry, elephants, and a citizen phalanx.

The Romans under Marcus Atilius invaded North Africa in 256 BCE. The Romans initially enjoyed success, but Xanthippus eventually defeated them. His military reforms resulted in a major victory at the Battle of Bagradas River in 255 BC, where the reformed Carthaginian forces decisively defeated the Romans.[67]

Despite this setback, Rome's determination did not waver. The Romans continued to rebuild their fleet, even after suffering tremendous losses due to storms and battles. The Roman Senate mobilized financial resources and manpower, often through private contributions, and demonstrated a firm commitment to the strategic goals of Rome.

Conversely, Carthage faced several strategic and resource challenges. The Carthaginians' inability to effectively capitalize on their initial naval supremacy was a critical factor. The war significantly strained Carthaginian

---

[66] Editors, H. (2013, June 12). Punic Wars. Retrieved from Hisory.com: https://www.history.com/topics/ancient-rome/punic-wars#first-punic-war-264-241-b-c.

[67] Lynch, P. (201, May 5). A Brutal and Bloody Affair: 6 Key Battles That Decided the First Punic War. Retrieved from Historycollection.com: https://historycollection.com/roman-military-might-6-key-battles-decided-first-punic-war/.

finances and military resources, leading them to seek aid, such as from Ptolemy II of Egypt, without success. The internal political dynamics of Carthage and the challenges of maintaining control over its African and Sicilian territories further complicated their war efforts.

Notable commanders such as Hamilcar Barca for Carthage and Gaius Lutatius Catulus for Rome played significant roles in various stages of the war. Hamilcar's guerilla tactics in Sicily were notable for their effectiveness in a situation where Carthage could not afford a large standing army.[68]

The war concluded with the decisive Battle of the Aegates in 241 BCE, where the Roman fleet achieved a significant victory over the Carthaginians. The subsequent Treaty of Lutatius was a turning point in the Mediterranean power balance. Carthage evacuated Sicily, handed over prisoners, and agreed to pay a substantial indemnity, marking the end of its dominance in the region. Sicily became Rome's first overseas province, signaling the rise of Rome as a major power and setting the stage for further expansion and future conflicts.

Second Punic War (218-201 BCE)

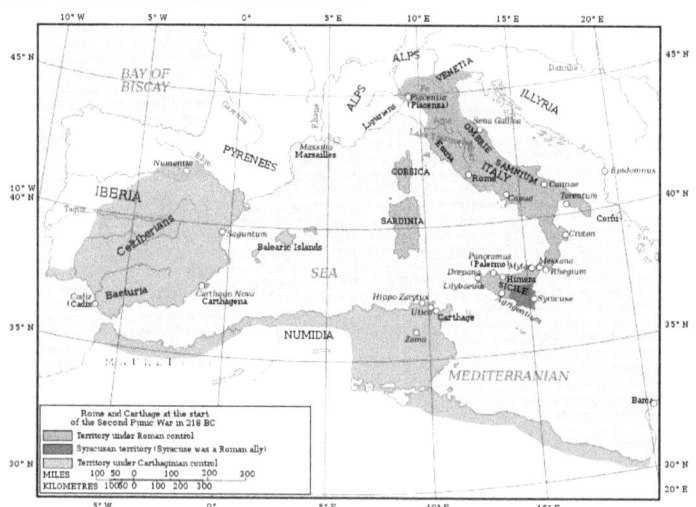

The western Mediterranean in 218 BCE.
Grandiosederivative work: Augusta 89, CC BY-SA 3.0 <https://creativecommons.org/licenses/by-sa/3.0>, via Wikimedia Commons;
https://commons.wikimedia.org/wiki/File:Map_of_Rome_and_Carthage_at_the_start_of_the_Second_Punic_War_2.svg

---

[68] Cartwright, M. (2016, May 26). First Punic War. Retrieved from Worldhistory.org: https://www.worldhistory.org/First_Punic_War/.

A legend describes how Hamilcar Barca made his sons swear vengeance on Rome for the humiliating defeat of Carthage in the First Punic War. Whether or not the father demanded this of his sons, one of them, Hannibal, came close to making his father's wish come true in the Second Punic War.

After the First Punic War, Rome and Carthage rapidly expanded their influence, particularly in the western Mediterranean. Because of trade routes, cities, and mineral sources, this region became the new arena of conflict between the two superpowers. The war's outcome would decide the dominant power in the Mediterranean.

<u>The Initial Spark</u>

The war was the culmination of tensions and strategic ambitions between Rome and Carthage. Carthage, which had been defeated and economically burdened by the First Punic War, sought to rebuild its power. Its focus shifted to Spain, a region abundant in resources, which would be crucial for paying off the heavy indemnity to Rome and restoring Carthaginian wealth.

The Barcid family, particularly Hannibal, played a pivotal role in this expansion. Hannibal's personal motivations, fueled by a desire for revenge against Rome, steered Carthage toward a path of confrontation. Hannibal saw conflict with Rome not just as a political strategy but as a personal and nationalistic crusade.

Rome was expanding its influence in the Mediterranean, especially in Spain. Roman interests in Spain were twofold: it wanted the region's rich metal resources, and it wanted to counter Carthaginian expansion. Rome's decision to confront Carthage was significantly influenced by its fear of a potential alliance between Carthage and the Celts in northern Italy. Such an alliance posed a direct threat to Roman security and interests. The Roman Senate saw the growing Carthaginian influence in Spain and the possible alliance with the Celts as a looming threat that needed to be addressed.[69]

The immediate cause of the Second Punic War was Hannibal's siege and capture of Saguntum, a city-state in eastern Spain allied with Rome. Saguntum's strategic and economic importance to Rome's plans in Spain

---

[69] DailyHistory.org. (2024, January 22). What Were the Causes of the Second Punic War? Retrieved from Dailyhistory.org:
https://www.dailyhistory.org/What_were_the_causes_of_the_Second_Punic_War.

made its fall intolerable to the Roman Senate. The Romans demanded Carthage hand over Hannibal for his transgression. Carthage refused, leading to an official declaration of war.[70]

A Military Genius

Hannibal was a general whose name is synonymous with military brilliance. His strategy was expansive and ambitious. He sought to form a global coalition against Rome by rallying forces that feared Rome's rising dominance. By invading Italy, Hannibal aimed to break the aura of Roman invincibility and attract allies, including Greek city-states and Italian rivals of Rome. However, this plan hinged on a critical factor: gaining and maintaining control of Italy, which proved to be Hannibal's greatest challenge.

Hannibal boldly decided not to invade Italy by taking a coastal route along the Mediterranean. Instead, he marched his army across the Alps. His successful trek through the Alpine passes took the Romans by surprise. The Carthaginian commander scored significant victories over larger armies at Ticino, Treba, and Lake Trasimene.

Hannibal's tactical brilliance was undisputed, as exemplified in the Battle of Cannae. Here, he orchestrated one of history's most remarkable military victories, decimating a vast Roman army and inflicting around fifty thousand Roman casualties. Despite this, he decided not to march directly on Rome after Cannae. This decision has been debated among historians for centuries. This choice, seen as a significant misstep, allowed Rome to regroup and ultimately turn the tide of the war.[71]

Despite his early victories, Hannibal faced insurmountable challenges in Italy. His army, though victorious on the battlefield, lacked the manpower and resources to maintain control over the territories. The inability to capture key port cities like Neapolis (Naples) and Tarentum (Taranto) severely hampered his efforts. Moreover, Rome's naval supremacy meant Hannibal could not receive adequate reinforcements or supplies, gradually diminishing his hold over Italian territories.

---

[70] Jones, M. (2024, January 3). The Second Punic War (218-201 BC): Hannibal Marches Against Rome. Retrieved from Historyooperative.org: https://historycooperative.org/second-punic-war-hannibals-war-in-italy/.

[71] Cartwright, M. (2016, May 29). Second Punic War. Retrieved from Worldhistory.org: https://www.worldhistory.org/Second_Punic_War/.

The Romans Adapt

The Romans realized after Cannae that a set battle with Hannibal was a bad idea and that new solutions needed to be tried. Under the leadership of Fabius Maximus, Rome adopted the Fabian strategy, avoiding direct engagement with Hannibal and instead focusing on cutting off his supply lines and isolating him within Italy. This approach of delay and attrition sought to capitalize on Rome's superior resources and manpower. By engaging Hannibal's allies and attacking where he was not present, Rome slowly started to regain the ground it lost.[72]

As the war progressed, its scope widened beyond Italy. Under leaders like Publius Cornelius Scipio (later known as Scipio Africanus), Rome's strategic offensives in Spain significantly weakened Carthage's position. Scipio's military reforms and his adoption of Hannibal's tactics facilitated Roman dominance in Spain. This expansion of the war and the subsequent loss of Spanish territories were detrimental to Carthage's war efforts. Scipio's advance on Carthage caused the Carthaginians to recall Hannibal to defend the homeland.

The Second Punic War culminated with Roman victories in Africa, notably the Battle of Zama, where Scipio defeated Hannibal, earning him the name Africanus. This marked not only the end of the war but also the decline of Carthaginian power and the rise of Rome as the preeminent power in the Mediterranean. Carthage was a beaten state, reduced to a shadow of what it once was.

Third Punic War (149-146 BCE)

The Third Punic War was the final episode of Rome's and Carthage's prolonged struggle. After Carthage's defeat in the previous wars, it found itself heavily restricted. The peace treaty imposed by Rome after the Second Punic War limited Carthage's military capabilities and imposed a heavy indemnity. Despite these limitations, Carthage began to recover economically, which alarmed many in Rome, who still viewed it as a potential threat.

A key figure in the prelude to the Third Punic War was Cato the Elder, a Roman senator known for ending his speeches in the Roman Senate with the warning, "Carthago delenda est!" ("Carthage must be destroyed!"). His concern was not merely the rantings of an old man.

---

[72] Cartwright, M. (2016, May 29). Second Punic War. Retrieved from Worldhistory.org: https://www.worldhistory.org/Second_Punic_War/.

Carthage's recovery threatened Roman commercial interests, particularly those of senators with investments in North Africa. There was also a deep-seated belief in Roman superiority and the perception of Carthage as a civilization that had to be subdued.

Cato's persistence gradually convinced his peers that eliminating Carthage was in Rome's best interests.

The Start of Hostilities

The immediate cause of the Third Punic War can be traced to a conflict between Carthage and the neighboring state of Numidia, a Roman ally. Carthage's decision to defend itself against Numidian incursions violated the treaty with Rome, which forbade Carthage from waging war without Roman consent. This provided Rome with the pretext to declare war.

Anticipating an easy victory, the Romans were met with staunch resistance from the Carthaginians. The prolonged siege of Carthage, led by Roman commander Scipio Aemilianus, eventually cut off Carthage's access to supplies and reinforcements. The Romans constructed a blockade, effectively sealing the city's fate.

As the siege tightened, the situation within Carthage became desperate. In 146 BCE, the Romans launched a final assault. They systematically broke through the city's defenses, and after intense street fighting, they captured and destroyed Carthage. The city was razed, its population enslaved, and a curse was said to be placed on anyone who tried to resettle the area. Carthage's fall marked the end of the Punic Wars and solidified Roman dominance in the western Mediterranean.[73]

---

[73] Cartwright, M. (2016, May 31). Third Punic War. Retrieved from Worldhistory.org: https://www.worldhistory.org/Third_Punic_War/.

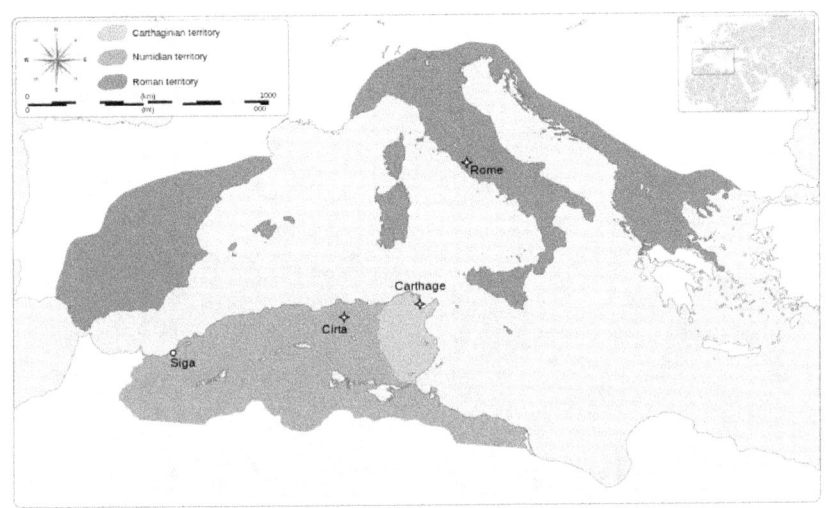

The western Mediterranean in 150 BCE.
Goran tek-en, CC BY-SA 4.0 <https://creativecommons.org/licenses/by-sa/4.0>, via Wikimedia Commons; https://commons.wikimedia.org/wiki/File:Western_Mediterranean_territory,_150_BC.svg

Carthage would rise again, this time as a Roman provincial city. However, the Punic culture, though maligned by Roman writers, showed remarkable resilience, continuing to influence the region long after the fall of Carthage. This trading empire had remarkable success for centuries and displayed a unique ability to regroup and flourish after a major defeat.

In Summary

The Third Punic War, with its dramatic siege and the final destruction of Carthage, stands as a testament to the ancient world's brutality and the lengths to which states went to eliminate their rivals. The war was not just a military conflict but also a culmination of economic, political, and ideological rivalries that had simmered for over a century. Cato the Elder's relentless advocacy for the war underscores the depth of Roman animosity toward Carthage.

The conflict's legacy is complex, marking the zenith of Roman power in the Mediterranean and a tragic end to a once-great civilization. This war serves as a crucial point of study for understanding the dynamics of power, rivalry, and imperialism in the ancient world.

Chapter 9: Empire of Ghana

West Africa had the Empire of Mali and the Songhai Empire, but these were developed after 1000 CE. There was one, however, that predated the millennium, and that was the Empire of Ghana. It is often referred to as Wagadou. It flourished from the 6th to the 13th century CE and occupied what is now southeastern Mauritania and western Mali; it was not part of what is modern Ghana.

The Empire of Ghana's history is rich and complex, characterized by its strategic position as a hub on trans-Saharan trade routes. Its origins, deeply rooted in the early medieval period, remain somewhat enigmatic with various historical interpretations.

The Ghana Empire at its greatest extent.
Luxo, CC BY-SA 3.0 <http://creativecommons.org/licenses/by-sa/3.0>, via Wikimedia Commons; https://commons.wikimedia.org/wiki/File:Ghana_empire_map.png

Monarchy and Aristocracy

The monarchy of the Empire of Ghana is shrouded in mystery, with its origins debated among historians. The first identifiable mention of the imperial dynasty was made in 830 by Muhammad ibn Mūsā al-Khwārizmī, with further details provided in the 11th century by the Córdoban scholar al-Bakri.

Historical accounts, such as those by the 11th-century writer al-Idrisi and the 13th-century writer ibn Said, suggest the rulers of Ghana traced their descent from notable figures, including the clan of the Prophet Muhammad. The king, often referred to as "Ghana," a title meaning "Warrior King," was not just a political leader. He also held a religious and cultural role. There were rules about how to behave in his presence, and these had to be obeyed. The guidelines for behavior suggest a high level of ritual surrounding the monarchy. The king had considerable authority over a precious commodity, as he had exclusive rights to own gold nuggets. The merchants were restricted to gold dust. This policy ensured the king could regulate the gold market and maintain its value.

The kings of Ghana relied heavily on advisors from the aristocracy. The ruling class maintained a luxurious and ceremonious court life. The king was adorned with gold and sat before the people in a high cap decorated with gold, surrounded by pages holding shields and swords decorated with gold and flanked by the sons of vassal kings in splendid garments.[74]

The Economy of the Ghana Empire

The Empire of Ghana traded extensively with its neighbors and distant markets. The empire's capital, Koumbi Saleh, was a commercial hub with a business district inhabited by Berber and Arab merchants.[75]

There were several prominent trade goods the empire had ready for market.

- **Gold**

    The principal product traded in the Ghana Empire was gold. Southern regions of the empire were abundant in gold mines,

---

[74] Cartwright, M. (2019, March 5). Ghana Empire. Retrieved from World History Encyclopedia: https://www.worldhistory.org/Ghana_Empire/.

[75] New World Encyclopedia. (2024, January 27). Ghana Empire. Retrieved from New World Encyclopedia: https://www.newworldencyclopedia.org/entry/Ghana_Empire.

making gold an essential component of Ghana's wealth. As mentioned, the kings of Ghana maintained strict control over gold production and trade.

- **Salt**

  Salt, sourced mainly from the Sahara, was equally vital to the empire's economy. Salt was not only a precious commodity due to its dietary necessity but also because it was indispensable in preserving food in Africa's hot climate.

- **Slaves**

  The Empire of Ghana participated in the slave trade, exchanging slaves for goods with Arab and Berber traders. This aspect of commercial trade was integral to the socioeconomic structures of the region at the time.

The empire traded in various other goods, such as hides, ivory, ostrich feathers, and horses. In exchange, they imported items like textiles, beads, copper, and manufactured goods from the Mediterranean.[76]

Trans-Saharan Trade

The Ghana Empire's economy was predominantly anchored in the lucrative trans-Saharan trade routes. This trade network, enhanced by the introduction of camels to the Sahara Desert in the 3rd century CE, transformed earlier sporadic trade routes into a more structured network running from Morocco to the Niger River. By the 7th century CE, the camel had revolutionized trade across the Sahara, facilitating the transportation of goods across vast desert expanses.

The kings of Ghana played a pivotal role in controlling the trade routes that crisscrossed the empire. They imposed taxes on goods entering and leaving the empire, forming a significant revenue stream that contributed to the kingdom's prosperity. The empire's strategic location, sandwiched between gold fields to the south and salt mines to the north, allowed it to act as a trading hub where these valuable commodities were exchanged.

The taxation system in the Ghana Empire was unique and innovative for its time. Instead of money, the king imposed a percentage fee on importers and exporters that was paid by their trade goods. Consequently, a given trade commodity was often taxed twice, once upon entry and again

---

[76] Cartwright, M. (2019, March 5). Ghana Empire. Retrieved from World History Encyclopedia: https://www.worldhistory.org/Ghana_Empire/.

upon exit from the empire.[77] In addition, Ghana received income from surrounding tributary states. The tax and tribute system added to the coffers of the treasury and helped the empire control trade in commodities such as salt and gold.

Ghana's location in the upper valley of the Niger River permitted it to have access to all the major trade routes. The trade in gold, salt, and slaves passed through the empire along two very important routes:

- The trade route that connected the capital of the Ghana Empire, Koumbi Saleh, to cities like Aoudaghost (Awdaghust) and Sijilmasa.
- The route to the iron ore and gold-producing areas in the south, particularly the Bambuk and Bure regions, which stretched into the empire's heartland.[78]

The wealth generated from trade led to significant urban development within the empire. Koumbi Saleh emerged as a major trade center, boasting numerous mosques and a vibrant mix of different cultures. This economic prosperity further facilitated the development of other urban centers across the empire.[79]

Islam in the Ghana Empire

There was a very significant cultural import that came from the trans-Saharan trade routes: Islam. Muslim merchants and traders introduced the religion to the Empire of Ghana in the 8th century CE, although it did not become a prominent religion until later. Commerce permitted Islam to develop and thrive, even though the monarchy retained its ties with the older religious customs.

The king relied on advisors and officials to manage the economy and monitor trade activities. This included Muslim merchants acting as

---

[77] Cartwright, M. (2019, March 5). Ghana Empire. Retrieved from World History Encyclopedia: https://www.worldhistory.org/Ghana_Empire/.

[78] Cartwright, M. (2019, May 13). The Gold Trade of Ancient & Medieval West Africa. Retrieved from Worldhistory.org: https://www.worldhistory.org/article/1383/the-gold-trade-of-ancient-medieval-west-africa/.

[79] LibreTexts. (2024, January 27). 12.6 The Ghana Empire. Retrieved from LibreTexts.org: https://human.libretexts.org/Courses/Lumen_Learning/Book%3A_Early_World_Civilizations_(Lumen)/Ch._11_African_Civilizations/12.6%3A_The_Ghana_Empire#:~:text=Ghana%E2%80%99s%20economic%20development%20and%20eventual%20wealth%20was%20linked,expansion%20to%20.

interpreters and officials, signifying the empire's economic complexity and its integration into the broader Islamic world.

Numerous scribes and ministers in the bureaucracy were Muslim, allowing them to have an essential role in the daily functioning of the empire. Islam brought with it the Arabic language, Islamic teachings, and scientific knowledge. The cities benefited culturally from the influx of learning that came with the Muslim merchants.[80]

The economic prosperity of the Empire of Ghana was also enhanced by its association with Muslim merchants. Muslim traders, particularly the Sanhaja Berbers, were central to the trans-Saharan trade network, facilitating the exchange of gold from West Africa for salt and other goods from North Africa.[81]

The kings of Ghana, while predominantly adhering to traditional religious beliefs, demonstrated a remarkable tolerance toward Islam, allowing for a symbiotic relationship between the two cultures. This approach of tolerance underlines the pragmatic nature of Ghana's rulers, who sought to harness the administrative and intellectual expertise of Muslims to enhance governance. Their understanding and respect for another religion demonstrate how cultures and religions can interact to their mutual benefit and improve the stability and prosperity of a nation.

The Fall of the Empire

In spite of great economic prosperity and a tolerant society, the Empire of Ghana eventually collapsed. It was not because of one catastrophe; a series of disasters hit Ghana. The ruling class was unable to come up with solutions that could have saved this civilization.

These were the principal reasons for Ghana's demise:
- External Invasions and Wars

    Regrettably, Islam brought challenges along with benefits. In 1076, the Almoravids, a Berber Muslim dynasty from the Sahara, invaded and defeated Ghana's army. This defeat weakened the empire's military strength and accelerated the spread of Islam,

---

[80] Encyclopedia.com. (2024, January 27). Empire of Ghana. Retrieved from Encyclopedia.com: https://www.encyclopedia.com/history/encyclopedias-almanacs-transcripts-and-maps/empire-ghana.

[81] Lane, M. (2024, January 21). How Did Muslims and Non-Muslims Interact in Ghana. Retrieved from Ncesc.com: https://www.ncesc.com/geographic-faq/how-did-muslims-and-non-muslims-interact-in-ghana/.

further exacerbating internal religious tensions. Following this, the Susu Kingdom attacked in 1203, eroding Ghana's military and economic authority in the region. These military defeats were crucial in diminishing the empire's ability to control its territories and maintain its economic dominance.

The final collapse of the Empire of Ghana can be attributed to the rise of the Mali Empire, which gradually became more prominent in the region. In 1240, the Mali emperor, Sundiata, conquered what was left of the Ghana Empire and incorporated it into the Mali Empire. This marked the end of Ghana as a political entity and the rise of a new regional power.

- Economic Changes

Ghana relied heavily on trade and the taxes derived from trans-Saharan trade. New routes were developed that bypassed Ghana. Additionally, the natural environment became a challenge.

- Climate Changes

Significant climatic changes happened in the 12th century, and the region became gradually drier. This prolonged drought affected agricultural production, undermining the empire's ability to sustain itself and its population. The agricultural decline would have a ripple effect on the economy, further destabilizing the already weakened empire.[82]

- Dissension within the Borders

Other internal factors were political instability and social unrest. The empire faced internal conflicts and growing dissatisfaction with the central government. There was a desire among member states for independence or alignment with other rising powers, like Mali.

Additionally, the empire grappled with the inherent conflict between traditional beliefs and the growing influence of Islam. These religious and cultural tensions weakened the social and political cohesion of the empire.

The final blows Sundiata inflicted were on an imperial state whose structure was shaky and whose foundations had been severely weakened.

---

[82] Cartwright, M. (2019, March 5). Ghana Empire. Retrieved from World History Encyclopedia: https://www.worldhistory.org/Ghana_Empire/.

The empire was no longer able to resist. What was left of the empire was incorporated into the Mali Empire. Ghana ceased to be a political entity, and the new authority in the region grew increasingly more powerful.[83]

<u>In Summary</u>

The Empire of Ghana is a remarkable saga in the history of West Africa, showing how control over strategic trade routes and resources with high consumer demand can sustain a powerful state. The empire's sophisticated economy and tax system facilitated its rise to power and prosperity while connecting West Africa to the rest of the medieval world. The decline of Ghana marked the end of an amazing empire located in the desert sands.

This discussion of Ghana is intended to remind the reader that the northern coast of Africa and the Nile Valley were not the only places where civilization flourished on the continent.

---

[83] Soto, N. (2024, January 16). Who Destroyed the Ghana Empire. Retrieved from Ncesc.com: https://www.ncesc.com/geographic-faq/who-destroyed-the-ghana-empire/.

Chapter 10: Slavery in Ancient Africa

An honest history of Africa must mention slavery. Slavery has plagued the continent for centuries and spawned the trans-Saharan slave trade and the later transatlantic slave trade.

The history of slavery in ancient Africa is complex and was shaped by the cultures and practices of various African civilizations. Forms of slavery included debt bondage, military slavery, the enslavement of war captives, and domestic servitude.

- Debt Slavery

  People who were unable to repay debts would be forced into servitude. Unlike other forms of slavery, debt slavery was often seen as a temporary and more humane solution for debtors. Debt slavery was common in West Africa among the Yoruba, Ga, Ewe, and Edo cultures. It was also common in ancient Egypt.

- Military Slavery

  Military slavery involved the recruitment and utilization of enslaved individuals as soldiers. This practice was prominent in certain African states, where enslaved soldiers formed an integral part of the military force. These individuals could rise to significant ranks and often held considerable power. In ancient Egypt, slaves were used as soldiers and guards. A later example would be the Mamluks, who eventually overthrew the Ayyubid dynasty and became the rulers of Egypt.[84]

- Enslavement of War Captives

    The capture and enslavement of prisoners of war was a widespread practice in ancient Africa. This form of slavery was the outcome of military conflicts and raids, and both Carthage and Egypt used prisoners of war as forced laborers. The slave trade in West Africa encouraged the use of raids and wars to gather a supply of prisoners to be sold.

Slavery in Ancient Egypt

A major source of enslaved people in ancient Egypt were prisoners captured from conquered lands during military expeditions. The victors often took captives back to Egypt to serve as slaves. Criminals and convicted individuals were sometimes sentenced to slavery as a form of punishment, and individuals could become slaves due to debts they could not repay.

Humans were a commercial commodity, and Egyptians would trade luxury items for captured humans. Slaves could also be acquired as gifts or tribute.

Slavery was hereditary in ancient Egypt, meaning children born to enslaved individuals would also be considered slaves.

A Slave's Life in Egypt

Slaves in ancient Egypt performed various tasks based on their assigned roles. They worked in agriculture, tending to fields and livestock, and in construction. Although slaves likely were involved in some building projects, modern-day scholars do not believe they worked on monumental structures like the pyramids due to the evidence of organized living quarters, a regular diet, and access to medical care and other necessities.

The living conditions of slaves varied depending on their roles and the social status of their owners. Of course, the working conditions could be harsh, but slaves did have certain legal rights and could own property.[85] Carthage allowed slaves to run businesses for their masters.

---

[84] Britannica, E. o. (2023, November 30). Mamluk. Retrieved from Britannica.com: https://www.britannica.com/topic/Mamluk.

[85] Historyrise.com. (2023, December 24). Facts About Ancient Egypt Slaves: Historical Insights! Retrieved from Historyrise.com: https://historyrise.com/facts-about-ancient-egypt-slaves/.

Slavery in the Kingdoms of Kerma and Punt

A significant challenge in analyzing slavery in the cultures of Kerma and Punt is the lack of records. We have to wait for archaeology to uncover information about the practice of enforced labor in these civilizations. We know that Egypt had a significant influence on the region. It is possible that slavery was conducted with customs that emulated those of the land of the pharaohs.

Slavery in Carthage

In Carthage, slavery had profound socioeconomic impacts. It facilitated large-scale agricultural and architectural projects, bolstered military campaigns, and was a cornerstone in trade relations.

Slavery was central to the Carthaginian economy, something that mirrored the practices of many other ancient civilizations. The enslaved were primarily conquered peoples and those bought from slave markets. The integration of enslaved people into Carthaginian society reflected the city's many military conquests and active participation in regional trade, including the slave trade.[86]

Slaves were employed in numerous professions. These might be domestic services or skilled labor in agriculture, craftsmanship, and maritime trade. Slaves were even used in the Carthaginian navy during the Punic Wars. The larger workshops in Carthage, which produced a range of goods from pottery to metalwork, employed both citizens and slaves. The presence of slaves in these workshops highlights their integral role in the Carthaginian economy.

The economic structure of Carthage was heavily dependent on slave labor. Slaves played a crucial role in the city's manufacturing sector, including textiles, pottery, and metalwork production. In agriculture, slave labor was instrumental in maintaining Carthage's agricultural output. Slaves were an essential part of the workforce. Slave labor allowed Carthaginian landowners to maximize agricultural production, contributing to the city's overall economic prosperity.

---

[86] LibreTexts. (2024, January 22). 4.2 Ancient Carthage. Retrieved from Libretexts.org: https://human.libretexts.org/Courses/Lumen_Learning/Book%3A_Early_World_Civilizations_(Lumen)/Ch._03_Early_Civilizations_of_Africa_and_the_Andes/04.2%3A_Ancient_Carthage.

The Status of Enslaved People

The relationship between slaves and their owners in Carthage was not uniformly oppressive. In some situations, slaves were allowed to run businesses for their masters with a degree of autonomy. This implies that while slaves were not free, they could engage in economic activities independently. Some slaves were even able to accumulate personal wealth, albeit likely under the oversight of their masters.

Despite slave revolts in the 4th century BCE, there is little evidence of widespread or continual unrest among the slave population in Carthage. This lack of significant unrest could be attributed to various factors, including the possibility of earning freedom or better treatment than other contemporary slave-owning societies.[87]

Slavery in Aksum

Slavery was an integral part of social and economic life in Aksum, as it was in many ancient societies. Slaves were primarily drawn from the Nilotic groups of Ethiopia's southern hinterland and the Oromo people. War captives constituted another considerable source of slaves. These individuals were assimilated into various societal roles, serving as concubines, bodyguards, servants, and treasurers. Despite the scarcity of detailed records, it's clear that slavery was deeply embedded in Aksum's social fabric.

The port of Adulis was a renowned hub for the slave trade, connecting the empire to a global market for slaves for many centuries. The involvement in such trade networks suggests external trade influenced the supply and demand of enslaved people as much as internal needs.

Aksum had a feudal society, with land ownership and agriculture playing pivotal roles. Slaves were instrumental in this system, working the land alongside free peasants. The empire's reliance on agriculture for its economy, with principal crops being grains like wheat and barley, necessitated a labor force that included slaves.

Aksum converted to Christianity in the 4th century CE. It is plausible that Christian morals and ethics might have influenced the treatment of slaves, but concrete evidence is limited.[88]

---

[87] Cartwright, M. (2016, June 16). Carthaginian Society. Retrieved from Worldhistory.org: https://www.worldhistory.org/article/908/carthaginian-society/.

[88] New World Encyclopedia. (2024, January 25). Aksumite Empire. Retrieved from

The Ancient African View of Slavery

We know about the slave trade in Africa from historical records, but many accounts date from after 1000 CE. Later West African empires, like the Ghana Empire, were deeply involved in the trans-Saharan slave trade, and later kingdoms were active participants in the transatlantic slave trade. However, the roots of slavery go back centuries before the Empire of Mali or the arrival of the Europeans. The early days are worth investigating.

The uniqueness of African slavery lay in its integration with kinship and societal structures. Unlike chattel slavery in the Americas, African slavery often involved complex relationships with certain rights and freedoms for the enslaved. The degree of leniency and the nature of treatment varied, often influenced by the slave's origin and whether they were born into slavery or acquired through purchase or war.

African societies utilized slavery as a means to enhance personal influence and societal connections, particularly in regions where land ownership was not a concept. This practice entrenched slaves within the master's lineage, occasionally allowing their offspring to ascend to significant societal positions, even to the chieftaincy. However, this integration did not erase the inherent stigma, and clear distinctions between enslaved people and the master's blood relatives were often maintained.

Moral opposition to slavery was nuanced. The indigenous forms of slavery, which were often less severe than the chattel slavery later established in the Americas, did not always elicit the same level of moral outrage. In some African societies, slavery was justified through cultural and religious beliefs. The enslavement of war captives, for instance, was often seen as a natural consequence of conflict. Moreover, the integration of slaves into the master's lineage in some cultures provided a form of social mobility, albeit limited, blurring the lines between pure exploitation and social integration.

While there was no widespread moral opposition to slavery akin to the later abolitionist movements, African societies exhibited a range of attitudes toward slavery, from acceptance as a social norm to forms of resistance and adaptation in response to internal and external changes.

NewWorldEncuclopedia.org: https://www.newworldencyclopedia.org/entry/Aksumite_Empire.

In Summary

Slavery in ancient Africa was not a monolith but rather a spectrum of practices influenced by cultural, economic, and environmental factors. Each civilization, from Egypt, Carthage, and Punt to Kerma and Kush, had its own distinct forms of slavery, shaped by its unique circumstances and interactions with neighboring regions. Understanding these nuances provides valuable insights into the complex account of ancient African history.

Conclusion

"Take up the White Man's burden—
Send forth the best ye breed—
Go bind your sons to exile
To serve your captives' need;
To wait in heavy harness
On fluttered folk and wild—
Your new-caught, sullen peoples,
Half devil and half child.
Take up the White Man's burden—
In patience to abide,
To veil the threat of terror
And check the show of pride;
By open speech and simple,
An hundred times made plain.
To seek another's profit,
And work another's gain.
Take up the White Man's burden—
And reap his old reward:
The blame of those ye better,
The hate of those ye guard—

The cry of hosts ye humour
(Ah, slowly!) toward the light:—
'Why brought ye us from bondage,
Our loved Egyptian night?'"

The White Man's Burden by Rudyard Kipling[89]

Europe carved up Africa in the late 19th century, justifying a naked land grab by insisting that the continent needed the gift of civilization that only it, Europe, could bestow. Africa was caught in a moment of weakness, and its nations could not adequately combat the technological and financial might of Great Britain, France, Germany, Italy, and Belgium. Africans would become part of empires whose people looked different and spoke alien languages.

The arrogance and condescension of these new masters was palpable. Europeans initially ignored the ruins of ancient imperial dynasties and assumed the native populations were primitive tribes or religious fanatics. Writers speculated that the Portuguese or Chinese built Great Zimbabwe, a city in Zimbabwe that is believed to have served as a capital during the Iron Age. Such notions stem from biased observations that the local population was incapable of academic discourse or building massive stone structures. It would take years of archaeological excavations before those ideas were dismissed as false.[90]

Ancient Africa was more than jungle and half-naked savages. European hegemony could not hide the continent's contributions to humanity over the centuries.

Metallurgy and Chemistry

The Age of Metals underscores Africa's invaluable contributions to metallurgy and chemistry. The skillful manipulation of metals by the Egyptians and the later Edo people, exemplified in artifacts like the Benin Bronzes, showcases advanced techniques in metalworking. Moreover, the ancient practice of alchemy in Egypt, which significantly influenced the Greeks and Asians, is a precursor to modern chemistry. This early

---

[89] Kipling, Rudyard (1899). The White Man's Burden. https://historymatters.gmu.edu/d/5478/.

[90] Koutonin, M. (2016, August 18). Lost Cities: Racism and Ruins—The Plundering of Great Zimbabwe. Retrieved from Theguardian.com:
https://www.theguardian.com/cities/2016/aug/18/great-zimbabwe-medieval-lost-city-racism-ruins-plundering.

knowledge of chemistry and metallurgy, vital to human progress, underscores Africa's role in advancing scientific knowledge.

Astronomy

African civilizations made groundbreaking strides in astronomy. The inhabitants of Nabta Playa created one of the world's first astronomical observatories, predating Stonehenge. Their Rock Calendar was a significant innovation for tracking celestial movements and is reportedly older than Stonehenge. Furthermore, the Dogon people of Mali were known for their detailed understanding of astronomical phenomena, notably the Sirius star system. These achievements in astronomy not only highlight Africa's scientific prowess but also its contribution to our knowledge of the cosmos.[91]

Egyptians integrated astronomy into their culture, with the best example being the Great Pyramid of Giza. The pyramid was aligned with celestial bodies. Its air shafts, pointing toward stars like Sirius and the Orion constellation, underscore the significance of these heavenly bodies in Egyptian mythology and religious practices. In addition, the alignments were used to mark the times of the year for planting and harvesting.[92]

Education

The Library of Alexandria comes to attention immediately when thinking about the advancement of knowledge. However, it was not the only African library; Alexandria was just one of many intellectual centers on the continent. The city of Timbuktu, part of the later Mali Empire, became a significant center of Islamic learning. Timbuktu had the University of Sankore, the Sidi Yahya Mosque, and the Djinguereber Mosque. Another academic center of ancient Africa was the Axumite imperial church. These prove the colonial notion of Africa being an illiterate continent false.

Mathematics

The mathematical practices of ancient Africa have contributed significantly to the global understanding of mathematics. An astonishing example of the use of mathematics in pre-modern Africa is the Lebombo

---

[91] Afrikaiswoke.com. (2023, September 15). 10 African Contributions to Civilization. Retrieved from Afrikaiswoke.com: https://www.afrikaiswoke.com/african-contributions-to-civilization/.

[92] Shuttleworth, M. (2024, January 28). Egyptian Astronomy. Retrieved from Explorable.com: https://explorable.com/egyptian-astronomy.

bone. This baboon fibula, discovered in the Lebombo Mountains of southern Africa and carved in prehistoric times, has twenty-nine deliberate notches that possibly represent an ancient lunar phase counter.

The Yoruba tribe of Nigeria developed a numeration system, a base-20 system that integrated subtraction for number expression and was operational up to two hundred. This system demonstrated abstract mathematical reasoning tailored to the needs of the tribe.[93]

We usually think of Mesopotamia and India regarding numbers, but Egypt left a mathematical legacy that significantly advanced the study of mathematics. A non-positional decimal system characterized ancient Egyptian mathematics. Their numerals, represented by distinct hieroglyphs for each power of ten up to one million, were effective for their needs and revealed an early abstraction of quantitative concepts.

The Rhind Mathematical Papyrus provides evidence of the practical nature of Egyptian mathematics. Along with other scrolls, the texts consider problems of land measurement, construction, and resource distribution.

The Egyptians showed an advanced understanding of algebra and used its methods to solve linear equations and arithmetic progressions. Their problem-solving techniques, including the method of false position, show an ability to approach mathematical problems systematically, showcasing advanced mathematical thinking. They had a deep understanding of geometry, calculating areas and volumes and applying these calculations to real-world problems.[94]

Medicine

Medicine in Africa goes beyond shaman chants and plants. Ancient African civilizations were pioneers in the field of medicine. They blended empirical knowledge and traditional practices to promote health and healing.

Procedures performed in ancient Africa before they were known in Europe include inoculations, mummification, limb traction, bone settings,

---

[93] Anplifyafrica.org. (2024, January 28). Africa Made Math: The Original Mathematicians. Retrieved from Anplifyafrica.org: https://www.amplifyafrica.org/africa-made-math-the-original-mathematicians/.

[94] Historyrise.com. (2023, December 25). What Advancements Did Ancient Egypt Make in Math and Science. Retrieved from Historyrise.com: https://historyrise.com/advancements-in-ancient-egyptian-math-science/.

brain surgeries, skin grafting, the filling of dental cavities, the installation of false teeth, anesthesia, and tissue cauterization. African cultures also performed surgeries under antiseptic conditions.

Ancient African societies employed many medical procedures that are used today. They utilized plants with salicylic acid for pain, kaolin for diarrhea, and extracts to kill gram-positive bacteria. Some plants had anti-cancer properties, could induce abortion, or were used to treat malaria. Africans discovered compounds like ouabain, capsicum, physostigmine, and reserpine, which had significant medical applications.[95]

Architecture and Engineering

The architectural and engineering feats of ancient African civilizations are a testament to their sophistication. From the towering pyramids and obelisks of Egypt to the grand stone complexes in Zimbabwe and Mozambique, African societies demonstrated advanced construction and urban planning knowledge. The stone structures of Great Zimbabwe are a testament to the ingenuity and skill of its builders. The later Empire of Mali, particularly its renowned city of Timbuktu, boasted impressive architectural structures, including grand palaces, mosques, and universities. These structures were not only marvels of engineering but also centers of cultural and intellectual exchange.[96]

Further Study

What we now know about Africa prior to the arrival of the Europeans refutes the colonial ideas of an uneducated continent. Nevertheless, there is still much more to learn about Africa. There are many mysteries waiting to be solved and secrets waiting to be uncovered. The investigation should be multi-faceted and include archaeological excavations, genetic research, and linguistic studies. This approach not only aids in constructing a more comprehensive historical narrative but also ensures that the research is inclusive and respects the region's cultural heritage.

Archaeological endeavors in regions like Great Zimbabwe and the kingdoms of the Sahel have the potential to uncover artifacts and

---

[95] Blatch, S. (2013, February 1). Great Achievements in Science and Technology in Ancient Africa. Retrieved from Asbmb.org: https://www.asbmb.org/asbmb-today/science/020113/great-achievements-in-stem-in-ancient-africa

[96] Exponent, E. (2023, November 14). Ancient Africa's Contributions to Modern Science and Built Environment. Retrieved from The African Exponent: https://www.africanexponent.com/ancient-africas-contributions-to-modern-science-and-built-environment/.

structures that can provide insights into these societies' daily lives, social structures, and technological advancements. Great Zimbabwe's buildings, with their intricate designs and construction techniques, could offer clues about the engineering skills of central Africa. Similarly, excavations in the Nile Valley and other historical sites could reveal new aspects of trade networks and cultural exchanges within Africa. Recent studies have identified traces of ancient African empires in the DNA of contemporary African populations. Further investigations will help explain the migration and interactions of people across the continent.

Linguistic analysis can reveal aspects of social organization, religious beliefs, culture, and the intellectual lives of civilizations that no longer exist. Breaking the language code of Great Zimbabwe may lead to some startling discoveries that could destroy contemporary ideas. That was the case with the Maya civilization. Initially, scholars thought the Maya were a peaceful society of stargazers. Their ability to finally interpret the glyphs found in Maya temples and monuments showed the people engaged in almost continuous warfare. What little we know about Great Zimbabwe might be wrong, and we must be ready to accept that possibility.

The religious beliefs, artistic expressions, and cultural practices of ancient African societies still need to be fully understood. Excavating worship sites, burial grounds, and artistic creations could offer a window into these societies' spiritual and cultural life. Looking further into the trans-Saharan trade, Indian Ocean trade networks, and intra-African trade dynamics could give us better insights into the continent's role in the global economy. Analyzing historic climate change has allowed us to better understand decisions made by the Maya and Khmer civilizations. Researching how ancient African empires adapted and responded to environmental fluctuations can offer insights into farming, climate change responses, and the impact of human activities on the environment.

The history of ancient African empires is a saga of human achievement and interaction. Further research of these societies is not just an academic pursuit but also a quest for a more inclusive and comprehensive understanding of human history. By exploring unanswered questions and uncharted territories, we stand to gain a deeper appreciation of the continent's rich heritage and its significant contributions to the story of humanity.

Part 2: Ancient Carthage

An Enthralling Guide to the Phoenicians and Carthaginian Civilization

Introduction

In 146 BCE, under the command of Scipio Aemilianus, the Romans completed the utter destruction of one of antiquity's greatest and most powerful cities and empires. The final few holdouts, barricaded in the inner part of the city, set the buildings on fire and threw themselves into the flames. It was a tragic end to a civilization that had once controlled much of the Mediterranean and whose influence and history stretched far from the center of what would one day become the nation of Tunisia in North Africa. The city was called Carthage, and the people were the ancient Carthaginians.

This book will tell the story of the origin, rise, and eventual downfall of Carthage. It is a great story and involves some of the most well-known people and places of the ancient world. The history of Carthage has long been overshadowed by its most famous rival, Rome. And it is through the Romans that much of Carthage's history is known. However, thanks to modern archaeological work and careful study of ancient sources, a fuller picture has emerged. Roman histories often attempt to paint Carthage as destined for failure, always as the perpetual enemy, but Carthage had many successes, great leaders, and a vibrant civilization. It was incredibly important for trade between the eastern and western Mediterranean and was the dominant power of the western Mediterranean up until the end of the 3rd century BCE. In fact, it is hard to imagine Rome becoming what it was without Carthage's empire first blazing the trail of conquests in North Africa, Sicily, the Iberian Peninsula, and even Italy. Would we remember Rome if not for the Carthaginians, a rivalry that spawned the greatest power of ancient Europe, North Africa, and Asia Minor?

The most visible remains of this once-great city are huge walls that were built in the 5th century BCE, which ancient sources claim once surrounded Carthage with a circumference of nineteen miles. We can also see two artificial harbors built sometime in the 3rd century BCE. One harbor housed all of the trade vessels that came to and from this trade center, and the other harbor was for Carthage's mighty navy. Archaeologists continue to excavate extensive burial grounds.

The remains of this metropolis are now silent, lying just north of the Tunisian capital of Tunis. The aged remains of beautiful mosaics bear testament to the once-lavish lives of the citizens who lived in large estates. Terracotta masks indicate the importance of theater and entertainment to the sophisticated populace. They loved music, poetry, commerce, food, wine, and even war when it was called for. They were not unlike their counterparts in Syracuse, Greece, Egypt, and Rome.

What had begun as a trading colony founded by the Phoenicians grew into a mighty empire. But it eventually fell into ruin. During the Roman Empire, Carthage was made an imperial city with a forum and baths; it went on to play an important role in the spread of Christianity in North Africa. Today, however, much of its glory has faded, and history books tend to only mention it in relation to the growth of the Roman Republic, but Carthage was so much more than that.

Chapter 1: The Phoenicians

In the waters off the coast of modern-day Lebanon, Syria, and northern Israel live a variety of sea snails known in ancient times as *murex*. These snails produce mucus that was used in the labor-intensive production of a certain kind of purple dye that was prized throughout the ancient world and came to signify wealth and a high rank. The people who lived in this area and extracted the purple dye were called Phoenicians by the ancient Greeks, which signified the color purple or crimson. In the forests of these lands also grew cedar trees. These two products, the purple dye and the cedar timber, became highly sought after in the ancient world.

The Phoenicians developed into fiercely independent and competitive city-states, much like the city-states of Greece. Chief among these cities was Arwad, Byblos, Sidon, and Tyre. We do not know what they called themselves or if they truly thought of themselves as a distinct ethnic group or nation. Early scholarship on the Phoenicians was done in the 17th century, and it was generally believed that their civilization emerged around 3000 BCE and that it lasted, in some form or another, until Alexander the Great conquered the Levant in the 3rd century BCE.

Their power did not go far inland and was instead focused on the sea. They were an early maritime power in the eastern Mediterranean and established trade routes between Asia Minor, Greece, Egypt, and beyond. They established trading colonies around the Mediterranean and are considered the dominant commercial power in the area from the Late Bronze Age to the 9th century BCE. Among their great accomplishments was the founding of a trade colony they called Carthage, which came to be a great empire in its own right. Their trade routes are believed to have fostered the foundations of Western civilization. Their contributions to world history cannot be understated, as they included advancements in trade and seafaring and one of the oldest alphabets in the world.

Did the people of the Levantine coastal cities, whom the Greeks called Phoenicians, consider themselves a distinct ethnic group? Were they, in any way, a unified people with a shared history, language, and culture? They were certainly not a unified kingdom like the people of the upper Nile or Mesopotamia, who were all under the rule of a single pharaoh or king. So, were they more like the Greek city-states, which were independent but shared a type of national identity and shared historical origins? Is it more accurate to say that instead of the Phoenicians founding Carthage, Carthage encouraged the idea of the Phoenicians being a nation for their own gain? The evidence is scarce and unclear.

A distinction must be made between the various faces of Phoenicia, specifically the people, the place, the language, and the culture. The Phoenician language is an extinct Semitic language that was originally spoken by the people around the cities of Tyre and Sidon in modern-day Lebanon. It became a common language spoken in trade around the Mediterranean during the Late Bronze Age and Iron Age. Colonies spoke their own dialects of Phoenician. Punic was the Phoenician dialect spoken in the city of Carthage, which is believed to have been a trading colony founded by people from Tyre. The identification of a Phoenician people, territory, or culture is a little harder to determine.

The Greek sources take us back to the realm of mythology to explain things. One of the earliest mentions of Phoenicia is the tale of Agenor, whose beautiful daughter, Europa, was seduced and kidnapped by Zeus. Some of the sources say Agenor was the king of Phoenicia and lived in the city of Tyre. Europa was picking flowers by the sea shore and Zeus, who always watched mortal women with a lustful eye, decided he wanted to have her for his own. He transformed himself into a majestic bull and persuaded Europa to climb on his back. He then swam out to sea, eventually reaching the island of Crete.

Agenor tasked his sons with locating what had happened to their sister, but it was an impossible task, as they could not discover a secret that Zeus wanted to keep. One son, Cadmus, traveled to mainland Greece and founded the city of Thebes. The sources, however, confuse the story and sometimes say that another son, Phoenix, traveled to the Levant and founded a land he called Phoenicia after himself. Also, the tales sometimes say that Europa was actually the daughter of Phoenix and not Agenor.

While Greek and Roman sources clearly identify Phoenician people as a distinct ethnic group, it seems likely that the people they called Phoenicians did not really see themselves as such. The historical record, specifically stone steles and grave markers, seem to indicate that these people typically identified themselves as belonging to a certain city. Someone would be called a "son of Tyre," for instance, which meant they hailed from that city. Ancient writings speak of fine goods being made by Sidonian craftsmen or fabric woven by Sidonian women. When the Phoenicians are spoken of as an ethnic group, they are usually described in a negative light, as they are depicted as a barbarous, greedy, bloodthirsty, and effeminate group of people. But, of course, these thoughts were written by rivals and enemies and should not be taken as accurate descriptions.

Levantine similarities might not be enough for the people of various cities to consider themselves one nation, but they are nonetheless noteworthy. The Phoenicians were all known for their maritime expertise. The various city-states of the Levant all had similar geographical features: a shoreline to the west and mountains to the east. Thus, it was only natural that they turned to the sea for their livelihood. While Egyptians and the people of Mesopotamia were sailing up and down their respective rivers on flat-bottom boats, the Phoenicians invented curved hulls that allowed them to venture into the sea more easily. The impression is that they were commercially minded from the very beginning. They harvested the sea snails that gave them the famous purple dye and obtained the cedarwood that became so important to Egypt and eventually the Assyrians.

However, the Phoenicians went beyond this and traveled to islands like Cyprus, Crete, and Kos, where they traded for copper, iron, pottery, and tin. They traded with Greece for olives. In doing so, they also traded cultural ideas. It is believed the Phoenicians gave the Greeks the basis for the Greek alphabet. They took on aspects of other cultures as well. Phoenician art is particularly eclectic and often contains Egyptian and Greek motifs side by side. This has led some to believe that they lacked an artistic style of their own, but careful inspection reveals that they did add their own flair to their art, often adding careful symmetrical details that proclaimed a work as being distinctly Phoenician.

In the realm of belief, the Phoenician religion is much more specific to a city-state. They worshiped Baal, a deity known throughout the Fertile Crescent, especially to the Canaanites. He was a primary god often associated with fertility. However, the Phoenicians in Tyre, for example, worshiped the "Baal of Tyre," who was more commonly known as Melqart and also "Baal of the Rock," which relates to one of the mythical founders of Tyre. One story says that there were two floating rocks off the coast of the Levant and a burning olive tree that had a snake wrapped around its trunk and an eagle in its branches that were not consumed by the flames. Melqart caused the two islands to remain in place as a favor to the mermaid Tyros and founded a city there that he named after her. The spot where the olive tree stood became a shrine to Melqart, who was worshiped in the city for millennia. Similarly, in the city of Byblos, they worshiped "Baalat Gubal," or the Lady of Byblos.

However, Phoenicians also seemed to worship El, the father or king of the gods, who was often seen as being equivalent to Kronos of Greek mythology. El was revered as the ancestor of all the gods in the Phoenician pantheon, regardless of the city-state. But it was the gods directly associated with the city-states that seemed to have had the most attention. Melqart was officially connected to the kings of Tyre and was used as a means of exerting influence on faraway trading colonies that were not directly under the throne's control. While the king acted as a lender and financier of trading journeys and colonial missions, he was also a religious leader, offering divine protection in exchange for obedience. The leaders of trading colonies, called "princes of the sea," who were often the heads of merchant firms or families that had extreme wealth and power, could not be managed in day-to-day affairs by the king. But through religion, they made sacred oaths, ensuring that the princes still acted in good faith.

Regardless of who Phoenicians worshiped, the most important element of their religion was sacrifices. Because of the lack of Phoenician or Punic writings on the topic, we do not know how often or in what context sacrifices were performed. One inscription mentions "the month of the sacrifice of the Sun." But nothing else provides a clearer context. However, it is known that sacrifices took many forms. Animals, food, oil, wine, flowers, incense, statues, and other objects were sacrificed to the gods. The small amount of information that exists about these practices bears a strong resemblance to sacrifices mentioned in the Old Testament of the Bible.

The Phoenicians shared some religious ideas, language, and technological advancements, but they identified chiefly with their cities and family. A prime example of this was the citizens of the city of Tyre. Tyre was not the first Phoenician city to establish trade routes throughout the Mediterranean Sea, but it became one of the best known and possibly went the farthest in search of trade goods. As previously mentioned, the city was supposedly founded by the god Melqart and dated back to the 3rd millennium BCE. Ancient Tyre consisted of two communities. The primary settlement was on an island, which was believed to be impregnable, and was the center of wealth and trade. The secondary settlement was on the mainland and provided the island with water and timber. Tyrian traders ventured far west in pursuit of goods, especially metals like silver and iron. They went as far as Cádiz, a trading colony they founded in the 12th century BCE, in what is today southern Spain, west of the Strait of Gibraltar. The traditional route taken to the Iberian Peninsula was essentially island hopping along the northern section of the Mediterranean, but the route home typically followed the coast of North Africa to the Levant.

For many years, Tyre was a satellite city to the Phoenician city of Sidon, but it broke away and became the dominant Phoenician city under the rule of King Hiram, who is mentioned in the Books of Samuel and Kings in the Hebrew Bible. He is supposed to have ruled from 980 to 947 BCE. According to the Bible, Hiram was a close ally of King David of Israel. Hiram helped to build David's palace in Jerusalem. The Tyrian king continued the close association with David's successor, Solomon, and helped supply materials and workmen to build the First Temple. It was said that Hiram and Solomon established a trade route to a land called Ophir, which was a great source of wealth and made both kings very rich. Speculation is rife on where Ophir actually was located, including theories that it was in Saudi Arabia, India, Sri Lanka, or even the Philippines.

From the writings of Josephus, who is said to be quoting Menander (a Greek dramatist), it is believed that Hiram had to put down a revolt in the city of Utica, a trading colony in North Africa. The Uticans refused to pay their tribute to their mother city, so Hiram had to "reduce them to submission." After Hiram died, the throne passed to his son, Baal-Eser I, who reigned from 946 to 930 BCE. Eight more kings ruled Tyre after this until the crown rested on the head of Mattan I. It is said that Mattan had two children: a son named Pygmalion and a daughter named Dido.

Chapter 2: Foundation Myths Surrounding Carthage

Ruins of Carthage.
Calips, CC BY-SA 3.0 <http://creativecommons.org/licenses/by-sa/3.0/>, via Wikimedia Commons; https://commons.wikimedia.org/wiki/File:Tunisie_Carthage_Ruines_08.JPG

There are several sources that give an account of the founding of Carthage. The main story that survives to this day is that the Tyrian king Mattan I left his kingdom to his son and daughter. The people of Tyre decided they did not like the prospect of co-rulers and put their support behind the son, Pygmalion. The new king's sister, usually Dido but sometimes given the name Elissa, was shocked to discover that the autocratic Pygmalion killed her husband, perhaps in an attempt to find her husband's hidden treasure of gold. Dido then cunningly asked to move into Pygmalion's palace. However, she asked the attendants given to her to throw bags of sand into the ocean. She told these attendants that the bags were filled with her husband's gold and that they must flee with her or face Pygmalion's wrath. They left Tyre and eventually came to a spot in North Africa, where they founded the city of Carthage. Dido ruled as its first queen.

This story is considered a myth or legend and is not the only legendary story concerning the founding of Carthage, though it is the most popular. In Virgil's *Aeneid*, the epic poem concerning the travels of the Trojan Aeneas, the hero stops in Carthage and hears the story of Pygmalion's murderous deed and Dido's flight. In this telling, Dido takes her husband's treasure with her and buys a plot of land in North Africa that is named Byrsa. Some sources claim that *byrsa* means "oxhide." This is a reference to the story that Dido bought enough land that could be covered with an oxhide from the local Berber people. Dido had the oxhide cut into thin strips and was able to claim a whole hill for her new city. However, *byrsa* in Punic (a dialect of Phoenician) means "fortress." This may have been an invention by later writers because *byrsa* is close to *bursa*, which in Greek means "oxhide."

The traditional date for the founding of Carthage is 814 BCE. However, archaeological evidence suggests it was not inhabited for another hundred years after this date. In Phoenician, Carthage means "New Town," and while Pygmalion is recognized as the historical king of Tyre, it is not clear that the story of Dido is anything close to the truth. The most likely explanation is that Carthage was founded, like its neighbor Utica, as a trading colony that was expected to pay tribute to the mother city of Tyre. However, because of Carthage's rivalry with the Greeks and, to a larger extent, the Romans, its founding has taken on a much grander narrative over the millennia.

The city was carefully picked, as it was situated on a triangular peninsula in the Gulf of Tunis with the Lake of Tunis behind it, which provided an abundance of fish and safe anchorage. The peninsula itself consisted of low hills and provided easy access to the sea, as well as protection against some of the wilder storms of the area. It was not far from the Strait of Sicily and provided a natural area from which to control the flow of goods in and out of the western Mediterranean. This indicates that the Tyrians carefully picked the spot for this city, just as they did with other trading colonies in Sardinia, Sicily, and Spain.

According to the legends, after Dido had cunningly obtained Byrsa Hill, the Tyrians dug to build the foundations of the city and unearthed an ox head, which was seen as a sign that the city would be prosperous but always enslaved. So, they moved to a different site, where they dug up the head of a horse, which was seen as a promising omen.

According to the Roman historian Justin, Carthage's growing wealth drew immigrants from neighboring Phoenician colonies and the nearby Berbers. This led to the Berber king, Iarbas, demanding Dido's hand in marriage. Dido was at first reluctant but then agreed to the marriage. She had her attendants build a large fire to burn the memories of her previous life in Tyre but then climbed onto the fire and killed herself so that she could be faithful to her dead husband.

In Virgil's *Aeneid*, Dido offers protection to Aeneas and his followers after they leave Troy following the Trojan War. Dido and Aeneas fall in love. Dido is convinced that they will marry, but the messenger god Mercury appears to Aeneas and tells him he must leave Carthage and continue to Italy. Aeneas leaves, and Dido, distraught with grief, kills herself on a funeral pyre. Aeneas can see the smoke of the pyre from his ship as he leaves, but he doesn't know the source of the smoke. Regardless, he believes it is a bad omen. With her dying breath, Dido asks for vengeance. Since Aeneas goes on to marry the daughter of the Latin king in Italy, with his descendants going on to found the city of Rome, this poetic device allows for the foreshadowing of the eventual wars fought between Rome and Carthage. However, Virgil's poem is not to be taken as historical truth, as he was certainly adding dramatic flair to his verses rather than giving an accurate account of the early days of Carthage.

It seems apparent that Carthage was founded by Tyrian colonists sometime between the 9th and 8th centuries BCE. Carthage was not meant to be a mere trading post but a substantial colony that could be part of the trade route from the Iberian Peninsula in the west to the Levant in the east and as a center for trade for North Africa, Sicily, Sardinia, and Italy. Unlike her neighbor Utica, there is no indication that Carthage revolted against Tyre. Instead, Tyre gradually lost power after the Assyrian domination of Phoenicia and Persia's eventual conquest of the region. Still, Carthaginian leaders sometimes traveled back to the mother city to provide tribute and sacrifices to the temple of Melqart, who continued to be a prominent god in Carthage.

Carthage's location and focus on commerce ensured early success. Based on burial evidence, after only a hundred years, Carthage had a population of close to thirty thousand, while most Phoenician colonies had populations of around one thousand. Pygmalion might have been the Tyrian king who sent colonists to establish the "New City," but there is no evidence to support or deny this proposition. It seems more likely that it was a king from a later generation. However, this would put the founding of Carthage during the Assyrian period, when the kings of Tyre were vassals who paid tribute to the Assyrian Empire. Hypothetically, the Tyrian king who founded Carthage might have been Ithobaal II or Hiram II. This is mere speculation, of course.

We do not even know what the Carthaginians believed was their founding story. Probably the closest source that we have are the writings of Philo of Byblos, who was a Phoenician born in the 1st century CE when Phoenicia was a province of the Roman Empire. Thus, he lived hundreds of years after the height of Phoenicia and the founding of Carthage. Philo's work on the history of Phoenicia is derived from the supposedly earlier work of Sanchuniathon, a Phoenician writer from an uncertain time period before the Trojan War. However, Philo's work seems to be mainly concerned with religion and the idea that the earliest religions were focused on hero worship and the worship of natural elements. There is nothing to shed light on the founding of Carthage.

Thus, it is difficult to say with any certainty when Carthage was founded, who the founders were other than Tyrian citizens, and what stories the Carthaginians told concerning their founding. If Dido/Elissa founded the city as a way to escape her brother, the king of Tyre, then it seems unlikely that Carthage would have had an established relationship with the city of Tyre. It would be more likely that these cities would be at odds. The story of Aeneas is even more likely to be complete fiction in regard to the origins of the rivalry between Rome and Carthage.

Chapter 3: Settlement and the Building of Carthage

We have firmly established that Carthage was a colony established by citizens of the city of Tyre. We know that Carthage was not intended to be a small trading colony but a large city designed to control as much of the trade in the western Mediterranean as possible. To varying degrees of frequency, the leaders of Carthage paid tribute to the city of Tyre and gave gifts to the temple of Melqart, the founder-god of Tyre, who became an important deity to Carthage as well. We know that Carthage's selection was not accidental, as the presence of the city on a peninsula with natural harbors was indicative of Phoenician colonies. Carthage, like other Phoenician cities, was focused on maritime trade, but it also had access to fertile land away from the coast, which helped to feed its growing population. Carthage also benefited from the presence of the Lake of Tunis, which provided fish and a safe harbor. Still, it remains something of a mystery how this colony went from being like many Phoenician colonies around the Mediterranean and the Atlantic to an imperial power and the greatest of all Phoenician cities.

According to the ancient historian Strabo, Tyre founded about three hundred colonies along the African coast. This number might be an exaggeration, but it shows that Carthage must have had many more neighboring colonies than we are aware of. The most well-known contemporary Phoenician colonies of Carthage were Cerro de Villar, Los Toscanos, and La Fonteta in Spain, Sa Caleta in Ibiza, Sulcis in Sardinia,

Utica in Tunisia, Motya in Sicily, the island of Malta, and Kition in Cyprus. Carthage was, at first, simply a link in a chain that stretched from Tyre in the Levant to Gadir, modern-day Cádiz, in southwest Spain, where Tyre was able to trade with locals for silver, the most common currency in that part of the world at the time.

At the site of a Phoenician shipwreck near a place called Bajo De La Campana, there was a rocky area off the coast of Spain where ships often ran afoul. One particular ship is of much interest. There is nothing to indicate that it had stopped at Carthage, but given that it was from the 7th century, it might have been on its way there when a hole was torn in its hull. It sank to the bottom of the ocean. Archaeologists have been excavating the site for years and have revealed promising discoveries in the past five years. The ship contained metal, almost a ton of it: tin, copper, and lead from mines in Spain, Sardinia, and Cyprus. Researchers uncovered a vast amount of pottery, the container of choice in ancient times. They had a limestone altar on board, carved by a talented sculptor and perhaps destined for a temple. There were also lead and bronze counterweights, which would be used in the weighing of items to be sold, bought, and shipped. They discovered a wooden comb, amber, and pieces of alabaster. There was also an assortment of perfume bottles, urns, and pitchers. Evidence was found to support the idea that the Phoenicians might have been the first to use pitch to seal their ships. The ship contained incense burners, oil lamps, and fine furniture with bronze legs. There were also elephant tusks and ostrich eggs, proof of a lively trade with North Africa.

Carthage would have been directly involved in the trade of such items. Included on the vessel were votive offerings of elephant tusks with Phoenician religious inscriptions. These tusks should have been in a shrine, but their presence on the ship indicates that the priests of gods like Ashtart (Astarte), a goddess of love and fertility from the Canaanite pantheon, and Eshmun, a Phoenician god of healing who was sacred to the people of Sidon, might have been selling offerings like these instead of dedicating them at their shrines as the worshipers believed they were.

By the time this ship sank, Carthage was a large and bustling city. The citadel of the city had been established on Byrsa Hill, and walls had been built around the end of the peninsula, making it very defensible in the event of a siege. Carthage, like other Phoenician colonies, was primarily focused on trade and acted as a weigh station for ships coming from the west. It was also a port that exported ivory, gold, ostrich eggs, and slaves from Africa. Slavery was a part of the Phoenician society, so it was also a part of Carthage. The Phoenicians were known to buy or capture slaves from Asia Minor and sell them to Egyptians and Greeks. The slave trade in the Mediterranean was already well established by the time Carthage was founded, and slaves came from all corners of the known world and were sent to lands that were foreign to them.

During the Assyrian invasion of Tyre and the city's eventual subjugation, many Tyrian nobles fled their home city and went to the far-off colonies to continue a life free of imperial influence. One of the cities they fled to was Carthage.

The Phoenicians also had a new competition in the eastern Mediterranean in the form of the Greeks. Greeks, who had learned from the Phoenician alphabet and had adopted Phoenician technology in their ships, were now sailing the same waters that had once been used predominantly by the Phoenicians. There were other growing powers as well. The Etruscans in Italy spread their influence, and places like Sicily, which had once been controlled by the Phoenicians, were now up for grabs. The Phoenicians traveled ever onward. There is no doubt they traveled past the Pillars of Hercules, the Strait of Gibraltar, and into the Atlantic. There has been some speculation that they went as far as Britain to get tin and might have sailed down the western coast of Africa. There are even vague suggestions in unverified sources that the Phoenicians knew of a land on the other side of the western sea, though this seems very far-fetched.

Essentially what developed in Carthage after its founding was a new identity. Like many other cities of the time, it became important early on to establish who was a citizen and who was not. Logic dictated that any important families from Tyre would have been first among the citizens. The exact nature of politics in Carthage is unknown, but since it was a colony, it was certainly modeled after Tyre. However, we do know that Carthage's government was largely an oligarchy and not a monarchy like Tyre. This is perhaps because the king was always in Tyre while his representatives were in the colonies. Aristotle complimented the Carthaginians on their government and said that the oligarchy must have been benevolent because it lasted for so many centuries without a despot taking control or an uprising by the masses.

Like the Roman Republic that came later, Carthage was ruled by two magistrates, which were called *suffetes*. Below this was a senate of twenty-eight members, possibly drawn from a larger body of three hundred. This senate could declare war, levy troops, and appoint generals. Eventually, it would come to be the most powerful branch of the Carthaginian government.

A new Phoenician dialect began to develop in Carthage called the Punic language. This name was, of course, not what the Carthaginians called their language; that is, unfortunately, unknown. The Romans called anything related to Carthage Punic. They called the Carthaginians *Poeni*, probably because of their descent from the Phoenicians. So, anything associated with them was *punicus*, which is known to us as Punic.

The language the Carthaginians spoke is long dead, so no one knows exactly what it was like. There are a few examples that survive in the comedy of Plautus called *Poenulus* or *The Little Carthaginian*. Almost all of the Punic writings and inscriptions were destroyed, but vestiges of the language were still spoken as late as the 5th century CE. Because of the loss of so much of the language, there is more speculative than concrete evidence when it comes to what the Punic tongue was like. Some scholars have even suggested that Punic might bear a strong resemblance to Arabic. Others have suggested that the language of Malta is similar to Punic. Apparently, there is a Carthaginian saying on the island of Malta that goes, "The plague needs a piece of silver; give it two, and it will leave you alone."

In the 8th and 7th centuries BCE, Carthage grew into a regional power in its own right. In about 753 BCE, legend has it that a new city was formed in central Italy on the banks of the Tiber River. It was called Rome. It is clear now, thousands of years after the fact, to see these two cities were set on a collision course with each other. But at the time, Carthage was clearly the greater of the two in population, influence, and wealth. If anyone in Carthage was aware of the formation of Rome, they probably took little note. Instead, Carthage was more aware of Rome's neighbors, the Etruscans, and the spread of the Greeks.

By the 6th century BCE, Carthage would have been hearing some unsettling news from its mother city, Tyre. The Neo-Babylonian Empire, sometimes called the Chaldean Empire, would go on to conquer the Assyrians and take control of Phoenicia. In 583 BCE, the Babylonians besieged Tyre. The siege would last for thirteen years and end with a partial Babylonian victory. Tyre most likely had to pay tribute and hand over control of some of the city's power in the Mediterranean. The

Babylonians had their own fleet and were known to engage in naval battles, but their strength was obviously not so great as to keep Tyre from receiving supplies for the first thirteen years of the siege. The city kept going. But to what extent this affected Carthage is unknown.

In fact, it might have even helped Carthage, as many Tyrians likely fled their home city and migrated to Carthage. Carthage might also have been sending supplies to Tyre to help its people survive for those thirteen years. It would seem that Carthage had plenty to give the mother city, but we do not know if Carthage was supplying Tyre free of charge. Given the commercial inclinations of the Phoenician people and the fact that Tyre was in no position to demand anything from Carthage, Carthage might have used the situation to its advantage, not in a malicious way necessarily but simply to extend its independence and to benefit the citizens of the growing city.

Carthage separated from the mother city in many ways but most notably in religion. Melqart had been the supreme deity of Tyre, but he was of lesser importance in the Carthaginian pantheon. The chief gods in Carthage were Baal Hammon and Tanit. Baal Hammon, whose name might mean something like "Lord of the Furnaces," was a powerful god who commanded extreme devotion. His consort, Tanit, was just as important as him. Her symbol of an outstretched figure is seen wherever Carthage left an imprint.

A stone monument with the symbol for the goddess Tanit.
https://commons.wikimedia.org/wiki/File:Karthago_Tophet.JPG

Baal Hammon's symbol is that of the crescent moon. To appease the god, the nobles of Carthage were required to offer sacrifices. Greek sources claim that the Carthaginians practiced child sacrifice. This was long considered Greek slander of an enemy until the discovery of a Carthaginian tophet.

A tophet is the location where child sacrifices might have been performed and where the remains of the sacrifices are interred. The Carthage tophet shows signs that it was in use for hundreds of years. Phoenician cities in the Levant were known to practice child sacrifice, but it seems that long after they had given up the practice, Carthage was still giving children to Baal Hammon.

Archaeological work at a large tophet on the outskirts of Carthage indicates that some of the children were stillborn and that some of the remains were actually animals. However, urns in later centuries held children who were three or four years of age. There are steles that indicate these sacrifices were made in times of great peril and that the sacrificed children came from the highest ranks of Carthaginian society. The inscriptions make a point to explain that the sacrifice was from a noble family and that the child was one of their flesh, not a substitute. The method of sacrifice is not clear, but the Greek sources indicate that the young victims were burned to death, which correlates with the idea of Baal Hammon as the Lord of Furnaces.

It is believed Carthage conducted child sacrifices throughout its entire history. This would seem barbaric to any modern person, but it is important to keep in mind that the Carthaginians truly believed they needed to sacrifice these children to protect their great city. It must have required supernatural resolve to go through with such a horrific act. Just as Abraham in the Bible was prepared to kill his son with his own hands, the Carthaginians were prepared to sacrifice what was most dear to them for the better of their city and its people. Yet, with all of that being said, it is a horrific practice and is hard to set aside as simply part of their culture, just as it is wrong to set aside slavery as just a part of the ancient world. With the benefit of historical hindsight, we know that those sacrifices did not ultimately save Carthage from destruction.

In the fires of Baal Hammon's furnace, Carthage forged a new identity, one that was removed from Tyre. The Carthaginians were prepared to shed the mantle of a colony and become a capital and center of an expanding empire. As the lights of Phoenicia were fading, the

Carthaginian sun was blazing against the horizon. This new entity needed land, power, and goods. It would not create itself in the image of its parent, Tyre, but instead in the image of the Assyrians and Babylonians, who had gained control of the Levant. When the Babylonians, under Nebuchadnezzar II, finally won the siege of Tyre after thirteen grueling years, the king of Tyre, Baal II, ruled as a vassal of the Babylonians.

However, this was not what led to the ultimate decline of Phoenician power in the Mediterranean. Instead, it was the decline in the demand for metals like tin, copper, and especially silver. The great Phoenician trade routes that ran from the Levant to the Iberian Peninsula dried up. Many colonies were abandoned. Islands like Sardinia, which had relied so heavily on the mining and sale of metal to hungry markets in the east, were thrown into chaos. The archaeological record shows many cities were not just abandoned but also burned to the ground, indicating there were conflicts between colonies and indigenous people. Fewer and fewer ships began to sail the paths from the Near East to Spain or from Spain to North Africa.

However, Carthage was not hit as badly, probably due to its investments in the trade routes not headed east to west but south to north. Carthage traded a wide variety of goods from North Africa to the northern Mediterranean and back again. Since the Carthaginians were not competing with the Phoenicians, their sudden absence proved to be the opening they needed to expand.

Chapter 4: Expansion, Independence, and Empire Status

The 7th century BCE saw the expansion of Carthage. It was no longer a city but instead encompassed a large area of what is today northern Tunisia. Carthage controlled farmlands, natural resources, and several towns. It traded with the local Berber people and exchanged customs and ideas with them as well. Carthage was becoming the center of the Punic culture, which relied heavily on its Phoenician origins but developed unique characteristics all its own.

Some archaeological remains have been found of some of the small towns within the new Carthage nation. The towns were plotted out in a grid pattern, even if they only had around one thousand inhabitants. The center of every town contained a temple, though which god or gods were worshiped there probably differed from town to town. Temples were often the largest local employers, with full-time and part-time priests, as well as musicians, barbers, singers, and cooks for ritual banquets. Some temples also practiced sacred prostitution. Houses were small and often built around peristyles in the Greek and, later, Roman fashion. The houses often contained built-in ovens for making bread and built-in washbasins in small rooms between the outside door and the living area, indicating that it might have been common to wash before entering the house.

The area around Carthage was renowned for orchards that produced pears, apricots, almonds, pistachios, figs, and pomegranates, which the

Romans called Punic apples. The climate of northern Tunisia today is generally mild, with wet winters and hot, dry summers. It was enough in ancient times to support the growing population of Carthage and the surrounding towns. Archaeological research shows that the Carthaginians enjoyed a diverse diet of barley, fish, fruits, nuts, cattle, and much more. The hinterland was also wooded and could provide materials for building ships.

Much of the shipbuilding and maintenance was done in two *cothons* of Carthage. A *cothon* is an artificial harbor constructed near the sea but connected via a manmade channel. These features were commonly associated with Phoenician construction. Carthage had two *cothons*. The first was rectangular and was used by merchant ships. The second was circular and used only for the powerful Carthaginian navy. These manmade harbors were surrounded by docks. The circular *cothon* had an island built in the center where the chief admiral of the navy could stay and review his ships and men.

The exact date for the construction of the *cothons* is unknown, but they would have been a massive endeavor involving thousands of laborers working many long days removing tons of soil, sand, and rock. The harbors had to be deep enough to accommodate the large hulled vessels and large enough to hold hundreds of ships at a time. They are a testament to Carthage's engineering skills. The only visible remains of ancient Carthage today are what is left of the city walls and the remnants of the artificial harbors.

Two Carthaginian expeditions passed the Pillars of Hercules (Strait of Gibraltar) sometime before the 5th century BCE. The first was supposedly conducted by a captain named Himilco, who sailed into the Atlantic and then turned north with a small group of ships, most likely looking for sources of raw materials that were known to exist on the Iberian Peninsula. However, Himilco's fleet went past the peninsula and arrived on the shores of Gaul, modern-day France, after a four-month journey involving harrowing encounters with sea monsters. In Portugal, they met the "Oestriminis," who reportedly had a commercial relationship with neighboring islands for tin and lead. The Carthaginians also visited Britain and Ireland before returning home.

Another expedition, this one of a much larger scale, was led by a man named Hanno and involved sixty-five oared ships with thirty thousand men and women. Many of these were settlers who were deposited along the coast of modern-day Morocco and Mauritania to establish crucial colonies in the area. It seems likely this was the main aim of Hanno's journey, but he continued into the Atlantic and headed south along the western coast of Africa. They went to the Niger Delta, witnessed active volcanoes, and saw a mountain called "Chariot of the Gods," which was most likely Mount Cameroon. In what would one day be Gabon, they encountered hair-covered savages, which were probably chimpanzees. They were unable to capture any males but did get three females; however, they were forced to kill them because of how fiercely they resisted their captors. According to legend, the skins of these females were displayed in the Temple of Tanit in Carthage until the Romans destroyed the city.

In 539 BCE, Cyrus the Great of the Persian Empire attacked and conquered the cities of Phoenicia. Tyre fell to the Persians, and many more Tyrians fled to Carthage and other cities. In the same century, a single family came to dominate Carthaginian politics and gained control of the military. They were known as the Magonids, and they controlled the city and burgeoning empire from the 6th to the 4th century BCE. The first head of this family is typically given the name Mago I. In Greek histories, he is stylized as a king, but Carthage did not have a monarchy. It appears that the power the Magonids enjoyed was allotted by the Council of Elders. Around the same time that Tyre was losing its independence, Mago sent his sons, Hasdrubal and Hamilcar, to Sardinia. Hasdrubal died, but Hamilcar was able to secure the southern half of the island for Carthage.

However, this was not a true conquest but more of an effort to maintain and improve imports from Sardinia, which Carthage relied on for agricultural goods and raw materials. Carthage founded two new towns in Sardinia: Caralis (modern-day Cagliari) and Neapolis. Melqart was worshiped in Sardinia as a cultural import from Tyre, but this became a connection between Carthaginian culture and the new Punic culture of Sardinia. The settlements on the island were largely autonomous, but Carthage became increasingly involved in their affairs and sent settlers from Carthage to the new cities. The settlements became fortified strongholds that controlled the countryside around them.

Sardinia is an excellent example of the various methods Carthage used in expanding the empire. During the 6th and 5th centuries BCE, Punic cities in Sardinia began to flourish thanks in large part to their connections with Carthage. The indigenous population of the island became more isolated and was pushed into mountainous regions. Punic cities in Sardinia began to produce luxury goods like amulets, jewelry, statuettes, perfume burners, and masks, which were then exported around the Mediterranean. Some of the elites of Sardinia were even given honorary Carthaginian citizenship. While the cities were ruled by independent municipal authorities, Carthage still held sway over the island. Supposedly, the Carthaginians had every fruit tree in Sardinia destroyed and banned the planting of anymore because it did not fit with their need for Sardinia to produce grain.

Just as, if not more, important than Sardinia's fertile fields and small gold mines were the Iberian Peninsula's mines. Carthage desired to control the trade of tin out of northwest Spain. Bronze, the primary metal of the age, was made from copper mixed with tin, and no ancient locale provided more tin than Iberia. By establishing trading alliances and founding settlements across southern Iberia and keeping the location of the tin mines secret, Carthage was able to establish a monopoly on the tin being extracted from the area. Carthage used its power and influence to put agreeable leaders in charge of the various people who traded in tin, ensuring that only the city could buy it at a low cost and sell it to the rest of the Mediterranean at whatever price it chose. This practice and Carthage's sometimes heavy-handedness caused some in Iberia to dislike Carthaginian domination. This fact would resurface during the wars with Rome.

For Carthage, however, the control of the tin market made them exceptionally wealthy and powerful. If they could not recruit soldiers and sailors to look into their interests, they were able to pay mercenaries to do the work instead. This was a very common practice in ancient times. In fact, the Carthaginian military between the 6th and 5th centuries grew from a citizen militia into an international military power made up primarily of foreign mercenaries.

It was said that once Cyrus the Great conquered Phoenicia, the Persians became interested in attacking Carthage directly, possibly due to their monopoly on tin and its tight control of the silver market. In order for Persia to attack Carthage, it would need a vast navy to transport the soldiers. However, the Persian navy was almost entirely run by Phoenicians and used Phoenician ships. The Phoenicians refused to participate in any attempt to conquer Carthage, which was originally a Phoenician colony. The Persians were forced to relent and give up on the idea. They then turned their attention to the Greeks, which would start a feud that changed the ancient world.

Carthage's trade networks stretched even farther than their physical presence. From across the Sahara, they obtained salt, gold, animal skins, and peacocks. They developed the auction system to trade with their African neighbors. They traded in amber, silver, and fur with the Celts, Celtiberians, and Gauls. Corsica had silver and gold mines. Malta and the Balearic Islands mass-produced products that were sent to Carthage and then sold in ports all over the Mediterranean. Carthage sold basic supplies to poor communities, often displacing local manufacturers, but they also produced high-quality luxury items that they sold to the Greeks and Etruscans.

According to Aristotle, Carthage also strengthened its foreign colonies by continually sending new settlers. These settlers brought the Punic culture and Punic business practices with them. Carthaginian settlements produced the purple dye and fine luxury goods known throughout the region, and these goods traveled along the trade routes that Carthage controlled. Yet, again according to Aristotle, Carthage sent any malcontents and others who had an issue with the leadership in Carthage to these far-off settlements. This meant that Carthage avoided civil wars and political infighting, which were common among nations at this time. The settlers were given independence and a higher status as citizens of Carthage living in a colony. While this might have undermined some of Carthage's control over her colonies, it proved to be a winning strategy for hundreds of years, as Carthage and her colonies grew.

In 509 BCE, Carthage entered into a treaty with the newest power of central Italy: the Roman Republic. Carthage was already trading with the Etruscans, and the Romans were looking to secure their trading interests. At the same time, Carthage was involved in a struggle with the western Greek powers and wanted a way around the Greek colonies of southern Italy into the rest of the peninsula. The treaty established a friendly relationship between the two cities. No Roman ships could enter the gulf of Carthage unless driven there by storms, and they could only buy what supplies were needed to sail out of the area. Roman merchants could operate in Sardinia and Libya but only under the supervision of a state clerk. Carthage agreed not to attack cities controlled by Rome or build fortresses in Latium. Carthaginians could not stay the night in Latium if they were armed. In Carthaginian Sicily, Romans had the same rights as Carthaginians. This treaty was essentially a promise made by each side not to attack the other directly, leaving Rome open to fighting the Etruscans and Greeks in Italy and leaving Carthage free to fight the Greeks in Sicily and elsewhere in the western Mediterranean.

By that point, the city of Carthage was massive. There were four residential districts that circled Byrsa Hill, a large theater, a marketplace, a necropolis, and large temples to Tanit and Baal Hammon. The aristocrats in the city, who controlled the commercial and military power, lived in vast palaces. There was a middle class of lesser merchants and foreigners who lived in modest but nice houses, and then the bottom class, who lived in apartments and huts outside the city walls. Carthage sat like a huge spider in the middle of a complex web that spun out around it and encapsulated all of the western Mediterranean. Every port and person was influenced by what some historians have referred to as the Carthaginian Empire. However, it is hard to put Carthage in the same category as the imperialistic powers of Assyria, Babylonia, Persia, or Macedonia.

The Carthaginian Empire, if it can be called that, was not uniform. When the Persians conquered a region, they typically put Persian satraps, or governors, in place to deal with any challenge to Persian rule. There would be garrisons of Persian troops stationed in every city under the empire's domain. Centuries later, Alexander the Great would do much the same thing, sometimes founding cities, which he usually named after himself, and populating them with locals and Macedonian and Greek veterans. When the Romans conquered a city, they would almost always introduce massive building programs to make that city look much like every other Roman city, with a forum, amphitheater, and temples to Roman gods. Yet, this was not the method Carthage would use.

Instead, the Carthaginians largely left cities and regions independent but made them dependent on Carthage through alliances and treaties. These cities would deal with Carthage in commercial matters, while Carthage would help in most military matters.

The Carthaginian army, therefore, had to remain highly mobile. A navy was required to protect trading vessels throughout a large patch of the Mediterranean Sea. These were, initially, strengths for Carthage since it did not need to spread itself too thin in an effort to keep every part of its "empire" in order. However, this meant that certain areas could become a weakness if they were threatened by another power or if they wanted to be free of Carthaginian control.

Chapter 5: The Sicilian Wars

In the 6th century BCE, Carthage maintained an alliance with the Etruscans but was ever wary of the actions of the Greeks, who were rapidly colonizing southern Italy and Sicily in what became known as *Magna Graecia* or Greater Greece. The Etruscans were unable to stop the colonizing efforts, and the Greeks eventually settled on the islands of Sardinia and Corsica. A group of Phocaean Greeks, who originally hailed from Anatolia, formed a colony in Massalia in southern France and at Alalia in Corsica.

Things came to a head in 540 BCE at a time when Carthage was conquering much of Sardinia and also dealing with issues with Greek colonists in Sicily. The Phocaeans began to prey on Carthaginian and Etruscan trade ships near Corsica, attacking the ships, taking the cargo, and killing the sailors. Carthage and Etruria sent about 120 ships to stop the Phocaean pirates, who had only 60 ships to defend themselves. All the ships involved in the sea battle were *penteconters*. These ships could be over 100 feet long and have 20, 50, or even 120 oars. The smaller Greek force was able to win the battle but at a high cost, losing almost two-thirds of their own fleet.

With a badly damaged fleet, the Phocaeans, knowing they could not withstand another battle, were forced to leave Corsica. Thus, it was a strategic victory for Carthage, which retained Sardinia while the Etruscans took control of Corsica. While the Greeks and Carthaginians had had plenty of skirmishes, this was the first large-scale battle and established distrust on both sides. These tensions transferred to the place where

Carthaginians and Greeks were already fighting for control: Sicily.

A Spartan prince named Dorieus was born sometime in the 6th century. He was the second born and became unsettled with his lot in life. So, he asked Sparta to support him in an attempt to found a colony in the west. He first tried to settle Libya but was driven out by a local tribe, which had Carthaginian support. He then set his sights on western Sicily, which he was told belonged to the descendants of the hero Hercules. Dorieus believed he was one of those descendants. He founded a colony there named Herakleia. However, the colony was attacked by an indigenous people from Sicily named the Segestaeans, who had help from Carthage. Prince Dorieus was killed in 510 BCE. His elder half-brother, the king of Sparta, died childless, which meant the throne would have passed to Dorieus. But since he died, it instead went to Leonidas I, who is famous for his last stand at Thermopylae in 480 BCE.

The situation in Sicily was more complex than it might first appear. There were essentially four different factions that were, at times, in competition or allied with one another. First, there were the indigenous people of Sicily, who were often allied with another faction, the Carthaginians. The Greeks were in two different groups: the Ionians and the Dorians. These two sides were part of a long-standing rivalry that originated in mainland Greece hundreds of years before when they were separate tribes. The Dorians typically came from the Peloponnese, while the Ionians were from Attica and Asia Minor. In Sicily, these two groups were often in competition with one another. This meant the Greek cities were often fighting each other.

Eventually, however, the Greek cities began to be controlled largely by tyrants who sought to consolidate Greek control of the island. The tyrant Cleander ruled the city of Gela on the southern coast of Sicily, replacing the existing oligarchy. He was murdered and succeeded by his brother, Hippocrates, who began an expansion phase that saw much of southern Sicily fall under his control. He was succeeded by his nephew, Gelon, who moved the capital of the kingdom to Syracuse. Gelon established an army of ten thousand men made up of recruits from Sicily and mainland Greece; he gave all these soldiers Syracusan citizenship. Gelon turned Ionian cities into Dorian ones through his campaigns, using executions and enslavement to ensure that Dorian Greeks gained control over most of the Greek cities in Sicily.

This was especially concerning to Greek cities in southern Italy, which feared Gelon would try to conquer them as well. Anaxilas, the tyrant of Rhegium, encouraged Greek refugees to take the city of Zancle in northeast Sicily. According to some accounts, these refugees were from Anaxilas's home city of Messenia, the island of Samos, or perhaps both. Zancle became the city of Messina (Messana), and Anaxilas was able to gain control of the city. Anaxilas also married the daughter of Terillus, the tyrant of the city of Himera on the central northern coast of Sicily, to secure his position against Gelon. Terillus was also friendly with the Carthaginians, specifically a late 5th-century general named Hamilcar.

At this point, it might be pertinent to note that Carthaginians often used the same names generation after generation; there are countless leaders named Hanno, Hamilcar, Hannibal, Mago, and Hasdrubal. This is not particularly unusual. There are many Romans named Gaius, Marcus, or Scipio, but they usually include additional names or nicknames. Macedonian kings and Egyptian pharaohs are identified with a name and number, such as Philip II or Thutmose III. However, not enough is known about Carthaginian history to give many of these leaders unique identifiers. For instance, the Hanno who sailed to the West African coast is often called Hanno the Navigator, but we do not know if he was a type of "king," naval leader, or simply a sailor of uncommon skill. The Hamilcar that appears to have been allied with Terillus was certainly a military leader, but he also might have served as a kind of king approved by the Council of Elders, as previously explained about the Magonid rulers.

In 480 BCE, Carthage responded to a call for aid from Terillus, the tyrant of Himera, after he was overthrown and deposed by a Dorian tyrant named Theron. This led to the Battle of Himera. Gelon and Theron faced the forces of Hamilcar. Carthage is said to have fielded an army of 300,000, though this is likely an exaggeration. The army of Gelon and Theron was believed to be about fifty thousand. In a small skirmish just outside the city, Hamilcar defeated a body of men under Theron. However, once Gelon arrived, the Carthaginians were defeated in a pitched day-long battle. Once Hamilcar saw that his army had lost, Herodotus tells us that he threw himself into a sacrificial fire near the battlefield. Another account states that Hamilcar was killed by Gelon's archers.

The fallout from the Carthaginian defeat was mild. Himera fell under Gelon's control, and Carthage had to pay two thousand talents of silver and build two temples where the details of the agreement were to be displayed. Even Hamilcar did not suffer a blow to his legacy, which was common for generals who suffered great defeats. He was generally regarded favorably and was honored with sacrifices in some Punic cities, perhaps due to his act of literal self-sacrifice. Carthage was hesitant to return to the island and stayed away from affairs in Sicily for the next seventy years.

Around the same time that Syracuse and Carthage were fighting against one another, the Persians were involved in an attempted invasion of mainland Greece. This invasion was deftly thwarted by the combined efforts of most of the Greek city-states. After Himera, Syracuse tried to present the idea that Carthage was the Persia of the west and that the battle in Sicily was akin to the battles in Greece. The Carthaginians were certainly seen as barbarians by the Greeks simply because they were not Greek. And since the Phoenicians were vassals of Persia, and Carthage was originally a Phoenician colony, it did make a certain amount of sense. However, many disregarded the Syracusan propaganda, including Plato and Aristotle, who believed Carthage represented one of the greatest contemporary governments in the world. Not everyone forgot the fact that Gelon had rejected a plea from Spartan and Athenian envoys to support them in the fight against Persia.

In fact, during the years after Himera, Athens appeared to have increased its trade with Carthage and also requested help from Carthage in political matters in Sicily. However, Carthage rejected the Athenians' plea. In Carthage, there were some political changes after the Battle of Himera. Hamilcar, being a Magonid, had acted largely in the interests of the Magonids and not necessarily for Carthage. Because of this, it seems that a more republican type of government was instituted. The Council of the Hundred and Four was created. This council of judges oversaw generals and the military to help rein in their independence. The appointments in the Council of the Hundred and Four were for life, and their power increased dramatically over the following centuries. However, after this political shake-up, the Magonids were still in power, indicating that they played a large hand in the reorganization. The Magonids would continue to hold the *suffete* roles as magistrates and generals for many years to come.

By 410 BCE, the Doric-Greek city of Selinus and the Ionian-Greek city of Segesta had become engaged in a bitter rivalry. Selinus defeated the Segesta forces in 416 BCE. Segesta had asked Carthage for help, but

Carthage denied its request. It then turned to Athens, which sent an expedition to Sicily that ended in disaster for the Athenians in 413 BCE when they were defeated by a coalition of Sicilian cities, which had help from Sparta. Segesta again asked Carthage for help, and this time, Carthage responded. They were led by Hannibal Mago, who attempted to end matters diplomatically. However, peace could not be reached between Carthage, Segesta, Selinus, and Syracuse. So, Hannibal Mago assembled a large army and took Selinus by force. He then won a decisive victory in the Second Battle of Himera, which restored Carthage's reputation. Hannibal Mago did not press on to Syracuse but returned to Carthage with his spoils of war in 409 BCE.

A Syracusan general named Hermocrates began to attack Punic areas in Sicily and captured Motya and Panormus before being killed in Syracuse in an attempted coup. Hannibal Mago responded by leading another army to Sicily in 406 BCE. This time, though, things didn't go well for the Carthaginians. While laying siege to the city of Akragas, they were hit hard by a bout of the plague. Hannibal Mago succumbed to the illness during the campaign. His successor, named Himilco, took the city of Akragas, captured several other cities, and repeatedly defeated the forces of Syracuse. However, the plague struck the Carthaginians again, so Himilco agreed to a peace treaty that left him in control of the cities he had captured. This would be the greatest extent of Punic control on the island of Sicily.

By 406 BCE, Dionysius I had been elected supreme commander of Syracuse, thanks in part to his steadfast defense against the Carthaginians in the previous war. Dionysius was first granted six hundred guards after he faked an attack on his life. He was able to extend these guards to one thousand. With this loyal force, made mostly of mercenaries, he proceeded to gain complete control of the city and establish himself as a tyrant. Unlike other Greek tyrants, Dionysius received the blessing of Sparta, which provided him with soldiers from some of its territories. Dionysius would prove to be the model for Greek tyrants and kings, including Alexander the Great. However, as a ruler, he is generally regarded as being the worst kind of tyrant: vindictive, suspicious, and cruel.

In 398 BCE, Dionysius broke the peace treaty with Carthage and laid siege to the city of Motya, which he captured. Himilco responded and recaptured the city and nearby Messina. In 397 BCE, the Carthaginian fleet, under an admiral named Mago, defeated the Greeks in the naval

Battle of Catana. Himilco then pressed his advantage and laid siege to Syracuse itself. At first, the siege was successful, but once again, the plague descended on the Carthaginians. The army collapsed in 396 BCE. Forced to withdraw, the Carthaginians lost the cities they had claimed but retained their territories in western Sicily. The island was split between Carthage in the west, Ionian Greeks in the north, and Doric Greeks in the east.

Dionysius regained his strength and sacked Solus in the same year the Carthaginians were ravaged by illness. Carthage did not immediately act because it was dealing with a revolt in its African territories. In 393 BCE, Himilco's successor, Mago II, attacked Messina but was repelled. Mago then led a reinforced army into central Sicily, where he was prepared to meet Dionysius at the Battle of Chrysas. The Sicels, the indigenous people of Sicily, allied with Dionysius and harassed the Carthaginian supply line, causing shortages. The Greeks under Dionysius revolted because he would not fight the Carthaginians directly. Consequently, the "battle" was settled with a peace treaty that gave Dionysius the lands of the Sicels. Carthage retained control of western Sicily.

Dionysius again broke his treaty with the Carthaginians in 383 BCE. Sometime between 378 and 375 BCE, Dionysius defeated Mago II at the Battle of Cabala. The details of the battle are scarce, and the exact location is unknown. It is believed that Mago died during the battle, though. Mago II's son, named Himilco Mago, succeeded his father and renewed the fight with Dionysius, defeating the tyrant in 376 BCE at the Battle of Cronium, close to modern-day Palermo. Dionysius's brother died in the battle. As a result, Dionysius was forced to pay one thousand talents in reparations and let Carthage maintain control of western Sicily.

Dionysius couldn't sit still. He again attacked Punic possessions in 368 BCE. This might have resulted in another drawn-out war in Sicily, except Dionysius I of Syracuse died in 367 BCE. His son, Dionysius II, did not desire to continue the aggression toward Carthaginian territories or allies. So, he settled a peace treaty that kept the spheres of influence roughly the same as they had been.

Dionysius II was completely inexperienced in public affairs and politics, so he leaned on his uncle, Dion, for guidance. Dion invited his teacher, the philosopher Plato, to Syracuse to help reform the government and make Dionysius II a philosopher-king. Dionysius II banished his uncle and ignored Plato's appeals. Dion eventually returned from exile and forced his nephew into his own banishment. Later, Dionysius II returned to Syracuse but was eventually removed by Timoleon, a member of the Corinthian aristocracy who had been sent to Syracuse to save it from despotism and tyranny.

Syracuse had been founded by the Corinthians, which was why the people appealed to Corinth for help against Dionysius II's tyranny. Carthage opposed Timoleon, but he was able to avoid its forces and restore order in Syracuse. Carthage responded by sending a large army, commanded by Asdrubal and Hamilcar, to finally defeat Syracuse and gain control of Sicily. However, Timoleon proved to be able to meet the attack by surprising the Punic forces at the Crimissus River, identified as the modern-day Freddo River in northwestern Sicily.

In June 339 BCE, Timoleon's forces attacked the Carthaginians while they were crossing the river. It began to rain, which hit the Greeks in the back but the Carthaginians in the face. The Greeks were able to break through the front ranks of the Punic army, which caused the Carthaginians to turn and flee. A few smaller battles happened after Crimissus, which stalled the war. The Carthaginians sued for peace, and Timoleon accepted. Carthage retained its territory on the Lycus River in the southwest of Sicily, while Syracuse was left alone. Many of the Greek tyrants of Sicily fell to Timoleon, and peace was restored in Greek Sicily until Timoleon's death.

It is perhaps important at this point to discuss why Carthage fought so hard to retain a foothold on an island mainly controlled by Greeks and indigenous peoples. The Carthaginians hoped to stop the Greeks, especially the Dorian-Greeks, from expanding their territory and influence farther into the western Mediterranean. Unlike Sardinia, Carthage never used Sicily for agricultural production or to obtain raw materials like metal. Carthage chiefly needed its Sicilian ports. These locations on the western coast of the island were crucial for Carthage to control the north-south trade routes to and from Italy. As long as the Carthaginians had ports on Sicily, they could supply ships that needed to stop along those routes and also keep their navies in those ports to combat piracy, which was always a problem. Some of the cities that Carthage founded in Sicily were heavily protected and had no connection to the rest of the island.

In 332 BCE, Alexander the Great crossed into Asia Minor and was in the process of acquiring a vast but short-lived empire. He laid siege to Carthage's mother city, Tyre, and captured the island city by building a large causeway to bring siege engines against the city walls. Some

Carthaginians were there, but Alexander spared them, telling them that Carthage would be next once he conquered Asia. The Carthaginians sent an emissary to Alexander's capital in Babylon to determine when they might expect the Macedonian king to arrive.

The emissary, Hamilcar Rodanus, first claimed to be an exile who wanted to join the Macedonian army. He was supposed to have sent secret messages back to Carthage, but the nature of these messages is unknown, and it is not clear if he was able to determine Alexander's plans. Rodanus returned to Carthage but was executed because the citizens believed he had betrayed them to Alexander. It is not clear whether Alexander truly had designs to conquer Carthage or not. Alexander died in Babylon in 323 BCE, thereby making his true intentions unknowable.

The situation in Sicily was unique for the Carthaginians. They had an army, made mostly of mercenaries, that answered to a general. The general was among the Carthaginian elite, but he had been elected by the Popular Assembly. Still, the supplying of his army had to be approved by the Council of Elders, and he could be audited by the Council of the Hundred and Four. He had considerable autonomy in the field, but his actions could be reviewed by the elite back in Carthage years after he had made his decisions. This made relations between Carthage and Sicily tenuous and complicated for both sides.

A cavalry commander of low-class origins named Agathocles stepped into this theater. He was a tyrant who had gained control of Syracuse after Timoleon's death. Agathocles styled himself as an Alexander for the west and saw Carthage as the western version of Persia. He massacred the oligarchs of Syracuse. Soon, he declared war on the Carthaginians, and they met at the Battle of Himera. The Punic army was led by Hamilcar, grandson of Hanno the Great. Agathocles was defeated at the battle and limped back to Syracuse, where the Carthaginians then laid siege. In a surprise move, he was able to break the blockade in 310 BCE and took an army to North Africa, where he landed on Cape Bon.

He defeated the Carthaginian force there and camped near Tunis. Agathocles began to capture several cities in North Africa. He allied with Ophellas, the ruler of Cyrenaica, and promised Ophellas that he could keep any African possessions they took from Carthage. When Ophellas arrived, Agathocles attacked his army and had Ophellas killed. He took control of what remained of the Cyrenaican army. In 307 BCE, Agathocles was decisively defeated and fled back to Sicily. He concluded a peace treaty with Carthage, which left him in control of several Greek cities on the east side of the island. Carthage maintained control of a portion of its ports in the west.

This peace remained until the appearance of King Pyrrhus of Epirus in Sicily, where he took control of the eastern Greek part. It was said that Pyrrhus had been requested to come there by Greeks living on the island, as they wanted him to deliver them from the Carthaginians. In 297 BCE, the Carthaginians were concerned that Pyrrhus would involve himself in Sicily. Pyrrhus had been in Italy, battling the Romans successfully but at a great cost. This is the origin of the term "Pyrrhic victory." The Carthaginians knew that the Greeks in Sicily were asking for assistance from Pyrrhus, so they sent a commander with 120 ships to Rome to offer help in defeating this potential foe. The Roman Senate declined the offer. However, there is some evidence that Rome and Carthage made another treaty at this time. It is also believed that at some point, the Carthaginians took Roman soldiers from Sicily and transported them to Rhegium to deal with a rebel Roman garrison. The Punic ships then waited to see if Pyrrhus made an attempt to cross to Sicily.

Pyrrhus did so in the late 3rd century BCE. He married Agathocles's daughter after the king of Syracuse died. Pyrrhus quickly attacked Carthaginian possessions, conquering Selinus, Halicyae, Segesta, and other cities. He besieged Eryx and eventually took that city as well. According to Diodorus Siculus, Pyrrhus took every Carthaginian city in Sicily until he was stopped at the last city, Lilybaeum, where the Carthaginians had finally been able to provide troops, grain, and catapults. Around this same time, it appears that the Greeks in Sicily were beginning to tire of Pyrrhus's rule, as he behaved as a despot and was suspicious of those who tried to help him. He received messages asking for his return to Italy, which he took as an excuse to leave. With Pyrrhus's departure, the Carthaginians became interested in regaining their possessions in the western part of Sicily, if not gaining control of the whole island. Unfortunately, their situation would prove to be much more dangerous.

Chapter 6: The First Punic War

Artist depiction of a Carthaginian hoplite.
User:Aldo Ferruggia, CC BY-SA 3.0 <https://creativecommons.org/licenses/by-sa/3.0>, via Wikimedia Commons; https://commons.wikimedia.org/wiki/File:Carthaginian_hoplite_-_Oplita_cartaginese.JPG

In the 280s BCE, a group of Italian mercenaries called the "Sons of Mars" or Mamertines took control of the strategically important city of Messina in northern Sicily. This city lay just across the Strait of Sicily from Italy and was an excellent base from which to control the flow of ships through the strait and from Sicily to Italy and back. When Pyrrhus was in Sicily, he had been asked to remove the Mamertines but had been either unwilling or unable to comply. After his departure and eventual defeat in Italy, Syracuse appointed Hiero II to be the commander of the city's troops. The Mamertines threatened Syracuse, and Hiero defeated them in battle but was stopped from taking the city of Messina by the Carthaginians. In 264 BCE, he attacked the Mamertines again after he had been declared king of Syracuse.

The Mamertines contacted both the Carthaginians and the Romans for help. By this time, Rome had defeated the Samnites, Etruscans, and the Greek cities of Italy and now controlled the entire peninsula. There is strong evidence to support the idea that Rome and Carthage not only considered each other allies up to this point but had also actively traded with each other. There were Carthaginians living in Rome and in other cities in Italy. Archaeological evidence shows that Rome's "African" district was occupied long before war broke out between the two superpowers.

Rome had certain advantages compared to other western Mediterranean nations. When the Romans conquered a city or land, they not only infused the Roman identity but also required a certain number of soldiers from their new territories. This meant the Roman army was made up largely of citizen soldiers and not mercenaries, which proved beneficial because the troops could be induced to fight for an ideal and not just a paycheck. Also, because of Rome's political structure, with senators and consuls holding office for a short time, it made it very difficult for Rome to sue for peace or work out any treaties with an enemy. No one in Rome had the personal power to surrender. This meant that even after several defeats, such as in their first battles with Pyrrhus, the Romans did not give up but kept fighting because they had no other option. This institutional tenacity would prove to be a hallmark of Rome's fighting prowess. And yet, Carthage was certainly the greater of the two when the Mamertines requested help against Hiero II.

The Carthaginians arrived first, and they may have been contacted first, but the Mamertines' plea to Rome was as fellow Italians. Rome was at first unsure of becoming involved outside of Italy, but it feared what would happen if Carthage had control of Messina. The Romans hoped to take control of Syracuse if they defeated Hiero, though. The Romans sent an army under the command of Appius Claudius Caudex to aid the

Mamertines, although they also wished to stop the Carthaginians from gaining any new territories on the island. Upon learning about the approach of the Romans, the Carthaginian general took the fateful step of leaving Messina and allying himself with Hiero. This combined force then besieged Messina (Messana). Rome and Carthage declared war on each other. It was 264 BCE, and the First Punic War had begun.

These opening hostilities were largely possible because Carthage, whose navy was much greater than anything Rome could muster, consistently failed to stop the Romans from crossing into Sicily. At one point, the Romans were even able to take a Punic ship, and they managed several large-scale crossings with mainly borrowed ships from their southern Italian territories. How this was possible remains something of a mystery. The Romans certainly used every trick they could think of to their advantage, but Carthage's navy was highly experienced in patrolling the waters. Luck cannot be completely discounted, of course.

Regardless, Rome's ability to land tens of thousands of troops on the island caused an immediate response. Many cities formed alliances with Rome. Hiero, who was isolated from support, sued for peace. Skirmishes between Romans and Carthaginians broke out, but not much was accomplished, and both sides claimed early victories.

Hiero became a friend and ally to Rome and was able to remain on the throne of Syracuse. The Punic general who had lost Messina to Rome and failed to stop the Romans from crossing over to Sicily was crucified for cowardice. The combined loss of Messina and Syracuse was a devastating blow to Carthage because it meant that Rome had secure ports where they could land troops. While no large battles had yet been fought, Rome had won a great strategic victory. While some might argue that Rome and Carthage had long been on a collision course toward each other, this is not entirely accurate. The truth was more subtle. Carthage had long been a great power in the area, and Rome had now made itself another great power in the same area. They eyed each other suspiciously and with jealousy. They both wanted to acquire more but also feared the loss of what they already had. Both sides saw each other (correctly) as adversaries in a game of empires. If either of them missed an opportunity or gave up an inch of influence, they opened themselves up to domination by the other.

Rome had already begun to identify itself as part of the Greek tradition. The Romans believed they were descended from the Trojan Aeneas, who came to be thought of as Greek even though he had fought against the Greeks in the Trojan War. In fact, the Trojans shared much in common with the Greeks, or at least that is how later writers and historians depicted it. The Romans had also come to accept the cult of Hercules into their religious calendar and believed that Hercules had figured prominently in their past. Some elite Roman families claimed to be descended directly from the great Greek warrior.

Carthage, on the other hand, had come to be associated with the Orient and the East, despite their geographical location. They had come from the Phoenicians, who were certainly not Greeks but instead "barbarians" from the Levant. This cultural divide between the Romans and Carthaginians was magnified in the years before the First Punic War. Therefore, the elites in Rome were already largely convinced of the Carthaginians' treachery and duplicity. Carthage might have felt something similar, but we can't know for sure because no writings from Carthage survived. The Punic culture owed much to the Phoenicians, but it was also largely its own creation and incorporated deities from Iberia and Sardinia, to name just a few. The Carthaginians most likely felt no connection to the Greeks, but their ancestors' stories went back much further. The Phoenicians were sailing the Mediterranean when the Greeks were still unrecognizable tribes. The Carthaginians most likely felt that their pedigree was more than adequate. The Romans were essentially invading foreigners, but the Carthaginians had no real claim to Sicily either. The two would be fighting over an island that wasn't a homeland to either of them. Yet, they each felt that the actions of the other were a legitimate cause for war.

In 262 BCE, Carthage decided to establish a base of operations at Akragas on the southwest side of Sicily. The Carthaginian strategy is not known, but it is clear they were pinning their hopes on their superior navy. Akragas was easily defendable and could be reached by Punic ships with ease. Rome essentially had no navy but instead relied on the ships of allies to transport its substantial land forces. Upon learning that the Carthaginians were in Akragas, the Romans besieged the city. The Carthaginians sent a force to relieve the besieged city. The Punic commander, Hanno, son of Hannibal, took his fifty thousand infantry units, six thousand cavalrymen, and sixty war elephants to Akragas after landing. However, Hanno seems to have had little confidence in his soldiers, as they camped for two months without attacking the Romans.

Finally, he could take it no longer and advanced on the Roman army, putting his elephants behind his soldiers, most likely to keep them from retreating. The Romans were able to push the Carthaginian lines back, and the elephants panicked, trampling on their own men. A considerable number of Carthaginians were lost, and their baggage train was taken. Upon returning to Carthage, Hanno lost his civil rights and had to pay a fine of six thousand gold pieces. The battle he lost was called the Battle of Agrigentum and is considered the first real battle of the Punic Wars.

Plans for a Roman navy began in 260 BCE after the Carthaginians began harassing the Italian coast. The Romans used the Carthaginian quinquereme, which had been captured very early in the war, as their model. Quinqueremes were large warships with three banks of oars, with two men on the top oar, two on the center oar, and one man on the bottom oar. Once the Romans began to build ships in earnest, they were finished in only two months. Rome's new admiral was consul Gnaeus Cornelius Scipio, and like every other Roman aristocrat engaged in military action, he didn't have the luxury to bide his time. He needed to act quickly. Rome's goal was now clear. If it could face and defeat Carthage's powerful navy, then the Punic presence in Sicily would be gone forever.

After Rome's victory at Agrigentum, it attempted to take other cities controlled by Carthage, but that proved difficult and costly. Cities would be taken by either side, then taken back by the other. Allegiances switched dramatically in a bloody stalemate that proved unsatisfying to both sides. This was why the Senate in Rome felt certain that the only course available to the Romans was with their new navy. They trained the oarsmen relentlessly and took their ships out often to go through various maneuvers so that the sailors' reactions would be automatic with no hesitation. Rome and Carthage ships met in brief skirmishes, with the Romans usually losing to the more experienced Carthaginians.

However, the Romans began to realize they might have the upper hand if they could turn a naval battle into something more like a land battle, which was where their soldiers could do what they did best. With that in mind, they began to implement the use of the *corvus* or "crow," which was a hooked gangplank that could latch onto the side of an enemy ship and allow it to be boarded.

The Roman admiral Scipio led seventeen ships in 260 BCE to the Aeolian Islands, where he was prepared to accept the surrender of the city of Lipara (modern-day Lipari). However, the Carthaginians arrived as well and trapped Scipio in the harbor. The inexperienced Roman crew abandoned their ships and were quickly captured, along with their commander. Scipio was ransomed back to the Romans but was not punished for the loss. He even became consul again in 254 BCE. Scipio was replaced as admiral by Gaius Duilius. It took some time for Duilius to arrive in Sicily, so the Romans made much-needed repairs to their hastily built ships, trained, and worked more with the *corvus*.

When Duilius arrived, he left Sicily in the hands of his lieutenants and led the Roman fleet in a full-scale assault on the Carthaginians. They met each other at Mylae in 260 BCE. The commander of the Carthaginians was Hannibal Gisco, who had been at the Battle of Agrigentum. Gisco saw the Roman fleet of 103 ships and approached them rapidly with his 130 ships. The Carthaginians, it would seem, were overly confident in their prowess at sea. If it had been a typical naval battle, they might have been well founded in their confidence. But the Romans were planning on a much different type of battle. As soon as the Carthaginians came within range, they dropped their "crows," and Roman marines quickly boarded the Carthaginian ships and dispatched everyone on board. According to ancient historians, thirty ships were taken in this way before the Carthaginians knew what was happening, but it was too late for the rest. Their momentum propelled them right into the arms of their destruction.

Gisco was barely able to escape in a rowboat. He was also able to escape punishment back in Carthage by sending a message asking if he should attack the Romans. When Carthage said yes, he claimed he was only following orders. The Romans were now emboldened and pursued Gisco to Sardinia, where they defeated another Carthaginian fleet. This time, Hannibal Gisco was not so lucky and was executed by his own subordinates.

Surprisingly, while the Carthaginian navy was suffering, their land army in Sicily was doing well. The Carthaginians were engaged in a war of attrition in the hilly Sicilian terrain. This did not work well for Roman generals, who wanted decisive action since their consulship only lasted one year. The Carthaginian commanders, who held their positions for much longer, could afford to play a longer game. The Romans would besiege Carthaginian strongholds but would have to give up after several months. Cities continued to switch sides sporadically throughout the conflict. The city of Enna, for example, changed sides three times in five years. Cities like Panormus and Lilybaeum stayed in Carthaginian hands consistently.

This still did not counteract their losses at sea. The Romans raided Malta and the Aeolian Islands and scored a victory against the Carthaginians off Cape Tyndaris on the northern coast of Sicily.

The Romans then decided to pursue a familiar course of action. They would take the fight directly to North Africa. This was a daring plan. Before this, the only Roman action outside Italy had been their crossing to Sicily. Now they were planning an invasion almost 373 miles across the open ocean. The Romans put together a fleet of 330 ships, with 120 marines assigned to each vessel and a certain number of oarsmen. The ancient historian Polybius tells us the Romans had a total of 140,000 men. The Carthaginians had an estimated 350 ships and 150,000 men. These massive navies met at Cape Ecnomus off the southern side of Sicily. Once again, the Roman *corvi* proved to be the defining element of the battle. The Carthaginians were laid out in a line, while the Roman ships were broken into four parts, making a triangle, with one section held in reserve.

The Carthaginian center crumbled first. The line collapsed in on itself, and the Romans were able to surround a large portion of the Carthaginian fleet. In all, ninety-four Punic ships were taken or sunk, with the Romans only losing twenty-four. It was a complete disaster for the Carthaginians. Their much smaller fleet regrouped, probably at Lilybaeum. They sent a new commander named Hanno to present peace terms to Rome, which were rejected. One commander, Hamilcar, stayed in Sicily, while Hanno took most of the fleet back to North Africa. The Romans continued on their mission and landed at a place called Aspis on Cape Bon, a peninsula in northern Tunisia, and quickly captured the city.

Rome perhaps second-guessed its decision to send two consuls and such a large army to North Africa, as it recalled one of the consuls, Manlius Vulso, back to Italy. This left the other consul, Marcus Atilius Regulus, with forty ships, fifteen thousand infantry, and five hundred cavalry. Regulus besieged the city of Adys, with the Carthaginians sending five thousand infantry and five hundred cavalry against them.

When the forces met in battle, the Carthaginians pushed the Roman lines back, but upon chasing after the Roman center, they found themselves surrounded. They turned and fled in disarray. Tunis was then taken by Regulus. Carthage was overrun with refugees fleeing the Romans.

Famine began to set in within the great city. Peace negotiations began, but Regulus demanded that the Carthaginians leave Sicily and Sardinia, pay ransoms for every Carthaginian prisoner, pay Rome's war expenses, and pay a yearly tribute. Regulus also demanded that Carthage get Rome's consent for any future declarations of war or peace and that Carthage be left with only one warship. The Carthaginians would never agree to such terms, which Regulus was counting on. He wanted to take Carthage itself and desired the plunder from such a great prize.

Carthage brought in new mercenaries, including a Spartan commander named Xanthippus. Carthage mustered twelve thousand infantry, four thousand cavalry, and one hundred war elephants. Xanthippus was put in charge of the entire force, perhaps showing that Carthage recognized the issue with their homegrown commanders. He attacked the Romans immediately and defeated them, thanks in large part to his superior cavalry. The Roman army was almost totally destroyed or captured; only about two thousand Roman soldiers were able to escape. Regulus was captured and died in captivity. North Africa had been saved. Xanthippus recognized his precarious position and the jealousy directed toward him, so he took his honors for the victory and left Carthage.

Rome still had control of the sea, though. Fortune favored Carthage in this one respect, as the Roman fleet was caught in a storm off the southern coast of Sicily in 255 BCE. Only 80 of 364 ships survived. However, things in Sicily were looking bad for the Carthaginians. The port of Panormus was taken in 254 BCE. Then, Thermae Himerae and Lipara fell in 252 BCE. Akragas was retaken, but the Carthaginian commander knew he couldn't keep it, so he had the city burned to the ground. An attempt was made to retake Panormus, but it was a failure, with twenty thousand Carthaginian troops lost.

Lilybaeum became the next Roman target. In 250 BCE, the Romans laid siege to the city by land and sea. The Carthaginians focused on breaking through the naval blockade with supplies and fresh troops. The hero of these blockade runs was a captain named Hannibal the Rhodian, who entered the harbor of Lilybaeum at least twice and challenged the Romans to battle, which they declined due to his fast and agile ship. However, one of the Punic quadriremes was stopped and captured by the Romans. This ship was then used by the Romans to hunt down Hannibal the Rhodian, whose own ship was captured and used by the Romans to completely seal off the harbor of Lilybaeum.

The constant warfare, the loss of Sicilian ports, and the dominance of the Romans at sea led to economic exhaustion in Carthage. In 247 BCE, Carthage was reduced to asking for a loan of two thousand talents from

Ptolemy in Egypt; the request was quickly denied.

Despite the devastation to Rome's navy in the storm of 255 BCE, Rome had finally been able to rebuild their fleet. Things remained a stalemate in Sicily. The one bright spot for Carthage was the actions of a commander named Hamilcar Barca, who conducted guerilla warfare of a mostly symbolic nature; he was not necessarily concerned with strategic goals. In Carthage, public opinion had shifted to a desire for peace. Rome had simply outlasted Carthage in its desire to continue hostilities. Carthage had never been able to adapt to Rome's highly aggressive strategy or develop a clear strategy of its own. Instead, the Carthaginians had largely been fighting a defensive war. They were not trying to win; they were simply trying not to lose.

The terms of peace that Rome offered were more appealing than the demands that Regulus had made. Carthage would need to surrender all its possessions in Sicily and its naval ports on neighboring islands. The Carthaginians could not be in conflict with Rome or her allies. They were also required to pay 3,200 talents or almost 100 tons of silver.

The war had lasted a grueling twenty-three years. Both sides had lost hundreds of ships and hundreds of thousands of soldiers, many lost at sea. The two sides had started off as wary adversaries with a history of treaties and trade. Now, they were bitter enemies. The Romans would speak of *Punica fides* or "Carthaginian loyalty," which meant the worst sort of betrayal. The peace after the First Punic War would last twenty-three years, but the stage had been set for an even greater war.

In the following years, Carthage's mercenaries and African allies turned against her in the Mercenary War, which lasted from 241 to 237 BCE. Rome nominally supported Carthage in the war but used the opportunity to take Sardinia and Corsica from Carthage. Carthage was able to suppress the rebellion thanks to Hamilcar Barca, who began to show a knack for great leadership. Consequently, his family grew exceptionally powerful. Hamilcar turned his sights on Hispania, modern-day Spain, instead of attempting to retake Sardinia, Corsica, or Sicily back from Rome. Hispania already had a Punic presence and was known for its excellent natural resources and good ports for expanded trade.

By the 220s BCE, thanks to its new territories in Hispania, Carthage had recovered from its war with Rome. Rome acknowledged Carthage's expansion in Spain and focused on governing her new burgeoning empire. From 225 to 222 BCE, Rome fought the Gauls in northern Italy and looked to expand into the territory of Illyria across the Adriatic Sea. However, things would take a turn, which would set Carthage and Rome once again against each other in a fight for their very existence.

Chapter 7: Hannibal Ad Portas ("Hannibal Is at the Gates!")

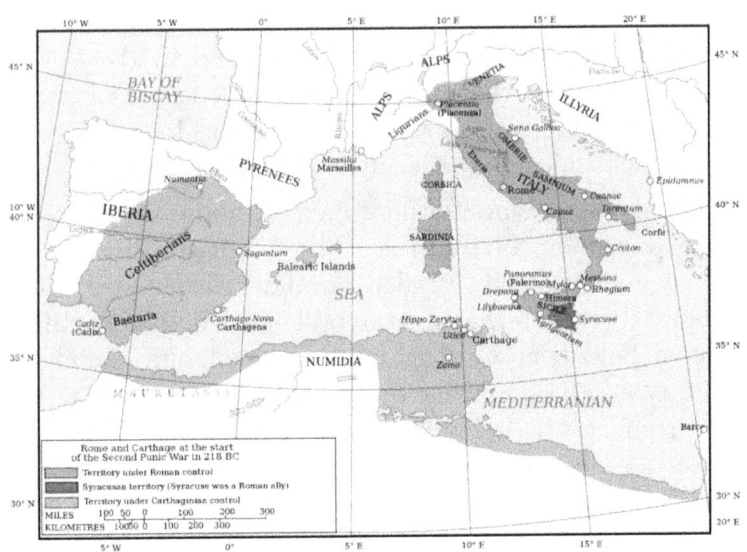

Carthage and Rome at the beginning of the Second Punic War.
*Grandiosederivative work : Augusta 89, CC BY-SA 3.0 <https://creativecommons.org/licenses/by-sa/3.0>, via Wikimedia Commons;
https://commons.wikimedia.org/wiki/File:Map_of_Rome_and_Carthage_at_the_start_of_the_Second_Punic_War_2.svg*

The "Mercenary War" that erupted just after the end of the First Punic War was significant in many ways. Hamilcar Barca retired from his role as commander of the Carthaginian military after securing the peace treaty with Rome, perhaps because he had been unhappy with the Carthaginian surrender. Another Carthaginian commander, Gisco, had the task of sending the many mercenaries employed by Carthage back to Cape Bon, where they expected to receive their payment. Carthage, most likely owing to a lack of currency, delayed handing out payments but instead sent the mercenaries to a town called Sicca.

As the mercenary numbers grew and as time drew on, the soldiers had plenty of free time to tally up just how much they thought the Carthaginians owed them, usually arriving at exceedingly large amounts. Feeling that the Carthaginians were ignoring their demands and because the mercenaries spoke a myriad of languages, which made it difficult for the Carthaginians to communicate with them, the mercenaries began to speak of rebellion. They were led by two mercenaries named Spendius and Mathos; they demanded that Gisco come to them and deal with them directly. The Carthaginians agreed to this, but the mercenaries captured Gisco and his guards and held them as prisoners.

Spendius and Mathos were able to gain the support of the Libyan subjects of Carthage, who had been heavily taxed by the Carthaginians during the First Punic War. Thus, the Mercenary War began, and Carthage, wanting nothing more than peace after its long years at war with Rome, found itself almost immediately in another struggle.

The mercenary and Libyan armies then set about besieging Utica and Hippo, close neighbors of Carthage. The Carthaginians suffered many losses early on and eventually recalled Hamilcar Barca to lead their forces. He moved quickly and ended the siege on Utica. He then met the army of Spendius in a field near Carthage and defeated him soundly. Mathos continued to besiege Hippo while Spendius escaped to Tunis. A group of Numidians from North Africa, led by a man named Naravas, came to offer their services to Hannibal Barca, who, despite his successes, was still outnumbered by the combined forces of Mathos and Spendius. Barca welcomed Naravas and promised him his daughter's hand in marriage if the Numidians assisted him.

Bust of Hannibal Barca.
https://commons.wikimedia.org/wiki/File:Mommsen_p265.jpg

    Hamilcar treated any prisoners he captured well, offering them the chance to return home or join his army. Spendius and Mathos became concerned this would lead to the disintegration of their forces, so they began to convince their confederates that Hamilcar's actions were a ruse. One of their commanders, a Gaul named Autaritus, encouraged the idea and convinced Spendius to have seven hundred prisoners, including the Carthaginian commander Gesco, tortured and killed by cutting off their hands and then extremities before finally dispatching them. When knowledge of this reached the Carthaginians, they became incensed and knew they could no longer give leniency to the rebels. In 239 BCE, the loyal cities of Utica and Hippacritae killed those in the Carthaginian garrisons and joined the rebels. The rebels then began to besiege Carthage itself.

The rebels ran out of supplies and were forced to end the siege of Carthage and fall back to Tunis. However, Spendius took an army of forty thousand men and harassed Hamilcar's army but eventually became pinned against a mountain range called the Saw. They ran out of supplies and were forced to eat their horses, then their prisoners, and then their slaves. Spendius and his lieutenants came to a parlay with Hamilcar but were arrested. The rest of the army attacked and were killed to the last man. Hamilcar had Spendius and his surviving officers crucified in front of Tunis, where Mathos remained.

Upon seeing the situation, Mathos left Tunis and met Hamilcar and another commander, Hanno, in battle at Leptis Parva. No details of the battle survive, but the rebels were crushed. Mathos was taken prisoner and dragged through the streets of Carthage, where he was tortured and then killed by the inhabitants. All of the cities that had sided with the rebels were won back by the Carthaginians, including Utica and Hippo.

The Mercenary War had unintended consequences that would prove pivotal to how Carthage planned to rebuild itself. In 240 or 239 BCE, the Carthaginian garrisons on the island of Sardinia had joined the mutiny, effectively ending Carthaginian control of this important island. When the Carthaginians sent a force to retake the island, that force joined the mutiny, and all the loyal Carthaginians on the island were killed. The rebels on Sardinia appealed to Rome for help, but Rome refused. In 237 BCE, the indigenous people of Sardinia rose up and took the island back, forcing the rebels to flee. These people then appealed to Rome. Rome accepted and took control of Sardinia. Carthage protested, stating that it was putting together a force to retake the island. Rome considered this an act of war and demanded that Carthage hand over control of Sardinia and Corsica and pay another 1,200 talents to Rome. After thirty years of war, the Carthaginians did not have the spirit to continue fighting, so they agreed to Rome's demands.

Hamilcar Barca, thus having regained North Africa for the Carthaginians, was sent to the Iberian Peninsula to expand and secure territories there. He brought his nine-year-old son, Hannibal, with him. Barca met his end in battle, and the command of the army in Spain went to his son-in-law, Hasdrubal. Hasdrubal ruled in Spain for eight years. He was able to expand Carthaginian territory mostly by means of diplomacy. He was assassinated by a Celt for what was said to have been something of a private nature. The command then fell to young Hannibal, the son of the great Hamilcar Barca.

According to ancient sources on the subject, upon taking the mantle of command, Hannibal had every intention of rekindling the war with Rome. The Carthaginians, for their part, felt abused by Rome in the ensuing peace, while the Romans remained suspicious that the Carthaginians would try to reclaim their empire.

Hasdrubal's and Hannibal's ascensions were a clear display of how things had changed politically in the Carthaginian world. When Hamilcar Barca died, his successor would have previously been picked by the Council of Elders in Carthage, but the Barcid clan had established so much dominance in southern Spain that the Carthaginian army took it upon itself to declare Hasdrubal the new leader of the army. The Public Assembly in Carthage, which supported the Barcids completely, quickly approved the appointment. The same thing happened when Hasdrubal was killed; the army declared Hannibal the new commander, and the Public Assembly approved the decision, bypassing the Council of Elders completely.

Hannibal was, in everything but name, the king of a region that encompassed much of southern Spain. He ruled from a palace in a city his brother-in-law had founded called New Carthage, modern-day Cartagena. While Barcid Spain enjoyed a silver boon and quickly paid off Carthage's debt to Rome with plenty to spare, the archaeological evidence shows Carthage remained in an economic slump during this time.

In 221 BCE, twenty-six-year-old Hannibal Barca took power. There were plenty in the Carthaginian elite who resented the apparent unregulated power of the Barcids. The coins minted in Barcid Spain during this time show a clean-shaven Hercules-Melqart with a club and laurel leaves on one side and an African elephant on the other—a reference to Hannibal's father and the Barcid clan in general. Hannibal spent the first two years as general dealing with issues in Spain and expanding Carthaginian control to the northwest, fighting the Celtiberians.

Early on, it became clear that Hannibal was as good a general, if not greater, than his famous father. In the spring of 220 BCE, Hannibal was faced with a force of Celtiberians greater than his own. He feigned a retreat across a river and set up camp. When the enemy took the bait, they crossed the river only to be ambushed by Hannibal's cavalry. The ones that made it through were then crushed by forty war elephants. Hannibal easily crossed the river and finished off the rest of the enemy's forces.

Hannibal then crossed the Hiberus River (modern-day Ebro River), took much of the territory there, and headed toward the city of Saguntum, which was a Roman ally. A debate arose within the city between pro-Roman and pro-Barcid factions. Roman envoys within the city, of course, sided with the pro-Roman faction and had many from the other side executed. The message was clear: an attack on Saguntum was a provocation of war.

Hannibal tightened his hold on the land surrounding the city, and the people of Saguntum sent appeals to Rome, which responded by sending emissaries to meet with Hannibal directly. The Romans, having kept abreast of Carthaginian activity in Iberia, knew they should talk with Hannibal and not waste time meeting with anyone in Carthage itself. The Romans met with Hannibal in his palace at New Carthage and told him plainly that he should not interfere in Saguntum. Hannibal replied that Rome had been the first to interfere in Saguntum, referencing the execution of pro-Carthaginians. He told the Romans that it was a Carthaginian tradition not to overlook injustice. The Romans stormed off and traveled to Carthage to express their protests there.

Hannibal was in a fine position to deal so high-handedly with the Romans. He personally controlled a vast territory in Spain that provided him with plenty of food and more than enough silver to pay his troops. He had a seasoned army of sixty thousand infantry, eight thousand cavalry, and two hundred war elephants. He was allied with many of the leaders around him, and he had married an Iberian to secure his political position. With this in mind, he disregarded the Roman threats and attacked Saguntum. It took eighteen months to conquer the city, during which Rome sent more envoys to Hannibal, but he sent them away without seeing them. The Romans who went to Carthage demanded to know if Hannibal's actions were sanctioned by the government. The Carthaginians deflected. The Romans asked if Carthage wanted peace or war; once again, the Carthaginians turned the question back on the envoys. The Romans decided on war, thus beginning the Second Punic War in 218 BCE.

It is believed that Hasdrubal had planned on crossing from Iberia into Gaul and then crossing the Alps, where he hoped to meet up with the Cisalpine Gauls to attack Rome. However, Rome had conquered the Gauls in northern Italy, and Hasdrubal had been assassinated, so Rome might have believed the threat had been avoided. However, Hannibal clearly wanted to continue where his brother-in-law had left off. After taking Saguntum, he sent plunder to Carthage, which gained him plenty of supporters there, though Hanno II, an old rival of Hannibal's father, voiced his opposition to the Barcids. He told the Council of Elders that Hannibal wished nothing more than to be a king and that as long as a Barcid controlled the army, there would never be peace with Rome. His words had no impact, if for no other reason than Hannibal controlled Spain, which had become Carthage's most profitable territory. The tribes in Iberia had pledged allegiance to the Barcids, not Carthage. Hannibal could not be detained or replaced. Wherever he went, Carthage went.

Rome was not yet ready to mobilize an army, and it had no idea what Hannibal had planned. Hannibal took his time after the fall of Saguntum to build up his army and stores for the grueling ordeal ahead. Hannibal left his brother, Hasdrubal, in Spain to defend it in case of a Roman attack and to keep the locals under a watchful eye.

Hannibal's plan sounded fairly straightforward. He would go by land north to Gaul and then east, thereby entering Italy from the north. This overland route would offer Hannibal the element of surprise because the Romans would not imagine Hannibal's army crossing both the Pyrenees and the Alps, the two highest mountain ranges in western Europe, to make war with them. It was a daring and incredibly risky plan, but Hannibal was a bold commander, and he knew this sort of gambit could provide a great payout.

Also, he did not have many options. After the end of the First Punic War, Rome's rule of the sea was unquestioned in the western Mediterranean. The Punic fleet at the outbreak of Hannibal's war was only thirty-seven ships. Furthermore, Hannibal was a land commander; he had no great admirals to rely on.

In 218 BCE, the Roman consuls were Publius Cornelius Scipio and Tiberius Sempronius Longus. Their plan was for Scipio to take 22,000 infantry and 2,200 cavalry and go to Spain to battle Hannibal, whom they assumed would still be there, while Longus took 27,000 men and a fleet of 180 ships to invade Africa.

Hannibal began his campaign by swiftly taking several cities and conquering tribes in modern-day Catalonia. This was particularly important because some of these tribes were known to be on friendly terms with the Romans. At that time, Hannibal then had about fifty thousand infantry, nine thousand cavalry, and several hundred war elephants. He split his force into three columns, which each crossed the

Ebro River. The crossing of the river and subduing the tribes in the area took a total of two months, during which Hannibal lost an estimated thirteen thousand men. The march through the Pyrenees and down to the Rhone River was largely uneventful. Publius Scipio had been given orders by the Senate to divert his course and meet Hannibal in northwest Spain, but he was not quick enough and missed the enemy. He learned in Massalia (modern-day Marseille) that Hannibal was not in Catalonia as he expected but was four days away from the Rhone.

The Romans attempted to meet Hannibal as he crossed the Rhone River. However, Hannibal was already making the crossing from the west bank. On the east bank was a Gallic tribe called the Cavares, who were prepared to attack the Carthaginian army when it crossed. However, Hannibal took Alexander the Great as his model, remembering when the Macedonian king crossed the Hydaspes River in India. Hannibal had one of his commanders take a northern route around the Cavares and attack their flank just as Hannibal's main army was making the crossing. In this way, Hannibal was able to crush the Cavares and cross the river without issue.

Hannibal had to get from the Rhone to the Alps as quickly as possible so that he would be able to cross the mountains before winter set in. If he could not do it in time, then the element of surprise would be lost, and the Romans would be able to raise an army to stop him from entering Italy. He had his cavalry skirt his right flank, which was the side near the sea, as he believed the Romans might land boats and attack from that direction. The cavalry could then hold the enemy off while Hannibal's infantry formed their lines. Hannibal stayed in the rear of his force with the war elephants, which now numbered thirty-seven, as he also believed the Romans might be behind him and come from that direction. The cavalry traveled about nineteen miles a day, while the infantry traveled twelve miles a day. For an ancient army traversing rough and unknown terrain, this was an exceptional speed.

Hannibal's army eventually reached the Alps. The route he took is still hotly debated, as it was in ancient times. There are at least five popular theories, with many other acceptable theories as well. It is believed that he might have taken the Little St. Bernard Pass, which goes from Savoie, France, to the Aosta Valley in Italy. The modern road that now goes across this pass is closed from November to the end of April. He also might have taken the Col de Clapier from Savoie, France, to the Piedmont region of Italy. There is the Col de la Traversette, where sediments appear to have been churned up around approximately the early 3rd century BCE; however, no Carthaginian artifacts have been found, nor the tell-tale bones of elephants. Another theory suggests Col de Montgenèvre, which was known to the Romans and would eventually be used by Julius Caesar when he began his campaign into Gaul. Also, there was a pass that went from Val-Cenis in France to Susa in Italy. Currently, there is no definitive answer.

The consul Publius arrived at the Rhone and found that the Carthaginian army had already crossed. By then, he could have figured out what Hannibal's plan was. He also would have been aware that the Carthaginian general was carrying out his strategy with great speed. Publius sent his brother to continue attacking the Carthaginians in Spain, while he planned to return to Italy and meet Hannibal when he descended the Alps.

Hannibal's journey through the Alps has become something more legendary than real, but it was certainly done, and it must have been a grueling ordeal for everyone involved, including the animals. Snow had begun to fall in many places. Men and beasts slipped from high paths and were dashed on the rocks below. Hannibal's ability to keep his men marching and to stop any mutinous actions is a testament to his ability as a leader. Many of the men in the army had never seen snow and had never crossed such mountains; it must have seemed impossible to them, but Hannibal kept them moving forward.

The men did not only have to contend with just the climate and terrain. They were also dogged by local tribes who hoped to gain booty and remove the outsiders from their homeland. Yet, as the Carthaginians rose higher in the mountains, these attacks stopped because they had reached a land where no man lived. They finally reached the crest of a huge mountain, where Hannibal was soon able to show his men the Po Valley stretching out before them. There, he told them, was where they would defeat their eternal enemy, the Romans. The spirits of his men lifted, and they began the dangerous task of descending the Alps.

When Hannibal's army reached the Po Valley and completed the crossing of the Alps, they numbered twenty thousand infantry, six thousand cavalry, and an unknown number of war elephants, which were now sick and famished after the crossing. They descended sometime in the fall of 218 BCE. After a short period of rest, the Carthaginians attacked the hostile Taurini, a Celtic-Ligurian tribe. They defeated them and raided their food stores. In late November, Publius Scipio and Hannibal met in battle. This would be the first time Hannibal faced Roman forces on Italian soil. It was at first a cavalry battle, with Hannibal having strength in numbers, but Scipio believed his soldiers were the better fighters.

When they met, a melee broke out. Hannibal's Numidian cavalry outflanked Scipio's men, causing the Romans to crumble and flee. Hannibal returned to his army and prepared for the main battle, thinking the cavalry battle was only a skirmish, but Scipio, perhaps feeling his men had lost morale, retreated down the Po River. This was not just a defeat for the Romans; the battle also caused all the local Gallic tribes to side with the Carthaginians. Hannibal's army increased dramatically in size after the Battle of Ticinus. The significance of this victory cannot be overstated.

Scipio fell back to the Trebia River, and Hannibal followed. Meanwhile, the Roman Senate had made the decision to abandon the plan for Consul Tiberius Sempronius Longus to attempt an invasion of Africa, instead ordering Longus to turn back from Sicily and come to Scipio's aid. Longus acted quickly and arrived at Scipio's camp before Hannibal could attack. The Romans are believed to have had about thirty-eight thousand infantry and four thousand cavalry. The Carthaginians had about twenty-nine thousand infantry and eleven thousand cavalry.

Since both consuls were with the Roman army, they alternated leadership every other day and camped in separate locations. Hannibal used this to his advantage. He waited until the inexperienced and rash Longus was in command to begin his attack. Scipio, who had been injured in the earlier engagement, had wanted to wait until after winter to battle Hannibal, but Longus wanted the glory of defeating the dreaded Carthaginian general.

On the morning of the Battle of Trebia, Hannibal sent out his Numidian cavalry to provoke the Romans. Longus fell for the trap in his eagerness to fight the Carthaginians. He sent his whole army after the Numidians, who wheeled around and took their positions at the wings of Hannibal's army. The Romans crossed the chest-high Trebia River, which was icy cold. The Carthaginians held back and waited for the Romans to come. The outcome was almost predictable. The infantry in the center met, and the fighting was fierce, with the Romans getting the better of it. However, the Carthaginian cavalry wings defeated the Roman cavalry quickly.

Meanwhile, a contingent of two thousand troops commanded by another of Hannibal's brothers, Mago, revealed themselves from their hiding spot to the rear of the Romans and attacked the unguarded rear infantry. The Romans broke and began to flee. The Roman death toll was estimated to be about fifteen thousand, which was a huge loss. Still, the fighting had been rough, and the Carthaginians lost about five thousand men, men that would be harder to replace than the Romans considering their location. Still, no matter how Sempronius Longus presented the battle to the Senate, it was clearly a devastating defeat. Both armies settled down to their winter quarters to wait for the spring.

Meanwhile, Gnaeus Cornelius Scipio, brother of Publius Scipio, landed with his fleet on the coast of Spain and began to attack cities allied with the Carthaginians. He was able to capture a Carthaginian general and an Iberian despot. Hannibal's brother, Hasdrubal, heard of these attacks and ventured north, destroying Roman ships and securing cities that had been taken by the Romans, although he did not face Gnaeus in open battle yet. Instead, he retreated south of the Ebro River and camped for the winter. Gnaeus Scipio stayed north of the Ebro and also settled down for the winter.

During the winter, Hannibal took various precautions to ensure his army would be ready come the spring. He was particularly concerned about the attitude of the northern Italian Gauls who surrounded him, some of whom had recently joined his army. He treated his Roman prisoners poorly, but he treated the Gallic prisoners well and eventually freed them to return to their homes. By doing this, he hoped to encourage support from the local tribes. However, Hannibal was aware that there might be spies and assassins in his midst, so he had several different wigs made of many different colors, which he would change regularly, along with different clothes so that people could not even recognize him easily. While Hannibal managed to survive the winter, along with most of his army, his war elephants did not do so well. When the weather changed, and it was time once again to be on the march, only one elephant remained.

In the spring of 217 BCE, Hannibal decided to head south. The new Roman consuls, Gnaeus Servilius and Gaius Flaminius, had separate armies and were prepared to stop Hannibal through the eastern or western route to Rome. Hannibal, however, decided to take a more difficult but more direct route through the mouth of the Arno River, which was a large marshland. The way was hard, especially on his Gallic allies, and because much of the land they crossed was covered in water, they were unable to sleep for days on end. Hannibal even lost his right eye from conjunctivitis during the journey.

The army arrived in Etruria. Hannibal wanted to lure Flaminius's army out of their encampment by destroying much of the land that they were supposed to protect. Hannibal attacked locations behind Flaminius's defensive position in an effort to draw him out of his protected location. Flaminius eventually realized he could not just sit passively by and went in pursuit of Hannibal. The Carthaginian army ambushed the Romans in a narrow pass on the shores of Lake Trasimene.

The Carthaginian army made camp but conducted tricky night marches to array themselves along the ridge above a narrow pass. Flaminius did not send scouts out before marching into the pass, which was not particularly unordinary. Hannibal waited until the Romans were fully within the trap before letting his soldiers loose. The combined Gallic, Iberian, and African forces slammed into the side and rear of the unexpecting Romans and decimated them. Of the twenty-five thousand Romans involved, only a few thousand escaped with their lives. Flaminius was supposedly killed by a Gaul. Gnaeus's cavalry units, which were unaware of what had happened to Flaminius's army, were scouting ahead when they were also defeated by Hannibal's forces a few days after the Battle of Lake Trasimene. Gnaeus pulled back his forces and retreated to Ariminum, modern-day Rimini, on the Adriatic coast.

When the news of the battle's outcome reached Rome, the city was overcome with panic. Fearing that Hannibal would arrive at the gates of Rome any day, the Romans took drastic measures. They dismissed the idea of electing new consuls but instead appointed a dictator: Quintus Fabius Maximus. He came from the esteemed Fabia clan, which claimed descent from Hercules and was among the first followers of Romulus and Remus, the legendary founders of Rome. Although Quintus Fabius was a dictator, he was not allowed to select his second-in-command. The Romans appointed a political rival, Marcus Minucius Rufus, to that position.

Hannibal, however, decided not to besiege Rome. After the march through the marshland and the subsequent battles, he knew his men and horses needed rest. He marched to the Adriatic and settled there for some time to feed his soldiers and animals from the abundant produce of the area. He also equipped some of his army with the weapons and armor they had taken from the Romans. A message was sent to Carthage, giving the details of his campaign and his victories against the Romans. The people of Carthage were elated and sent troops to both Spain and Italy. Hannibal then marched his army across Italy, devastating the countryside.

In the meantime, Fabius had been able to muster four legions for the emergency and marched out of Rome to Rimini, where he relieved Gnaeus of command and sent him back to Rome to prepare for any possible Carthaginian attacks by sea. Fabius then approached Hannibal's army and set up camp. Upon seeing the Romans, Hannibal brought his army out and arrayed his men for battle, but the Romans did not come out to meet him. Fabius had learned from his predecessor's mistakes. He adopted a strategy in which he would not meet Hannibal in all-out combat but would attack his supply lines and harass the enemy in a war of attrition. This would eventually be called the "Fabian strategy." The Carthaginians were an army prepared for battle, and their success lay in victory on the battlefield. Fabius realized that the Romans were in an entirely different position. They had almost limitless supplies and men but would almost certainly be defeated in a traditional engagement. However, Fabius's second-in-command, Marcus, openly criticized the dictator for what he considered to be weakness and cowardice.

Hannibal did everything he could to try and draw Fabius into a battle. He even ravaged all the land around Fabius's country estate but left the dictator's land untouched, adding to a rumor that Fabius was somehow working with Hannibal. However, a year passed without a decisive battle.

In the following year, 216 BCE, Fabius's dictatorship ended, and the Romans mustered eighty-seven thousand troops. The Romans elected two consuls: Gaius Terentius Varro and Lucius Aemilius Paullus, who had opposing views on how the war with Hannibal should be conducted. Paullus favored the Fabian strategy, but Varro wanted to defeat the Carthaginians once and for all. Eventually, in late July, the Roman army tracked Hannibal down to a small town named Cannae. On August 1st, Hannibal offered to engage the Romans in an open battle, but Paullus was in command that day and refused. On the next day, he offered the same again; Varro was more than willing to meet the Carthaginian army.

The Romans established themselves in a linear formation, while Hannibal put his troops in a crescent shape, with his least reliable soldiers in the center. The Romans pushed through the center but then found themselves enveloped by the Carthaginian forces, who then closed in and defeated the numerically superior Romans. The loss at the Battle of Cannae did not decide the war but caused some Italian allies to abandon Rome and go over to the Carthaginian side. With this victory, the road to Rome now lay open, but it appears Hannibal's primary goal was not to lay siege to Rome, which would be long and costly. He certainly wanted to continue to win over Rome's allies in Italy, but it seems that he sought to establish terms of peace after Cannae since he sent several messengers to Rome to ransom prisoners. However, Rome rejected the offer and forbade the paying of ransoms for prisoners and publicly announced its intention to fight until the bitter end.

For the next few years, things followed a similar pattern. Rome continued to levy more troops, eventually allowing criminals and the poor to be soldiers. In 214 BCE, the Romans had eighteen legions; the next year, they had twenty-two. In total, Rome had about 100,000 soldiers, not counting allied troops, but they were broken up into forces of about 20,000. Thus, they could not face Hannibal directly but were able to hamper his movements. Most of southern Italy, which had formerly been Greek cities, went over to the Carthaginian side. Macedonia sent emissaries and established an alliance with Hannibal. There was even a pro-Carthaginian rebellion in Sardinia, but the Romans were able to stamp it out quickly.

Fabius became consul and continued his strategy. Eleven years after Cannae, war raged around southern Italy. In 207 BCE, Hasdrubal Barca followed his brother and crossed the Alps into Cisalpine Gaul. In 205 BCE, another of Hannibal's brothers, Mago Barca, landed his troops in northwest Italy after he had been defeated by Roman forces in Iberia.

However, in 204 BCE, Publius Cornelius Scipio, the Roman general that had defeated Mago, carried out his planned invasion of Africa. Scipio was the son of a former consul also named Publius Cornelius Scipio, who had died fighting Hasdrubal Barca in Spain. He was the only person to ask to command the army in Spain, as it was considered unwinnable. After defeating Mago, Scipio rejected the idea of returning to Italy, instead feeling the best option was to take the war to Carthage. When he arrived in Africa, the Numidian commander, Masinissa, allied with the Romans. Scipio quickly defeated two Carthaginian armies. Due to this sudden change in events and the fact that the city was in danger of being taken, Carthage recalled Hannibal and Mago back to Africa. Hannibal and

Scipio met at the Battle of Zama in 202 BCE.

Hannibal had thirty-six thousand infantry, four thousand cavalry, and eighty war elephants. Scipio commanded twenty-nine thousand infantry and over six thousand cavalry. They both deployed their infantry in the center in three lines and their cavalry in the wings. Scipio and Hannibal had both studied each other and knew their strengths and weaknesses. Hannibal held back his center to avoid being encircled by Scipio's wings. Scipio knew that the war elephants could charge but only in straight lines. So, he had his men leave gaps in their lines where they could let the elephants pass through without doing any real damage.

The fighting was fierce; it seemed Hannibal had certainly met his match in Scipio. The Carthaginian cavalry was routed, and the Roman cavalry was able to encircle Hannibal's army. Hannibal was finally defeated. It was the end of the Second Punic War.

Chapter 8: Carthago Delenda Est ("Carthage Must Be Destroyed")

Hannibal was able to escape the Romans. He went to Carthage and advised the Council of Elders to begin peace negotiations immediately. The peace terms the Romans proposed included the loss of all territory outside their home in North Africa. Additionally, Carthage was forbidden from fighting any wars outside Africa and even then had to seek permission from Rome. The indemnity was a hefty ten thousand talents of silver to be paid over fifty years. That was ten times the amount in the treaty of 241 BCE. Carthage also had to give up its war elephants and could have no more than ten warships. The Council of Elders accepted the terms. Scipio would forever bear the name "Africanus" for his conquests on the continent. The Roman Senate approved the terms, and the treaty was ratified in North Africa. Carthage's fleet was burned before the city, and Scipio returned to Rome, where he enjoyed a triumph.

Hannibal remained in charge of part of his army, which he set to work planting olive orchards. He then entered politics. Hannibal soon gained popularity among the common citizens by correcting corruption within the government. He proposed a new law in which members of the Council of the Hundred and Four would be decided by elections. He then conducted an audit of state revenues and found evidence of embezzlement from officials. As a result, Hannibal soon made enemies with the political elite. He was a populist leader and began a construction program to improve the city.

The Council of Elders began to be concerned that Hannibal was attempting an autocratic takeover of Carthage. The council sent reports to Rome, saying that Hannibal was scheming with the enemy, Antiochus of the Seleucid Empire. Roman envoys arrived to investigate, and Hannibal fled to the court of Antiochus, as it was the only place he could find safety.

Once there, Hannibal proposed an attack on the Italian Peninsula. The Carthaginians once again sent reports to Rome of Hannibal's activities, and he found himself on the outskirts of Antiochus's court. The Seleucids attempted to expand their empire but were defeated by the Romans in 190 BCE, so Hannibal once again fled, drifting to and from various Hellenistic courts. He finally arrived in Bithynia, but his presence was discovered by the Roman general Titus Quinctius Flamininus. Before he could be handed over to the Romans by Bithynian soldiers, he took the poison he always carried with him. Hannibal died in 181 BCE.

In 180 BCE, Carthage made a remarkable recovery, as it had been freed from the troubles of empire-building and war. The Carthaginians were able to settle their debt to Rome after only ten years, but the Romans denied their request. Carthage was able to supply millions of bushels of grain to Rome and certainly had plenty left over. Carthage's agricultural economy grew rapidly, while Rome had to rely on help from allies due to constant warfare. The Carthaginians also improved their shipyards. The circular port was able to hold at least 170 vessels, though this would have been far beyond what had been stipulated in the peace treaty made with Rome.

It seems these harbors, which were possibly built at this time, were created to be invisible from the seaside of the city. The port was built far inland and would have been impossible to see from ships sailing past the city. Still, the Romans had emissaries who entered the city regularly and would have known about the construction of these harbors. It seems more likely that the inner harbor was not used exclusively for warships but also for Carthage's commercial fleet.

Carthage had a bigger problem with King Masinissa, the Numidian who had been of such great service to Scipio. Masinissa, as a Numidian, was certainly jealous of Carthage's power and took advantage of the results of the Second Punic War to grow his power. He used his position to keep the Romans wary and suspicious of the Carthaginians. Masinissa often seized some of the agricultural output of North Africa as his own. Tensions between Carthage and Numidia resulted in envoys being sent to

Rome, but Rome tended to almost always favor their allies, the Numidians. In fact, one of Masinissa's sons, Gulussa, traveled to Rome to tell the Senate to beware of Carthage, which he said was preparing a large fleet to defeat the Romans. This accusation never came to anything, but it helped fuel the fire of anti-Carthaginian attitudes in Rome.

In 162 BCE, Masinissa overran farmland in Syrtis Minor, a territory that Carthage had owned for centuries. Rome ruled in favor of the Numidian king and forced Carthage to hand over the trading towns along the coast and pay the Numidians five hundred talents as well. Masinissa did this again with some land in the Thusca region. Carthage once again complained to Rome.

Rome sent an envoy led by Marcus Porcius Cato, who was eighty-one years old at the time. Cato had served in the Second Punic War, and his hatred for Carthage was as strong as his political will. He arrived in Carthage in 152 BCE. Cato ruled in favor of Numidia, but he was also appalled by what he found in Carthage. The city was teeming with vigorous men and overflowing with wealth. There were weapons of every description. He saw crops growing in abundance in the countryside. The envoys found stored timber, which they believed might be for the warships Carthage was supposed to be building.

When Cato returned to Rome, he set about convincing his fellow senators of what actions needed to be taken. He ended every speech with "Carthago delenda est" or "Carthage must be destroyed." He felt that Carthage was not only on the verge of building back its armies and wealth but that it had also learned from its previous mistakes and would annihilate Rome. Cato was opposed by a faction led by Scipio Nasica, nephew of Scipio Africanus, who believed that the complete destruction of Carthage would destroy Rome's equilibrium. Without a clear adversary, Rome would become drunk with greed and power. It is from later writers that we hear of Scipio Nasica's arguments, and those later writers, of course, knew that the Roman Republic would eventually fall into civil war, with the republic being replaced by an empire. Scipio might have simply felt that there was no clear justification for war against Carthage. But this did not seem to concern Cato.

By the end of the 150s BCE, it had become clear to Carthage that its treaty with Rome offered no protection but only obligations. The Carthaginians could not rely on Rome to help them in their dealings with the Numidians. A group led by Hamilcar the Samnite and Carthalo gained popular support in Carthage for their belief that the city needed to defend itself. Masinissa sent two of his sons to demand that pro-Numidian leaders be established in the city. His sons were not allowed in Carthage, so they were ambushed by Hamilcar. War was declared between Carthage and Numidia.

After a brief battle, the Carthaginians were surrounded, starved out, and then massacred. Masinissa took another large piece of Carthaginian territory as a result. The greater issue was that the Carthaginians had violated the peace terms established in 201 BCE; they had declared war without Rome's approval. Rome had since resolved its wars in Macedon and Greece, so it now had a large army it could use to attack Carthage and answer Cato's demands. In 150 BCE, Rome mobilized an army for North Africa. Carthage sent envoys to Rome, but by the time they got to Italy, the army had already set out for Sicily. The Carthaginian envoys were greeted with a cool welcome. When they explained that they were going to execute those who had led the war against Numidia, the Romans asked why they were not already dead. When the Carthaginians asked what they could do to atone for their crimes, the Senate told them simply that they must satisfy the Roman people. Cato rallied the Senate, demanding to know why they should forgive Carthage after all the times its people had acted cruelly and broken trust with Rome.

Rome, putting up a farce of possible reconciliation, asked Carthage for three hundred noble children as a sign of good faith. At the same time, an army of eighty thousand infantry and four thousand cavalry, led by consuls Lucius Marcius Censorinus and Manius Manilius, was headed to North Africa. The army disembarked at Utica and told the Carthaginians how war could be avoided. The Carthaginians sent envoys and were told by the consuls that they must surrender all their weapons. Carthage handed over weapons for twenty thousand men and two thousand large catapults. The Romans then told them they could live freely under their own laws but that they must move their city and allow the current one to be destroyed. The envoys tried to argue against this destruction, but their pleas fell on deaf ears. They had to return to Carthage to deliver the unfortunate news that the city they loved would be razed to the ground.

However, the Carthaginians would not accept Rome's terms, and they began to prepare for war. Every building was turned into a workshop to make weapons. Women cut their hair for rope to make catapults. All the slaves were freed, and Hasdrubal, who had escaped execution, was placed in charge of the entire operation. Rome prepared to besiege the city. The siege began in 149 but dragged into 148 BCE. Hasdrubal had been able to get his army out of the city and was disrupting Roman supply lines in the Carthaginian hinterland. Thus, the Romans were still unsuccessful in 147 BCE.

But this was the year that Scipio Aemilianus, the adopted grandson of Scipio Africanus, rose to the consulship and was put in charge of the African campaign. Scipio acted quickly and corrected what he felt was lax discipline within the Roman ranks. He centered his army around Carthage and led a daring night attack with four thousand men. His forces were able to get past the defenses and enter the city. However, he soon realized his position was undefendable, so he returned to the rest of his army.

Things within the city had deteriorated, though. Realizing that there was no chance for surrender, anyone who spoke against those in charge was put to death. Roman prisoners were killed on the city walls in full view of the Roman army. Scipio attempted to cut off Carthage's harbor by building a large mole, or causeway, across it, but the Carthaginians simply dug another trench from the harbor to the sea. A newly built navy sailed out of this opening and attacked the Roman ships in the Battle of the Port of Carthage, but it was forced to withdraw. Many ships sank or were captured. Scipio also attacked the Carthaginian army in the field, overran its camp, and killed many of the soldiers.

Scipio's command was extended for another year. In the spring of 146 BCE, he launched a full-scale assault that successfully breached the city walls. Over the next six days, the Romans and Carthaginians fought in the streets, setting fire to many of the buildings. There was a terrible slaughter until Scipio began to allow the Carthaginians to surrender themselves instead of simply killing them. This was true except for nine hundred Roman deserters who were trapped in the temple of Eshmun. The deserters, knowing all hope was lost, set fire to the temple and died inside.

The Carthaginian leader, Hasdrubal, eventually surrendered to Scipio. Upon seeing this, his wife took his children into a burning building as she cursed her husband. This was not just the end of the Third Punic War but also the end of ancient Carthage, one of the greatest cities in the western Mediterranean and once the center of a great empire. Carthage would lay in ruins for a hundred years, only to be rebuilt as a Roman city. The city survived into the Middle Ages, but it was never truly Carthage again.

Chapter 9: Government and Military

Like any other nation or empire, the Carthaginian government and military changed over time. In the beginning, it was believed Carthage was an oligarchic government. The city was ruled by an aristocratic elite called the *b'lm*, or the princes. This group controlled every important judicial, governmental, religious, and military decision in the state. The ancient Greeks apparently believed the Carthaginians were ruled by kings, but this seems to have been a misunderstanding, probably due to the fact that the princes were led by a single dynastic family, such as the Magonids or Barcids. The Carthaginians seemed to have a tendency to give political power to a son after the father had died, but it was different from a monarchy, in which power automatically went from father to son, etc. There was not a clear line of succession in Carthage. We can see this when Hamilcar Barca died; instead of power going directly to Hannibal, it instead went to his older and presumably more competent brother-in-law, Hasdrubal. It was not until Hasdrubal was assassinated that Hannibal was able to gain power.

Even when a son rose to be the greatest among the princes, he was not an autocratic ruler. There were various councils that were able to, more or less, check his power. There was, of course, the Popular Assembly, which appears to have been a part of Carthage's political landscape sometime after the loss of Syracuse to Gelon, but it initially did not have much power. This body was composed of citizens of Carthage, and there were various qualifications that changed over the years, such as age, property ownership, and wealth. However, the particulars of who could and could not participate in the Popular Assembly are not completely known due to the loss of all of Carthage's records when the city was burned by the Romans. However, the Popular Assembly saw a great increase in power thanks to the rise of the Barcids after the Sicilian Wars. Hamilcar was able to secure the general command of an army in Libya simply by popular vote, something that would have been unheard of a generation before. The ordinary citizen, or *s'rnm*, now had a taste of influence that they would not give up.

There was also the Council of Elders, which seems to have been a very old institution within the city. This was, as the name suggests, a council of venerated older members of the elite class whose power waxed and waned as the years went by. They could decide who controlled the army and conducted foreign affairs and had control of the treasury.

After the loss of Syracuse to Gelon, another council was formed: the Council of the Hundred and Four. This council appointed special commissioners, called *pentarchies*, who dealt with a wide range of affairs of state. The Hundred and Four was a council of judges that, according to Aristotle, were the highest constitutional authority. They had the ability to judge generals, along with many other powers. This was particularly important because generals had a great deal of autonomy in the Carthaginian government, and the Hundred and Four provided a check to their power. The Hundred and Four also controlled the senate, the generals, and the *suffetes* or *shophets*. The *shophets* were civic leaders. The name is Semitic in origin, as is the concept. Like the consuls of Rome, there were two annually elected *shophets* who acted as judges and senate presidents. They also brought issues before the Popular Assembly. Eventually, the term was used more broadly, as there were *shophets* in various locations around the Carthaginian Empire.

As has been noted, the Carthaginian Empire was not the rigid, clearly defined nation that one might think of when one thinks of an empire. Carthage gave plenty of autonomy to her possessions and relied on treaties and alliances as much as full-scale conquest. Carthage does not appear to have been in the habit of leaving garrisons in cities it conquered as the Romans and Greeks did. This was both beneficial and detrimental to Carthage since it did not need to extend its people and resources across a wide area, but it also made it easier for cities to revolt. Whole regions could be lost quickly, like Sardinia and Corsica.

For many centuries, Carthage relied heavily on its navy to protect its commercial vessels and ports and to keep its various territories in check. This, of course, changed during the Punic Wars. However, its land army was just as important and was involved in as much activity as its forces on the sea. The two areas had to often work in concert, such as when troops needed to be transported or when cities were being besieged. This meant that generals needed to have supreme authority while they engaged in military actions. Carthaginian generals did not have to wait for approval from the senate before they acted as their Roman counterparts did, but they were in danger of later prosecution from the Hundred and Four if it was deemed their actions were in error. For this reason, many Carthaginian generals were executed after serious losses.

The primary problem with this system was that the Hundred and Four could act cruelly and arbitrarily, so a general had no way of knowing if his actions would be excused or if he might be put to death after a particular battle or war. By the time of the Barcids, however, thanks to support from the Popular Assembly, generals were able to escape prosecution. When they were away from Carthage, they could essentially act as monarchs in their given territories, as Hamilcar, Hasdrubal, and Hannibal did in Spain.

The army of Carthage was incredibly successful when they were commanded by a competent general. These generals were typically selected for a particular campaign or war and almost always came from elite families. Generals were generally autonomous, but the Hundred and Four or the *shophets* might order a general to call a truce or sue for peace. Some families in Carthage also had their own private armies, which they could call upon for overseas operations. Thus, an army could have two or even three different commanders, a situation that caused many difficulties. Due to the pressure of command and the possibility of harsh punishment, many unsuccessful commanders committed suicide rather than face judgment back in Carthage. However, they could still face punishment after death. For instance, the Hundred and Four crucified the corpse of general Mago in 344 BCE.

The Carthaginian army consisted of heavy armored infantry drawn from the citizenry. They numbered 2,500 to 3,000 and were known for their white shields. They were called the Sacred Band. Infantry and cavalry units were also pulled from allies, notably the Libyans and Iberians. They were paid for their services but might not have been considered mercenaries. Additionally, Carthage employed what is typically considered mercenaries, that is, soldiers for hire. Mercenaries came from all corners of the empire and beyond, such as Gaul, Iberia, Greece, Sardinia, and Tunisia, to name a few. The Carthaginians also employed the Numidian cavalry, whose men carried small shields and threw poisoned darts. The Numidians would, of course, play a crucial role in the lead-up to the Third Punic War when they opposed Carthage. The Carthaginians also had a unit of Egyptian-Libyan women who rode chariots into battle.

The Carthaginians often used the armor of their fallen enemies. After the Sicilian Wars, they commonly used bronze Corinthian helmets and heavy hoplite armor. Their shields were typically circular, though Celtic soldiers had rectangular oak shields. Shields were often decorated with designs from the Punic religion or, in the case of Hasdrubal Barca, self-portraits. Hannibal wore gilded bronze-scaled armor that had belonged to Hamilcar, his father. Soldiers typically carried straight or curved blades with a dagger for backup. The armor and weapons varied greatly due to the many different origins of the units that made up the Carthaginian army.

There were archers, but they were used less than in other contemporary armies. However, there were typically archers on top of the war elephants. There were slingers as well, with the most famous being the Balearic slingers, who used almond-shaped lead shot. The Punic army also used catapults and crossbows.

The Carthaginians were perhaps most famous for their use of war elephants. These massive creatures were used as much for their psychological effect as their importance on the battlefield. Elephants were trained to charge, but they could be unwieldy. In many instances, they turned and trampled the men in their own army rather than the enemy. They were often covered in armor, with spears attached to their trunks. The elephants used were native to North Africa and are now extinct. They were not large enough to carry any structure on their backs but instead had a rider and a bowman or javelin thrower. The elephants were typically placed in front of the infantry when battle lines were formed.

The Carthaginian army was used to great effect by Hannibal in his Spanish and Italian campaigns. He did not rely too heavily on the war elephants but instead used his cavalry to outflank his enemy. He was also a master of the ambush and was able to catch the Romans by surprise on various occasions and use this to his advantage. Hannibal appears to have planned out every detail and communicated his plans to all parts of his army so that they could work together as one unit and exploit the weaknesses of his enemy.

Despite the arguments of Greek and Roman historians, the Carthaginian army was in no way inferior due to their use of mercenaries or because of the natural disposition of the Carthaginians themselves. Hannibal was not an aberration but the product of a system designed to maintain one of the greatest powers in the western Mediterranean.

Chapter 10: Society, Economy, and Religion

The Carthaginian society was born, first and foremost, from its Phoenician origin. The language they spoke was derived from Phoenician, the gods they prayed to were, at first, Phoenician gods, and their commerce was built around the Phoenician model. The Phoenician cities of the Levant were primarily maritime cultures. Carthage seems to have adopted that in many ways, but the Carthaginians did venture into their own hinterland for territory and did not rely on a network of ports from which to trade. They were expansionists to a large degree, which was nothing particularly unique in the time and place they lived. They were not, as some have suggested, solely interested in commerce and currency. The Carthaginians had very keen concepts of duty, honor, and loyalty.

The Romans might have thought the idea of Punic loyalty was a joke, but the Carthaginians were not in any way more scheming or two-faced than the Romans themselves. It was the Romans, after all, who pretended to consider peace during the Third Punic War when they had already sent an army to raze Carthage to the ground. The Romans might have thought Carthaginian generals had too much power and were verging on being tyrants, but a few generations after Carthage was destroyed, Rome would be rocked by a civil war caused by the dictator-for-life Julius Caesar.

Still, it is true that the Carthaginians exploited native populations for their own gain, but this was just as true for every one of their neighbors. Syracuse might have felt that Carthage had no claim to Sicily, but Syracuse was founded and populated by the Greeks. The indigenous people of Sicily suffered at the hands of both of these powers. Every nation of the ancient Mediterranean practiced slavery, and Carthage was certainly no exception.

Depiction of Baal Hammon.
https://commons.wikimedia.org/wiki/File:Bardo_Baal_Thinissut.jpg

The chief gods of Carthage were Baal Hammon and his consort Tanit. Baal Hammon was a weather god and the god of fertility. He was the chief of the gods and was often associated with the Greek Cronus and Roman Saturn. Many parents sacrificed their children to Baal Hammon.

He was derived from the Phoenician god Baal, hence his first name, while his last name remains something of a mystery. He became the primary god of Carthage after the link between Carthage and Tyre ended.

Tanit was closely associated with the Phoenician goddess Astarte and was considered the co-chief god along with Baal Hammon. She was a war goddess, virginal unmarried mother, and nurse. At times, she was associated with the Roman Juno as a goddess named *Dea Caelestis*. She was sometimes associated with the crescent moon. In art, she was often depicted naked and riding a lion or with a lion's head. She was also associated with the dove, the palm tree, and the rose.

The largest site yet discovered of evidence of Carthaginian child sacrifice was a tophet near the temple of Tanit, the Tophet of Salammbo. However, the remains found at the tophet indicate children of very young ages. Some scholars have suggested this is evidence that it was a site for the burial of children who died of natural causes, not child sacrifice.

The Carthaginians also worshiped the Phoenician god of healing, Eshmun, who was associated primarily with the Levantine city of Sidon. Their chief god before the break with Tyre was Melqart, who they still worshiped afterward. Melqart was the primary god of Tyre, so he became popular all around the Mediterranean world. He was often associated with Heracles, also called Hercules, and had worshippers in Sicily, Sardinia, and Spain.

Hannibal was a faithful follower of the cult of Melqart. He believed he had a vision sent to him by the god before he set out on his journey through the Alps. He dreamed of a giant serpent causing destruction along its path and was told this was the foretold destruction of Italy.

The Phoenician goddess Astarte was also popular. She was closely associated with Ishtar, a Mesopotamian goddess. She was associated with war, sex, royal power, healing, and hunting. She was often shown as a combatant on horseback or on the prow of a ship extending her arm forward; thus, she was most likely the inspiration for ship figureheads.

A thunder god, also associated with plague, war, and protection, was worshiped in Carthage. His name was Resheph. Resheph was a very old god who is believed to have made his way from Egypt to Canaan to Phoenicia and finally to Carthage. The Carthaginians also worshiped an ancient Mesopotamian sun god named Utu, who provided justice and protection to travelers. Carthage adopted the Greek goddesses Demeter and Persephone in the 4th century BCE. They worshiped many Egyptian gods, such as Bes, Bastet, Isis, Osiris, and Ra. In Sardinia, they worshiped a deity named Sid Babi, who was believed to be the son of Melqart.

Carthage ruled over an eclectic empire, and Carthaginian society reflected this. Dominating everything was the elite Carthaginian class; some families could likely trace their heritage back to the beginning of the city or to the mother city, Tyre. All the important political and religious positions were held by this group. But they only represented a small portion of the Carthaginian population. Carthage was home to skilled artisans, wealthy merchants, laborers, mercenaries, and slaves. In every city under Carthaginian control, there would have been various populations of foreigners who were part of the commercial and cultural exchange happening in the western Mediterranean. At its peak, the city of Carthage was home to 400,000 people. It was a cosmopolitan city that blended old, new, rich, and poor.

However, most people only wanted to know about the riches the city held. Roman writers called it the richest city in the world, and this might have been true for a time. Precious metals, art, jewels, glass, ivory, and alabaster were constantly coming in and out of Carthage's large harbors. The elite were, above all else, amazingly wealthy. In fact, land ownership was not required to be counted among the aristocrats; all that one needed was to be extremely wealthy. Therefore, it is possible that enterprising individuals could make use of the vibrant markets in Carthage and make themselves rich and then turn that into political power. Aristotle thought the preoccupation with wealth was unhealthy.

The aristocrats also had control of religious life in Carthage. The head of the priests was also a member of the Senate and was on the Council of the Hundred and Four. That incredibly powerful position could only be held by someone with extensive wealth and the backing of other aristocratic families. However, the priestly positions were often hereditary and required an austere life.

Priests were noticeable for their shaved heads. However, due to the destruction of Carthage in 146 BCE, we do not know what the initiation rituals were for priests or if they served for life. There were female priests as well, but very little is known about them. Priests may have had a hand in education or maintaining the libraries of Carthage, but this is speculation.

Citizens were exclusively males, and they could participate in the Popular Assembly, which was relatively powerless until the rise of the Barcids. However, political positions were not paid in Carthage, so there is the question of who could afford to engage in politics and forgo a trade. The citizens were separated into various groups, possibly families or if they fought together in a battle. There were certainly powerful trade guilds in the city as well. These groups held regular banquets, where they discussed important matters and enjoyed each other's company. Unlike other ancient societies, the Carthaginians were not expected to perform military service, save the members of the Sacred Band.

Despite a few previously mentioned instances, the Carthaginians did not, as a rule, resort to rebellion very often. There are many theories for this. It seems most likely that because Carthage remained relatively prosperous for much of its history, the general public never felt particularly motivated to challenge the oligarchy that ruled them. Citizens might not even have been taxed, so not much was asked of them. They were able to work and earn enough to live fairly comfortably, so they never felt it was necessary to overthrow the government that was protecting them. Also, it has been suggested that because political appointments were unpaid and because military service was not compulsory, Carthaginians might not have really known how to effect change even if they wanted to. Of course, this is, again, speculation. Because we lack records of Carthaginian history written by the citizens' own hands, we do not know the exact nature of the struggles the citizenry might have faced.

Carthage was certainly a male-dominated society. Women could not be citizens, and inscriptions that refer to women typically mention her in relation to her father or husband. Women lacked not only a voice in Carthaginian history but also names.

Carthage was home to many artisans, metal workers, potters, and glass makers. The raw materials might have come from various places in the empire, but they were shaped and molded within the walls of the capital city. The artisans made weapons, statues, and pillars. They made cloth and dyed it the famous purple. Many workers lived in the same neighborhood, in a potter's district, or in a metal workers' conclave. Workshops used citizen labor and slaves. Carthage was famous for the wide-eyed, grinning masks it produced.

Just as important were the sailors, dockworkers, and porters who labored in the various harbors and on board the massive fleets of commercial vessels that traveled from port to port within the empire and beyond. There were cooks, scribes, shopkeepers, doctors, and fishermen in every corner of the Carthaginian Empire. There were also interpreters who could help foreigners and Punic speakers conduct business.

Slaves were a normal part of Carthaginian society. They were used in the countryside and in the city for menial and important tasks; they even served in the navy during the Second Punic War. Citizens could not become slaves, as was the case in Rome. But slaves could become free, though they most likely never enjoyed the benefits of being a citizen. Slaves had general autonomy and ran businesses for their masters. Carthaginian inscriptions indicate that slaves could accumulate their own wealth, as some inscriptions were paid for by slaves. At the end of the

Third Punic War, slaves were given their freedom to help protect the doomed city.

Perhaps Carthage's greatest success was its trade. Like their Phoenician forefathers, the Carthaginians were particularly focused on establishing trade networks around the Mediterranean to accumulate wealth. They were renowned for their ability to sell anything to anyone at a price that made them a profit. The location of Carthage was most likely picked because of its excellent harbor and the fact that it lay on two incredibly important trade routes. One route went from Spain to the Levant, and the other went from North Africa to Sicily and Italy. Being in such a spot meant that Carthage was perhaps destined for prosperity, but the Carthaginians did not rest on that alone. From the city's founding, they embarked on trading expeditions all around the Mediterranean and even out into the Atlantic. They established trade routes from North Africa to Sardinia, Spain, Corsica, Malta, Cyprus, and Sicily.

Due to the expedition down the West African coast by Hanno the Navigator, Carthage may have traded with indigenous people in western Africa and possibly as far as Britain if the story of Himilco can be believed. These territories provided Carthage with a multitude of important goods, none more important than silver, which was the standard currency of ancient times. Carthage followed what would become the standard of trade to our present day. The Carthaginians were able to buy things like metals at very low rates, ship them somewhere that had no such natural resources, and sell them at a remarkable profit. They continued this strategy for their entire history. It worked exceptionally well.

Carthage formed colonies where these raw materials were being extracted. The colony's sole purpose was to ensure that the flow of the commodities continued unabated. Rebellions and revolts disrupted the flow, as did wars with outside enemies. This is perhaps why Carthage was quicker to resolve issues with diplomacy and agreed to pay fines regardless of whether the outcome was just since it was more important that trade continued.

The Carthaginians didn't just explore the sea; they are also known to have established trade routes across the Sahara as well. They also traded with Greece, Egypt, Hellenistic kingdoms, and Rome. Was there a better place to sell silver and bronze than in places like Greece that relied on silver and bronze but had very little in their own country? The Carthaginians turned up everywhere. They traded in markets in Athens,

Rome, Delos, Rhodes, and Syracuse. They sold their goods in Tyre, Sidon, and Byblos, becoming the child who beat their parent at their own game.

Carthaginian coins are of particular interest to scholars since they are one of the few artifacts of Carthage that remain in existence. During good times, Carthaginian coins were made of gold, silver, electrum (a combination of gold and silver), and bronze. During hard times, coins were made of bronze, though it seems soldiers were always paid in bronze. It also seems that trade was not just conducted by private individuals but also by the state. The powerful Carthaginian navy was used to protect commercial vessels and trading routes. If the navy found a foreign ship in what was believed to be exclusive Carthaginian waters, that ship was sunk. Pirates were dealt with in the same way.

The Carthaginians most likely traded a wide variety of items. This was used to comic effect in a Greek play, in which a Carthaginian character, Hanno, is said to have a cargo of pipes, shoe straps, and panthers. The Carthaginians certainly traded in gold, tin, silver, copper, lead, iron, wool, amber, ivory, and incense. They also traded slaves. They were known for their luxury items like fine art, textiles, furniture, carpets, and cushions. They also traded in olives, olive oil, salted fish, wine, pomegranates, nuts, herbs, and spices. The problem, of course, was competition. Due to competition, they lost the war in Sicily and then the Punic Wars, which cost them everything.

Conclusion

The story of Carthage is truly one about reaching great heights only to fall from that lofty perch. However, its complete destruction by Rome does not discount its domination of the western Mediterranean for centuries.

Its story is perhaps best exemplified by the most famous Carthaginian of all: Hannibal Barca. Hannibal, who was intelligent and proud, took on tasks that seemed impossible, but he accomplished them and continued to reap victories. However, Hannibal finally met Scipio and lost everything his family had built and everything Carthage had achieved through long years of struggle and perseverance in a single battle. It is what is written on every gravestone and every clock face: all things come to an end. And just as Rome brought the end of Carthage, it, too, was heading toward its own demise.

Though the story of Carthage may have ended poorly for anyone who called themselves a Carthaginian, and though that history has been obscured almost beyond understanding, there is still greatness that shines through. There is still, somewhere in the mists of time, a great city of traders, artists, aristocrats, and priests, and there are still harbors filled with ships heading off into the dark sea destined to make a fortune.

Part 3: African Mythology

Enthralling Myths, Fables, and Legends from Africa

Introduction

Let's begin with two important facts about Africa: Africa is huge, and Africa is very varied. Africa's nearly twelve million square miles of space is enough to fit in the US and China and still have room for half of Europe. (The Mercator map of the globe, which is the one mostly used in atlases, vastly underestimates Africa's true size.)

Africa's landscape is also incredibly varied. There are huge deserts, such as the Kalahari and the Sahara, and there is the long fertile strip called the Nile Valley. There are savannahs, wetlands like the Okavango Delta, and high mountains like Kilimanjaro and the Drakensberg. There are tropical rainforests, rich floodplains, the dramatic landscape of the Rift Valley, and the Great Lakes. African stories reflect this variety of landscape and its creatures, as well as the variety of foods that grow in the different regions, including yams, tubers, bananas, millet, and rice.

Africa also has an immense diversity of people. There are over six thousand different distinct groups speaking two thousand different languages (many people are multilingual, speaking several local languages and French or English too). While we often think of Africa as an untouched continent, unlike, say, Europe or North America, it has been influenced by numerous different cultures over time. There were the Greeks and Romans in Egypt, Islamic cultures from the Middle Ages onward, and Christianity through the Orthodox Coptic and Ethiopian Churches, 19th-century missionaries, and modern Pentecostal evangelists.

Often, traditional stories have been adapted for a new culture or religion, and traditional rites have been reconciled with Christianity or

Islam. For instance, many sangoma healers in South Africa practice Zulu rites but also belong to a church, saying, "God is God, but our ancestors are our ancestors."

Even before the 20th century and the advent of African mega-cities, Africa had developed urban cultures like the Mali Empire, the Benin city-state, and trading cultures in the Sahara and Sahel. In Zanzibar, a cosmopolitan trading culture linked Africa, Arabia, and India. But Khoisan hunter-gatherers, Fulani cattle herders, and Kenyan pastoralists still live in a traditional way, though, in many cases, their lifestyles are threatened by encroaching development and sometimes by climate change.

Though many 19th-century explorers saw Africa as a timeless, eternal continent where nothing ever changed and no civilization had ever been created, Africa has seen numerous great civilizations emerge, starting with ancient Egypt and the Kushite Kingdom of Meroe. Africa was home to the Ethiopian Kingdom of Aksum, the Ghana Empire, the Mali Empire, the Songhai Empire, and the court culture of Ife. Statues and carved heads of great delicacy were made in Ife nearly a thousand years ago; some of them are still displayed on altars, with a festival held in their honor every year. Great Zimbabwe was built by the ancestors of the Shona people in the 9th century and abandoned by 1500; the huge stone Great Enclosure was the center of a city home to some eighteen thousand people.

However, many of these civilizations were not literate. Myths and histories were transmitted orally, with some myths being passed on in the form of performances, such as masked dances. Often, stories and songs were interactive, involving audience participation, and they passed down moral lessons. Proverbs were also immortalized in designs, such as the adinkra textile motifs of Ghana, and through rituals like divination.

Islam brought widespread literacy in Arabic, so stories could be written down, but it also might have changed some of the myths to make them more palatable to a Muslim audience.

Oral tradition was not in any way a free-for-all; the tradition had guardians and keepers, including storytellers, griots (court musicians and poets), and members of sacred societies. In some cases, secret and esoteric aspects of myths were jealously guarded from outsiders; in others, stories were told publicly to underline the importance of a lineage or deity. For instance, Malian griots still sing the Sunjata epic, transmitted through the Kouyate family that goes back to Sunjata Keita's griot, Balla Fasséké, in the early 13th century.

However, rarely has any central authority attempted to create an "authorized version" since so many African myths exist in different forms and are sometimes contradictory. For instance, in one cult, the god Eshu Elegbara is said to be the son of Ogun, the iron god, but this is a minority view. According to another story, he was born to a man called Osunsun and his wife as they were on their way to the market. In yet another story, the enfant terrible Eshu is said to have been born miraculously to the elderly woman Ketu. And yet it's also true that Eshu and Ogun were created by Olorun, the creator. African myths slip, slide, and entangle themselves.

Even when the story is the same, the details may vary. There are more than forty different transcriptions of the Sunjata epic (*African Myths of Origin*), and more versions are continually being created in film or novel form, in children's books and even in books like this one. Spellings often vary, and sometimes, a myth is told by a number of people but with slight changes in names or in the detailed events of the story. This becomes even more confusing with African myths that reached the New World; Nigerian gods turn up in Brazil and Cuba, for instance, but the goddesses show a disconcerting tendency to merge with aspects of the Virgin Mary. Some gods take on the attributes of Christian saints, while river goddesses tend to become sea goddesses. Trickster stories about Anansi and Br'er Rabbit became part of African American and West Indian cultures and, in some cases, were adapted to their new setting.

So, don't expect everything to tie up neatly. African mythology is a fluid universe that continues to evolve to this day. But its roots go way, way back. Let's begin at the beginning with the story of how the world was created.

Chapter 1: African Creation Myths

The simplest of all creation myths is that once upon a time, there was nothing, and then a god created the world so there was something. That is the view of the Banyarwanda of Rwanda.

But other origin myths are more complex. In some cases, creation is a multi-stage process carried out by a number of different deities. Oftentimes, the creation myth not only helps people understand the world but also explains why death exists and why the spiritual and physical realms are no longer the same.

The Senufo of Côte d'Ivoire tell how Kolocolo (Kolotyolo), a god of light and sky, created the world to be inhabited by animals and immortal entities known as the madebele. When the madebele challenged his authority, Kolocolo banished them from the sky and created human beings. These new beings chased the madebele into the bush and took over their farms and houses.

Ever since, diviners have been needed as intermediaries to placate the madebele and use them as messengers to and from the spirit world. The Senufo are exclusively farmers (their blacksmiths, wood carvers, and brass casters live in their villages but belong to other ethnic groups), so the distinction between the village, with its cultivated fields, and the wildness of the bush is crucial to their thinking about the world.

Many creation myths explain why the sky is now so distant. In Sudan, the tale is told of Abradi, the creator who lived in the sky. In the beginning, the sky was close to the earth, and it was easy to come and go between the two. But because the sky was so close, people on Earth had to bend their heads. One woman, who was angry at having to bend over her cooking pots, pushed the sky away with her stirring rod, and Abradi, sulking, moved the sky as far away as he could.

The Nigerian Efik have a similar supreme creator, Abassi. He created the world, and then he made a man and a woman. But he didn't want the man and woman to live on Earth, as he feared competition. When his wife finally convinced him to let them live on Earth, he made two conditions: they must accept the food he gave them, eating with him every night, and they must not have children. However, the woman started tilling the fields to make her own food, and eventually, she and her husband stopped eating with Abassi. They also began to have children. Abassi feared he was forgotten.

Abassi's wife, Atai, who must have felt responsible for his disappointment, wanted to find a way to ensure that he would never ever be forgotten. So, she created death. Men have never forgotten this.

It is intriguing that the Dinka people of Sudan have a myth that combines elements of both of the previous stories. The primordial woman Abuk was only allowed by the supreme creator to plant one grain of millet a day. Feeling rebellious, she decided she would plant more, but she hoed too hard and struck the god with her hoe. The god was so angry that he cut the rope between heaven and Earth.

The Uduk people of Ethiopia have a similar myth in which the creator Arum made the heavens and Earth and linked them together with a huge tree, with its roots in the earth and its branches in heaven. But one day, an old woman cut the tree down. Humans could no longer visit heaven, and death came into the world. (Traditional settlements in Ethiopia and Somalia have trees at their center, and Ethiopian churches are often surrounded by walled forests, so it is perhaps not surprising to find a tree having such an important role.)

Shona mythology tells of Mwari, the creator; he is also called Musikavanhu, "maker of people," Mutangakavara, "he existed at the beginning," or Dzivaguru, "the great water." He filled the world with creatures, and his power can still be seen in the generation of new life and in the blessing of rain. He is both male and female, and he unites other opposites, such as light and darkness and earth and sky. But like so many other creator gods, he is distant. No one can call on Mwari for help without going through the intercession of a spirit medium who is possessed by the ancestors or by other spirits.

Intriguingly, when Christian missionaries translated the Bible into Shona, they used "Mwari" as the word for God.

A much more complex account of creation comes from the Dogon people. There are simple versions, more complex versions, and a rather esoteric version that French anthropologist Marcel Griaule received from a blind hunter and Dogon holy man named Ogotemmeli.

The short version states that Amma created the earth, the sky, and the Nommo spirits before creating other spirits, animals, and people. The earth and sky were separated by a metal post, and they were close together. People did not grow tall, and the hyena put his pawprints on the moon. When the earth and sky quarreled, Amma knocked the post away.

Women were responsible for the separation of the sky from the earth. One day, a woman knocked the sky with her pestle while pounding millet. Amma sent a blacksmith down to the earth on a chain to teach men how to make fire. When Amma was angry and made a drought, the blacksmith pounded on his anvil to make it rain.

Another version tells how the sky god Amma created the Nommo. The Nommo divided himself into four sets of twins. (The Dogon believe twins are magical, as does much of Africa.) One of the twins rebelled against Amma, and another one was sacrificed to atone for the sin. His body was dismembered and scattered throughout the territory, and where pieces of his body fell, there are now shrines.

The ancestors did not die but transformed themselves into snakes. However, Lebe's son became a snake before his father, breaking the natural order. As a consequence, when it was time for Lebe to become a snake, he could not make the change. He died and was buried. When the Dogon decided to migrate, they wanted to dig up Lebe's bones but found a huge snake in the tomb; this snake led them to the Bandiagara escarpment, where they now live.

There is an even more complex version involving primordial incest, three sacred words, and many more stories, which was related to Griaule by Ogotemmeli. This also includes the assertion that the Dogon knew about the invisible star Sirius B, which has been interpreted by author Robert K. G. Temple as evidence that they were in touch with an alien civilization. (Most historians don't find this theory plausible.)

While Griaule was already an expert on Dogon life and religion when he had his series of interviews with Ogotemmeli, basing an analysis of an entire culture on one man's words is like basing the entire history of

Christianity on a single text, such as Augustine of Hippo's *Confessions*. Quite a few scholars disagree profoundly with some of Griaule's ideas and even more profoundly with Robert Temple's!

The Dogon people's concern with how death came into the world is echoed by a number of other African myths. One Zulu story tells how the creator decided men should live forever and sent a chameleon to tell them the good news. However, he saw how the humans multiplied and saw them make war on each other, which gave him second thoughts. He called the lizard to him. "I have decided men should die after all," he said. "Go and tell them."

Now, the lizard is fast, and the chameleon is slow, so the lizard got there first. Thus, humans never had a chance; they have always been mortal.

The Bambara of West Africa trace creation to the root sound *Yo*, which was uttered in the void and brought into being the creators: Teliko, Faro, and Pemba. The water spirit Faro created seven heavens, and then she rained to fertilize them. The air spirit Teliko created twins, who were the ancestors of the first humans. And Pemba created the earth, and out of the earth, he made himself a wife, Musokoroni.

However, Musokoroni was a spirit of disorder, and she rebelled against Pemba. Among other evil deeds, she brought death to the world. Eventually, Faro took over from Pemba as ruler of the cosmic balance since Pemba had been unable to maintain it. (Other accounts say that the supreme god sent a flood to cleanse the earth, and Faro rescued humans in her canoe.)

The Maninka creation myth is different, though it shares some aspects with the Bambara account. The creator Mangala created an egg, which contained seeds and two pairs of beings, male and female. Pemba, one of these beings, broke out of the egg and descended to Earth with the seeds, which he planted. However, the earth was impure and sterile because there was no moisture, and he used his own blood to fertilize the earth. The male aspect of the other being was sacrificed, creating water; this was Faro, represented by twin catfish. He brought with him plants, animals, and four pairs of humans. The ancestor of the griots and the ancestor of the blacksmiths then descended separately from heaven, and finally, Pemba's female twin, Muso Koroni, joined Pemba.

Pemba continued to be rebellious and destructive, even more so after Muso Koroni arrived. Eventually, Faro had to deal with him. The Niger

River shows the track he took toward Pemba's hideout in the delta.

Far more charming is the Kono creation story from Sierra Leone. There was no light in the world until Sa gave birds the ability to sing. The sound of birdsong brought light to the world.

The Jewish creation story doesn't give God any motivation for creation. God just creates. But African creator gods are often motivated by boredom. The Bambuti pygmies say that Khvum (Khonvoum) the creator was bored of being alone. There was no one to make or share his food, so he filled his bag with nkula nuts and made them into people.

The Bunyoro, who live near Lake Victoria, also see boredom as the motivation for creation, though this time, there are two primordial beings involved. They tell how, at the beginning, there were two brothers, Ruhanga and Nkya. Nkya was bored, so Ruhanga separated the earth from the heavens and made the sun. Earth and heaven remained close together, with Nkya living on Earth and Ruhanga in heaven. Nkya got burned, so Ruhanga made clouds to cover the sun and then made the moon so there was light in the darkness. Nkya wanted shade, so Ruhanga made trees and threw water down from heaven as rain. But Nkya complained that the rain was cold, so Ruhanga made him a shelter and showed him how to use tools.

Nkya had four sons. The oldest was Kantu. The others were nameless, so Nkya sent them to Ruhanga to get names. Ruhanga set them tests and then named the boys Servant, Herdsman, and King. However, Kantu was angry that Ruhanga did not give him the kingship, so the sons had a falling-out with each other. Nkya, fed up with life on Earth, returned to live with Ruhanga and knocked away the supports that kept heaven and Earth together.

The Yoruba have several different explanations of creation. First, there is a story that tells how Orisa-nla the creator lived with his slave Atunda in a formless void. But one day, Atunda, fed up with playing second fiddle, rebelled against his master. He rolled a huge boulder down a hill. The god shattered into a myriad of fragments, each one becoming a separate god or orisha.

Then, there is the story of how Olodumare the supreme being asked Orisa-nla to make a world out of magic earth. Oris-nla did so, but it was Olodumare who breathed the soul into each animal and human to complete creation.

Or there is the story of how Olorun (Supreme God) chose Oduduwa as his assistant, giving him a cockerel (a young rooster), a handful of soil, and a palm nut. Oduduwa came down from heaven on a chain and found a mass of water. He threw the soil down to create the earth and then set down the cockerel, which scratched at the earth to create rivers, seas, hills, and valleys. After this, Oduduwa planted the palm nut, which grew into a sixteen-branched tree, with each branch representing a Yoruba kingdom.

Creation didn't go too well, though. According to one story, Eshu Elegbara was jealous. He had thought Olorun would pick him to help create the world and was upset that Oduduwa had been chosen instead. So, he got his rival too drunk to do the work properly.

There's also an interesting Yoruba story that suggests women have a much bigger part in creation than the Judeo-Christian canon. Seventeen odu (gods) came down to Earth, and they worked to prepare a sacred grove for each of them. However, they left Osun out. She sat quietly by, plaiting her hair with a comb. Because they left her out, nothing they did was successful, so they returned to heaven and complained to Olodumare about their lack of success. Olodumare, counting them, found only sixteen odu. "What happened to Osun?" he asked and told them they needed to recognize her.

In another story, the supreme god doesn't actually mean to create anything; instead, he vomits the universe into creation. The Kuba people in Congo say that the god Mboom (also known as Bumba or Mbombo) was in darkness and vomited up the sun, moon, stars, animals, birds, fish, and humans. These animals, in turn, vomited up others. The crocodile vomited snakes, the goat vomited horned animals, one man vomited up ants, and another vomited up plants.

Even this story comes in different versions. Some say that Mboom initially worked with the god Ngaan, but they quarreled. Ngaan then created water creatures and harmful creatures, such as crocodiles and snakes. And there are later episodes in which Mboom's nine sons, each called Woot, create the arts and crafts and human knowledge. For instance, one forges iron.

Look back to ancient Egypt, and you will find several different accounts of creation. Different myths seem to have developed or gained prominence over time as different gods were adopted by the ruling dynasties. Local cults also had different myths, which had to be reconciled (or not) once Egypt became unified.

In Heliopolis, for instance, the sun god, Atum, spat (or, according to other accounts, masturbated) into the water, which created Shu and Tefnut (air and water). Their children were Geb and Nut (earth and sky), and their children were Osiris, Isis, Set, and Nephthys. These eight gods, together with Atum, made the Ennead or Great Nine.

But in Hermopolis, it was the Ogdoad—eight gods, or rather four pairs of male and female deities. The gods had frog heads, and the goddesses had serpent heads. The Ogdoad inhabited the primeval waters. The union of the Ogdoad created the mound from which the sun, Ra, emerged to light the world. The Ogdoad resemble other African multiples like the Nommo and the Woot, and like them, the Ogdoad are not distinguished in any way, though this hasn't stopped scholars from trying to give them different functions.

In Thebes (today's Luxor), it was Amun who created the universe. His call broke the silence, and at his cry, the primeval mound arose, along with the Ogdoad and the pantheon of the gods. (The priesthood of Amun neatly took over the tradition of Hermopolis but set its god neatly on top.)

In Memphis, Ptah was the creator god. He was said to have "crafted the design of the world in his heart," according to one hymn, and brought the world into being through speaking it aloud.

Then, there is the story of how the sun god Ra existed alone in a watery void. The Benben mound (later seen as a pyramid) emerged, with a lotus flower out of which Ra stepped. He then created the deities of air (god Shu) and water (goddess Tefnut) by union with his own shadow. He created life by uttering the secret name of every plant and animal. Humans were created from his tears and sweat.

The Atum and Ra myths were reconciled with that of Ptah through the idea that Ptah had created Atum and Ra through his original thought. This seems typical of other African myths since there are different levels of the creator, with a more distant original creator god who delegates much of the specific work of creation to junior gods.

By the way, Atum is also the god of endings. In the Coffin Texts of the First Intermediate Period, quite early in Egyptian history, he tells Osiris that after a million years, the universe will revert to the state of the primordial waters. Only he and Osiris of all the gods will remain, doing so in the form of water snakes.

In all of these myths, the original state of being is the primeval water. That seems appropriate for Egypt, a land whose very existence was based on the Nile flooding. But which of these stories is the *right* one? Egyptians don't seem to have been overly bothered; their stories were as fluid as the Nile itself.

But then, many African myths accept that there is more than one way of explaining creation. For instance, the Fang people in Cameroon say that the first being, Mebege, created the world, but they also say that the world was created by a spider that came from heaven on its own spiderweb. That may not make sense to you, but it does to them.

Chapter 2: Gods and Goddesses I

Africa has a wide range of gods and goddesses, and that's been the case for the last five millennia, at least. The first gods we can definitely identify in Africa are those of ancient Egypt. There are more than 1,500 of them, some widely worshiped and others restricted to a single locality. They often (though not always) have animal heads on human bodies. They're also often presented in the form of a definitive set of myths, but Egyptian mythology actually developed over time, and different localities had different versions. Upper and Lower Egypt, which were originally separate kingdoms, often had separate deities or gods with different emphases or different attributes.

Some gods were identified with a particular location, like Montu at Thebes, Sobet the crocodile god at Kom Ombo (where there is an impressive collection of mummified crocodiles in the temple museum) and at Faiyum, and Khnum the ram-headed god at Elephantine. (Montu was eventually demoted by Amun as the main god at Thebes, being described as the son of Amun and the goddess Mut.)

The earliest well-attested Egyptian god is Ra or Re, the sun god. He is found in inscriptions of the Old Kingdom by the Fifth Dynasty after the pyramids of Giza were built. Ra is often shown as a falcon carrying the sun disk on his head or is depicted just as a sun disk. He is said to have been the first pharaoh of Egypt.

As the sun god, Ra carries the sun on his solar barque (ship) during its daily journey through the sky and then over the horizon (akhet) into the underworld (Duat) at sunset. He emerges again at dawn after a night of struggling with Apep, the underworld snake.

Later, Ra was merged with other gods, with there being gods like Amun-Ra, Ra-Atum, and Ra-Horakhty (merged with Horus, another falcon-headed god). He was given Khepri (scarab) and Khnum (ram) as his morning and night manifestations.

Amun was a creator god and the patron god of Thebes. His cult came to prominence in the New Kingdom with the Eighteenth Dynasty, which based its capital in Thebes and vastly extended Amun's temple in Karnak. Amun is shown with blue skin and is associated with the air. He is transcendental and self-created. His name means "hidden" or "invisible." His titles included lord of truth, father of the gods, maker of men, creator of all animals, lord of things that are, and creator of the staff of life.

Ptah is shown as a mummified man with a green face, and he is part of the triad of Memphis, together with his wife, the lion-headed Sekhmet, and their son, Nefertem.[97] Ptah, as creator, incubates the idea of the world and is able to manifest it by speaking it forth, which makes him a god revered by craftsmen. He is actually quite a good father for an architect since he symbolizes the transformation of mental plans into physical reality.

Later on in the history of Egypt, the god Osiris became important, alongside his wife Isis and son Horus. Osiris is specifically a pharaonic god; the pharaoh becomes Osiris when he dies, and many mortuary temples of pharaohs include statues of the pharaoh-as-Osiris, for instance at Abu Simbel. Originally, Osiris was worshiped at Abydos, which was a major royal necropolis very early in Egyptian history, along with Anubis, the jackal-headed god.

Osiris is the god of death, taking the title "Lord of Silence" (that is, of the underworld), but he is also a god of fertility. His green skin symbolizes putrefaction and the green of growth. He is shown with the false beard of a pharaoh and with crossed arms, holding a crook and a flail.

Osiris's story is one of death and resurrection. He was murdered by his evil brother Set (or Seth), who cut him into pieces and then scattered the pieces all over Egypt. This, according to Egyptian thinking, would have stopped Osiris from being able to go to the afterlife. However, Osiris's

---

[97] The sage Imhotep, who designed Djoser's magnificent step pyramid and funerary complex, was eventually made into a god. Since he came from Memphis, the idea eventually arose that he was another son of Ptah.

wife, Isis, traveled around Egypt to find the pieces of his body. She was able to revive the corpse and became pregnant, giving birth to Horus.

Little figures of Osiris were filled with dirt and then planted with wheat and watered. One of these was found in the tomb of Tutankhamun. These figures symbolized new life.

Isis, Osiris's wife, was the mother of both Horus and the pharaoh. Pharaoh Seti I is even shown being breastfed by Isis in his temple at Abydos, and other pharaohs showed themselves in this way as well. Isis wears a throne on her head and is, in a way, a personification of the throne, a symbol of the power of kingship.

During the Ptolemaic period and under the Romans, Isis's cult became popular outside Egypt, as she was seen as one of the most important mother goddesses. In one hymn of this period, she is described as the creator "through what her heart conceived and her hands created."[98]

Set, Osiris's brother, was the god of storms, deserts, and disorder. Egypt divided itself into the Black Land and the Red Land—fertile land and desert. Set was the lord of the Red Land. However, he also had a positive role, as he accompanied Ra's barque during the night to protect him against the snake Apep. Set was the father of Anubis, the underworld judge. Few reliefs show Set, but when he does appear, he is shown in black with an animal head with flat-topped ears and a forked tail.

Horus avenged his father, Osiris, and expelled Set from Egypt, becoming pharaoh. Shown as a falcon or as a falcon-headed man, Horus was a sky god associated with kingship and healing. His temple in Edfu had a roof terrace for sky rituals and narrow staircases up which the golden idol of the god would be taken to "recharge."

The ruling pharaoh was seen as a manifestation of Horus, with one of his official names being known as the "Horus name." In some early accounts, Horus is mentioned as the son and helper of Ra. Other inscriptions say he was the son of Nut and Geb (the earth and sky), which would make him the brother rather than the son of Isis and Osiris. However, by the Ptolemaic period, the Osiris version had become definitive.

Horus was tasked by Isis with protecting the people of Egypt against Set, who was ejected from the Egyptian throne. In other words, he was

---

[98] Žabkar, Louis V. Hymns to Isis in Her Temple at Philae. Brandeis University Press. 1988.

tasked with protecting the fertile land and the civilized order against the barren desert and nomadic barbarians. It's likely that the story of this struggle represents early power struggles between different smaller kingdoms. Horus is often associated with Lower Egypt (the Nile Delta and Cairo), while Set is associated with Upper Egypt (the rest of the Nile Valley).

These were the major Egyptian gods; there were many others, but they were typically seen as less important. Thoth, shown most commonly with the head of an ibis but sometimes with the head of a baboon, was the son of Set. He was the god of the moon, wisdom, scribes, and the written word. Together with his wife Ma'at, he stands on Ra's solar barque. Thoth was seen as a magician and the judge of the dead. In many ways, Thoth represented balance, and Ma'at represented truth, order, and law. In fact, the word Ma'at means measure or order.

Ma'at is often seen as a tiny figure accompanying a king or as a hieroglyph. She wears a single feather in her headband. Her task was to regulate the constellations in the sky and the seasons on Earth. Her feather was important because it was the weight that was used to balance the scales in the Duat when the souls of the dead were to be weighed. Kings often used her name as part of their regal name. For instance, Ramesses II took the name Usermaatre Setepenre (the Ma'at of Ra is powerful, chosen of Ra), while his father Seti I took the name Menmaatre (the Ma'at of Ra is established).

Ma'at was the first deity that Ra created. It was the king's task to maintain Ma'at (justice or, more generally, order) in the double kingdoms of Egypt. So, though she doesn't get much notice in most books of Egyptian mythology, Ma'at was actually a very important god.

Anubis, the jackal-headed god of the underworld, is always black, which was an auspicious color in Egypt and symbolic of regeneration, like the fertile soil of the Nile Valley. In the Old Kingdom, Anubis was the most important god of the dead, but eventually, Osiris became more important. Anubis became the patron of mummification and a psychopomp (one who leads the dead soul to the underworld). When Set turned himself into an angry leopard to attack Osiris, Anubis took a hot iron rod and branded Set's skin; that is how the leopard got his spots and is also why priests who celebrated funerary rites wore leopard skins.

Hathor was an important goddess. She was sometimes shown as a cow and sometimes as a woman with cow ears, cow horns, and a sun disk. She was the goddess of the sun, sexuality, and music. The jingling sistrum was used in her worship. (It's also intriguingly used in the worship of the Ethiopian Church.)

Hathor is known as the Eye of Ra and is the divine counterpart of the queen (or Great Wife, to give her the Egyptian title). She was said to be the consort of Ra and the mother (or consort) of Horus. As the Eye of Ra, she had a wrathful aspect, carrying out Ra's commands.

In one story, Ra sends Hathor to punish humans for rebelling against him. In her anger, she turns into the lioness-headed goddess Sekhmet and massacres thousands of people. When Ra sees this, he decides to save the rest of humanity. He does this by dyeing beer red so that it looks like blood. The bloodthirsty Sekhmet drinks the "blood," becomes drunk, and passes out. As she sleeps, she turns into the peaceful Hathor again.

Khnum, a ram-headed god, was associated with water and procreation. He was said to mold human children out of the Nile's silt and place the tiny babies in their mothers' wombs. He was worshiped on the island of Elephantine (Aswan) together with his consort, Satis, and his daughter, Anuket. Khnum was the guardian of the source of the Nile.

Taweret was a very popular goddess, though she did not have a high status. She was the hippopotamus goddess and the protector of women in childbirth. (That's logical, as hippos are very protective mothers.) Many Taweret amulets have been found; these would have given many women confidence as their due date approached.

Finally, Aten was originally an attribute of Ra, the sun disk he bore on his head. However, under Akhenaten and his immediate successors, Aten was made into a transcendent god. He was already being worshiped under Amenhotep III, but Akhenaten made his worship obligatory and exclusive. Aten's temples, unlike the dim sanctuaries of other gods, were in the open air, and Aten was shown not as a human but as a simple disk, sometimes extending multiple rays ending in hands as a sign of blessing. Whether the abstraction of this god was too much for the Egyptians or whether Akhenaten's family lost a power struggle against the priesthood of Amun, Aten didn't last. The regular gods were soon reinstated after Akhenaten's death.

Nubia, farther south of the Nile Valley, was, at times, part of Egypt. At one point, Nubia actually provided Egypt with a dynasty of pharaohs (the Kushite or Black Pharaohs). It's not surprising that the Nubian religion was largely influenced by the Egyptians, with the two religions sharing many of the same gods. For instance, Amun was worshiped at the Kushite capital of Napata, and Mut (a mother goddess) was particularly popular.

There were also a number of specifically Nubian gods. Dedwen, or Dedun, was the god of the four directions and also the god of incense. Under the Kushites, he became aggregated with Osiris. The lion-headed Apedemak was particularly popular in the Meroitic period (300 BCE–350 CE) when the Nubians tried to get rid of Egyptian influences in their culture. He was the god of war and kingship.

In the Horn of Africa, Aksum in Ethiopia is now a major site of the Ethiopian Church, but before the 4th-century conversion to Christianity, Aksum had its own religion. There's only fragmentary information available, but it appears the religion of this early empire was originally a Semitic religion similar to the pagan religions of southern Arabia. The original triad of the sun, moon, and Venus was slightly altered in Aksum and became sea, earth, and Venus (Behr, Medr, and Ashtar) instead. There was also a war god named Mahram, who was specifically the protector of the Aksumite ruler. So, in a way, Aksumite myths were not "African" but Middle Eastern. (Later, Arabia would have a much more profound influence on Africa through the spread of Islam.)

The Berbers or, to give them their proper name, the Imazighen nowadays are mostly Muslim, but archaeology has found traces of their original beliefs. Ancestor worship was a key part of their religion. Often, they went to sleep overnight in tombs, where they believed they would have dreams that divined the future.[99]

The Greek historian Herodotus mentions the Berbers worshiping the sun and moon, and Saint Augustine of Hippo says they worshiped rocks. They seem to have been eclectic and even magpie people, taking gods from Egypt and later from Greece and Rome.

The Akan religion of the Ashanti people in Ghana is still practiced by some Ghanaians, though the country is largely Christian. Many people blend some aspects of the Akan religion and thought with a professed Christian belief.

The Ashanti believe that the supreme god, Nyame, created the world but is no longer involved with it. He has two other names—Onyankopon Kwame and Odomankoma—and has sometimes been confused with the

---

[99] Their use of tombs as worship centers may have left its mark on the cult of marabouts, Muslim saints, whose tombs are often visited by the faithful and which is specific to North and West Africa.

Christian Trinity. However, he is a single god with three aspects, not three interlinked godheads.

Nyame's consort is the earth mother Asase Yaa or Afua. She is the earth mother and the mother of the dead, so she has two different aspects, one as an old woman and the other as a beautiful young woman. Asase Yaa is worshiped in the open fields, not in temples.

There are various stories of why Nyame withdrew from the earth. One says that he was annoyed by someone pounding yam and climbed back into heaven. Asase Yaa tried to reach him by making a tower of mortars, but the tower collapsed. Nyame and his wife have been separated ever since, as has the earth and heaven.

Of more direct importance in the Akan religion are the abosom, the lower deities, which are similar to the Vodou lwa (loa or loi) or to the orishas in the Yoruba religion. These include the river god Tano, the thunder god Bobowissi, and the bush god Bia. Anansi the spider is another of the lower gods.

Below the gods are the various spirits. There are tree spirits, animal spirits, and spirits that animate amulets. Below these but of still great importance to individuals are the ancestor spirits, Nsamanfo. They are venerated, often by having libations poured on their graves, and can be a source of advice or assistance but only to their own lineage (except in the case of former kings, whose entire kingdom is their "family").

The Dogon recognize Amma, the sky god, but he is distant from them. More relevant to daily life are the primordial spirits known as Nommo and Lebe, the first ancestor and the first man to die. Lebe, as a huge snake, led the Dogon to their home on the Bandiagara escarpment. They are worshiped through sacrifices.

Some gods are dual in nature. The Efik refer to Abassi Onyong (the god above) and Abassi Isiong (the god below), and the Lugbara people in Uganda, Sudan, and Congo have two similar gods: Adroa and Adro. Adroa is the transcendent sky god, while Adro is an earth god and, as the "bad Adro," is associated with death. Bad Adro's children are spirits who follow people at night; you must never look backward when you are walking at night, or they will kill you.

The fact that the supreme god is so distant from the world makes it necessary to have diviners or priests who can bridge the gap through sacrifices or through visions and trances. The Turkana in Kenya believe that contact between Akuj and the people can only be made through a diviner called an emuron. All diviners come from the same clan, though the office isn't hereditary. Akuj is the provider of rain and has a dual aspect since he is both a benevolent god who brings rain to fertilize crops and a dangerous god who brings thunder, lightning, and floods.

Chapter 3: Gods and Goddesses II

One of the most complex and developed pantheons in African mythology is the orisha pantheon of the Yoruba people. Many of its gods are also well known outside of Africa since, along with the Akan gods, knowledge of them crossed the Atlantic with slaves. They are known in New World spiritual paths like Candomblé and Voodoo (or Vodou). In some ways, the Yoruba pantheon fills in the missing link between the distant creator god and the subsidiary deities who concern themselves with life on earth, making it a theologically complex creation.

It is also a fluid pantheon. Some gods have different names in different areas of Yorubaland, as well as new names in the Americas. Some gods even cross genders; in some traditions, the goddess Olokun is male. Different religious societies tell different stories about the gods and give gods different tasks. So, it's difficult to condense the Yoruba pantheon into a rigid structure. Nonetheless, although the details differ, the overall shape of the pantheon is the same, whoever's telling the story.

Olorun or Olodumare is the creator god and prime mover who infused the world with *ase*, or life force. Like other creator gods, he has withdrawn from the world. His offspring, Orisa-nla, is the Maker who created the physical part of the world for Olodumare to give life to.

Orunmila, the god of fate, was present at the creation and knows everything that is and will come to be. He is the god of wisdom and is in charge of divination. Osanyin is the god of herbal medicines and healing, and Ogun is the god of iron, steel, and war. Oaths are taken on a machete in Ogun's name, and he is the patron of hunters, blacksmiths, warriors, and ironworkers. Nowadays, he has become the god of taxi drivers and truckers.

Shango is a wrathful and energetic god who creates thunder and lightning. He is also a royal ancestor of the Yoruba and the most feared of the Yoruba gods, which is why he is always called on at the coronation of Yoruba kings. While Lady Oshun was married to Orunmila and shared the patronage of divination with him, she fell in love with Shango at a drum festival and became his third and most favored wife.

An important god is Eshu, who is a mediator between the creator Olodumare and his world. He reports to Olodumare on what is happening on Earth and checks that the right sacrifices are being made. He always has a place in a Yoruba shrine, no matter which god it is devoted to. Eshu is also a trickster, though he usually has a reason for his tricks. For instance, his tricks show people that the way they are behaving is not right.

Oshun is the river goddess and a seductive woman who is wealthy and generous. She is given bracelets and ornaments of brass in Nigeria, where it once was an expensive, imported metal. In the Americas, where brass is not so valuable, she is given gold. Her color is yellow. Oshun represents the healing powers of coolness and water and is worshiped in a sacred grove on the banks of her river. She is also the goddess of love and pleasure.

Oshun is sometimes disruptive. She once refused to make sacrifices, so Eshu sold her three dolls filled with magic that made them dance. She gave him all the brass she had to buy the dolls, but when she got home, she found that Eshu had taken the magic away. The dolls were nothing more than wood. Somehow, money never stays long with Oshun, but she always manages to get more; just like the river, she is always flowing.

She is also sometimes imprudent, to say the least. In the city of Oro, Oshun had so many children that there was no room in her house for her to sit down. However, she is willing to go to great lengths to defend her people. When the city of Ido was besieged by enemies and the people were taken away as slaves, Oshun rescued her people. They didn't know their way back to Ido, so Oshun turned herself into a river and flowed back to Ido, carrying the people along in the water.

Yemoja is another water goddess, the deity of the Ogun River. She is also the patron of pregnant women. While Oshun is flirtatious and sexy, Yemoja is a mother. Her name means "mother of fish children," and she is the mother of all the orishas. She is sometimes shown as a mermaid, though in Nigeria, she is strictly a river goddess and yields the sea to the god Olokun. In Cuba and Brazil, on the other hand, Yemoja has become the sea goddess. Her color in Yorubaland is usually white; in the Caribbean and the Americas, it is light blue.

There are over a thousand divinities in the Yoruba pantheon. Some accounts put the number as high as six thousand. Some of these gods are local, such as the goddesses of the different rivers; there is Oya (the Niger River), Yemoja (the Ogun River), and Otin. Some are deified humans; these might be rulers of city-states or people who did great things, such as Moremi, the woman who saved the city of Ife. No disrespect is meant to any gods who have been missed, but space is limited!

The Igbo, who live around the Niger River in southern Nigeria, espouse the Odinala religion. Chukwu is their supreme creator god, but as is often the case in African religions, he is seen as a distant god who doesn't occupy himself much with the affairs of the world. His daughter, Ala, is an earth goddess and fertility goddess. She is also the ruler of the underworld and the mother and queen of the ancestors. This combination of fertility and underworld roles is not unusual in African mythology and is another way in which many African goddesses (and some gods, such as Osiris) have dual aspects.

Gods can be dangerous. Ala is usually benevolent, but she can turn violent if she is offended. She maintains justice and morality and can inflict serious punishment. Her particular emblem is the royal python, which is greatly respected by the Igbo. Pythons are allowed to wander wherever they like, including in the villages and even into houses. If one is killed by accident, it is given a proper funeral.

Naturalist J. A. Skertchly, in his account of his travels in Dahomey, tells of the "fetish house" where the royal pythons lived. Should anyone kill a python, even by accident, he would be placed in a hut that was then set on fire. If the man tried to save himself by running from the flames, the women who guarded the shrine would club him to death. Anyone meeting a python in the street had to worship it by pouring palm wine on the ground, and if a python crawled up to a baby, the child would be given to the snake as its new priest and brought up in the temple. The pythons, in short, ran the place.

The agbara or arusi are lesser spirits that represent natural forces. Amadioha is sometimes shown as Ala's consort and is the god of thunder and lightning. Like Ala, he is a god who visits justice on malefactors, either with lightning bolts or by sending a swarm of bees after them. His color is red, and he is often shown as a light-skinned man of high rank. He brings wealth to his personal devotees and is often prayed to for redress, for help against infertility, and for material betterment.

Ikenga is a horned god, and a statue of him is found in many Igbo households. The image of Ikenga represents the power to achieve success. While an American might read self-help books to get by in the world, an Igbo will make sacrifices to his (and sometimes her) Ikenga.[100] Ikenga is also the patron of blacksmiths and industry.

However, Ikenga doesn't always get respect. The relationship between gods and humans is different from the submission to God that is expected in the Abrahamic religions. Ikenga has to work for his keep; otherwise, people are likely to say, "If the Ikenga's not working, just chop him up for firewood!"

Njoko Ji is the god of yams. This is not an unimportant task, as the yam is one of the main foods in Igboland, and the New Yam Festival is one of the major events of the year. While most Igbo nowadays are Christians, Igbo festivals like the New Yam Festival (Iri ji) and masked dances are still performed. Sometimes, they are treated as "traditions" rather than religion to reconcile them with the Christian faith.

A great empire to the west of Yorubaland was that of Dahomey (now in modern Benin), inhabited by the Fon people. The Fon pantheon, or Vodun, has certain similarities to the Yoruba gods, but it is organized in a more complex way, with several different pantheons under the supreme god Nana Buluku, who is both male and female.

The sky pantheon is headed by the twin god Mawu-Lisa, the creator of the material world. Mawu is female and represents the earth, the west, the moon, and the night. Her time is sunrise. She is gentle, forgiving, nurturing, and fertile. Lisa is male and represents the sky, the east, the sun, and the day. His time is sunset, and he can be strong and ruthless. Mawu-Lisa's son Agè is the god of the wilderness, the forest, and the hunt.

Gu is another sky pantheon god. He is the fifth son of Mawu-Lisa. He is the god of iron, weapons, tools, craft, and war; this is a potent combination in West Africa, where the Edo Kingdom of Benin, the

---

[100] While Ikenga is mostly found in men's shrines, women who have high status may also have an Ikenga.

Yoruba Kingdom of Oyo, and the Fon Kingdom of Dahomey all came to power between 1400 and 1700 through aggressive conquests. All three cultures share a similar iron and weapons god (Ogun in the Yoruba and Edo cultures), showing how central the smelting of iron was to weaponry and to the expansion of these states.[101]

The thunder and sea pantheons are headed by Sogbo, or Hevioso, an androgynous sky-dwelling god. Sogbo gave birth to all the other gods of the thunder pantheon and sent them to live in the sea, which was ruled by Agbè and his twin wife, Naètè. The sea gods control storms and rain, and the youngest of them, Gbade, is a trickster who enjoys making the noise of thunder.

Then, there is the earth pantheon, headed by Sagbata, a son of Mawu-Lisa. Sagbata took as much as he could of the sky's riches to Earth, but he could not take the rain, which Sogbo kept under his control. That is why Earth doesn't always get the rain it needs, as the two gods don't always get on well with each other.

However, Legba, Mawu-Lisa's youngest son, found out from Sagbata that there was a drought on Earth. He sent a little bird (Wututu) to tell Sagbata to make a huge fire. Meanwhile, he told Mawu-Lisa that Earth was burning up and would burn heaven too if he didn't stop it. Mawu-Lisa told Sogbo to let all his stored-up rain fall as quickly as possible. Ever since then, Wututu has lived on Earth and can be sent as a messenger to Mawu-Lisa if there isn't enough rain.

Legba is an unpredictable trickster god. Though in the previous story he seems to act benevolently, it's also said that he was responsible for the drought because he'd previously told Sogbo to stock up on rain. Because of his unpredictability, he's one of the gods who is always propitiated by the Fon just to keep him on their side.

The Maasai, the cattle-herding nomads of Kenya, have a rather different view of things compared to the complex West African pantheons. That might reflect the fact that their world is rather less complex than the city-states, trading entrepots, and empires of the West. They have just two gods: the supreme god En-kai and his wife Olapa, who represent the sun and moon. Some say that En-Kai is an androgynous

---

[101] Barnes, Sandra T & Ben-Amos, Paula. "Benin, Oyo, and Dahomey: Warfare, State Building, and the Sacralization of Iron in West African History." *Expedition Magazine* 25.2 (1983). Penn Museum, 1983.

god.

En-kai made the first man, Naiteru-kop, and gave him the earth to live on. One night, En-kai told all the people to leave their kraals (compounds) open. Some did, but some didn't. Those who did found cattle in their compounds in the morning, and they became the Maasai. The others had no cattle and became the ancestors of other peoples. But it may not surprise you to know that there are other versions of the story of how the Maasai got their cattle. There will actually be another one in the next chapter!

Chapter 4: Animal Fables

Examine earlier books of African folk tales, and you will find many of them full of stories about animals. That doesn't mean that animal stories are a huge part of African mythology and folklore; it probably has more to do with the fact that early European collectors found them easier to sympathize with and understand than historical tales or myths of African gods and heroes. Tales about humans make assumptions about social norms, many of which, like polygamy, the prevalence of half-sibling relationships, veneration of ancestors, and initiation ceremonies, were antipathetic to early Africanists and differed widely from Western society.

The animals in African stories were often interesting to Europeans because they were distinctively African animals. Early Africans in the area inhabited by the Khoisan (Bushmen) painted elands (spiral-horned antelopes) and praying mantises on rocks thirty thousand years ago, and San/Khoisan mythology still centers on these creatures. Khaggen, the praying mantis, is a shape-changing trickster with a rock hyrax (a rabbit-like animal) wife and an adopted porcupine daughter. The eland, on the other hand, is a power animal that can help a San shaman go into trance.

Power animals were often "master animals," the main food animal of a people. For instance, the buffalo was the master animal of the South African Baronga, who believed they had a special pact or covenant with the buffalo. Breaking that pact brought dire consequences.

Some animals were teachers. The Greeks had Aesop's fables, in which animal stories were used to make a moral point. For instance, Aesop praises the ant for its industrious nature. But the Berber and Kabyle story tells how an ant taught men how to farm. A man and a woman saw an ant trying to remove the husk of a grain of wheat and learned from it how to thresh wheat, how to make flour, how to cook it, and how to sow it. They sowed it at the wrong time of the year, though, and the seeds failed to sprout, so the ant had to come back and tell them the right season for sowing.

Sometimes, animals had knowledge that men wanted but weren't willing to teach them. According to the Bambuti (Pygmies) of the central African forests, chimpanzees were once human but fell out with the others and withdrew to the forest. This wouldn't have mattered except for the fact that only the chimpanzees had the secret of fire. A Bambuti decided to make friends with the chimpanzees and visited them often. The chimpanzees would give him bananas and let him warm himself by the fire, something that he very much appreciated. However, they never volunteered to show him how to make fire.

The Bambuti thought up a plan to steal the fire. One day, he turned up to the chimpanzees' village wearing a long fake tail. He sat down as normal to eat some bananas and chat, but as he sat by the fire, his tail—made out of pounded tree bark—began to burn. He jumped up and down in pain as if the tail was real. "Help! Help!" he cried. The chimpanzees thought that was the funniest thing they'd seen in a while, and they were so helpless with laughter that they didn't notice when he began to run. He got all the way back to his village before the chimpanzees understood what he'd done. He had stolen the secret of fire, and the Bambuti have had it ever since.

Snakes are often important in African stories, like the Igbo's Royal Python. The Lunda people believed the python Chinawezi governed the earth and all bodies of water, including rivers, streams, pools, and watering holes. The Woyo of the Lower Congo see Bunzi, the snake daughter of the Great Mother Mboze, as the rainbow (which does look like a snake) and rainmaker.

A Fulani story from the Sahel tells how a woman had twins. One was a boy, and one was a snake that had ninety-four scales, each the color of a different type of cattle. The boy was called Ilo. She didn't give the snake a name, but she hid him under a pot.[102] When she died many years later, Ilo built his brother a hut to live in and brought him milk every morning for

---

[102] Another version of the story gives the snake a name: Tyanaba.)

his breakfast. Ilo looked after their cattle. The brothers became wealthy, and they had a big herd.

The snake told Ilo that he must never marry a small-breasted woman because if such a woman ever saw the snake, he would have to leave. Of course, Ilo fell in love with a small-breasted woman, but he didn't forget what his snake brother had said. He built a big wall around the snake's hut. No one could see over it, and the snake was happy and secure.

But one day, curiosity got the better of Ilo's wife. She took a big pot and used it to stand on to look over the wall. There, she saw the huge snake lying on the ground, soaking up the sun.

The snake slithered down to the river, followed by all the cattle from his brother's compound. He explained to Ilo what had happened and said that he had to go and that the cattle would follow him. However, he would share fairly with his brother; Ilo could keep as many cattle as he could touch with a stick. The rest would follow the snake into the water.

Ilo cut himself a stick from a blackwood tree that stood nearby and touched as many cattle as he could before the herd disappeared into the river. And that is why Fulani herdsmen always use a walking stick made from blackwood.

A snake also figures in the alternative story of how the Maasai got their cattle. In the beginning, the Maasai had no cattle. The Dorobo (non-Maasai people) possessed them all. A Dorobo man lived with a snake and an elephant and its calf. One day, the Dorobo found a cow. The snake sneezed and gave the man a rash, which made the man angry, so he killed it. The elephant and its calf used the waterhole and made the water muddy. The cow couldn't drink. The Dorobo was angry, so he killed the elephant. But the calf escaped and found a Maasai man called Le-eyo. The elephant calf took Le-eyo back to the Dorobo's hut.

The god Naiteru-kop came down and told the Dorobo to get up early the next morning to make a compound and to find a calf and sacrifice it. Le-eyo overheard this, so he got up earlier and made a compound and a sacrifice. A leather cord came down from heaven, and a herd of cattle started to come down the rope into the enclosure. The Dorobo cattle came out of their compound and mixed with the others. Since the Dorobo had no way of proving which were his, Le-eyo took them all. Since then, the Dorobo have been hunters, and the Maasai have herded cattle.

It is an interesting story since the rope from heaven resembles many African creation stories, but the "world on a rope" motif is also rather reminiscent of Jack and the Beanstalk.

In Rwanda, a similar tale is told about Gihanga, one of the early kings of Rwanda. He discovered that cows came out of a lake and set off with his men to capture them. However, having been warned by his diviners not to take his son, Gafomo, he sent his son off on an errand. Gafomo was suspicious and followed his father's expedition in secret. When they arrived at the lake, Gafomo hid in a tree.

Gihanga's men captured many of the cows that came up out of the lake. But when the bull came out, Gafomo was frightened and cried out. The bull turned back into the lake with the rest of the cows.

The San, however, have a different story to tell. In the old days, King Mamba, the snake, owned all the cattle. Heise was a friend of King Mamba's, but nothing he could do would get the king to give him even a single cow. So, Heise built a big fire and dared King Mamba to jump over it. To show him, Heise jumped first, easily clearing the fire and landing on the other side of it with a thump.

King Mamba was rather arrogant and thought he could do anything better than this puny human, so he gathered his coils together and leaped straight into the middle of the fire. Snakes are not good at jumping, after all. Once Heise saw the mamba completely burned to ashes, he grabbed the cows!

Animals are found in Egyptian mythology too. For instance, the great snake Apep inhabits the night world and tries to stop the sun god Ra from sailing his boat toward morning. Apep is a force of evil or disorder. However, the snake goddess Wadjet is the protector of Lower Egypt. She's often shown on the front of the pharaoh's crown to symbolize her protection of the land and its ruler.

The hippopotamus is also prevalent. Usually, the hippopotamus was seen as a dangerous creature belonging to the watery marshes, a symbol of disorder and destruction. The pharaoh was often shown harpooning a hippo, which was a sign of his mission to maintain order in the land. But the goddess Taweret shows the positive side of the hippopotamus: the mother's protectiveness.

There is a Nigerian tale that tells why the hippopotamus lives in the water. Once, the hippos lived on land like other animals. The Hippo King was second only to the Elephant King, and he had seven big, fat, wonderful wives. He was a generous host, always giving huge feasts.

At one of these feasts, the Hippo King stopped his guests from sitting down. "None of you even know my name," he said, "but you come and eat here nonetheless."

(This was true. Only his seven wives knew his name, and they weren't telling.)

So, the guests went away ashamed. All except Tortoise.

"If I find out your name, what will you do?" Tortoise asked the Hippo King.

"I'd be so ashamed if you did. I'd have to go and hide in the river!"

Now, Tortoise knew that the king and his wives all went down to the river in the morning to bathe. So, he dug a hole in the middle of the path they took and hid under the sand. Four of the wives passed by with the king, and Tortoise popped up right in front of the fifth wife, who stubbed her toe on his hard shell.

"Ow!" she howled. "Isantim, come and help me!"

The king came lumbering back to see what was the matter, but he didn't see Tortoise, who had dug back underneath the sand.

A month later, the Hippo King had another feast. He laid out excellent food and huge jars full of palm wine and invited everyone to partake freely.

But Tortoise shouted out, "I know your name, Isantim!"

And the hippopotamus had to go and live in the river, along with his seven cumbersome but lovely wives. They may come out of the river at night, but they're too ashamed to come out in the daytime!

Although real creatures like elands, snakes, elephants, and cows appear in African myths, Africa also has plenty of mythical creatures. Some are monsters (they'll get a chapter to themselves later), but some are benevolent, like Chipfalamfula, the "River-Shutter," a big fish who is said to have the ability to control a river's flow. He can cause floods, but he also saves drowning people. In one story from Mozambique, he saved a little girl by letting her climb down into his belly when she was nearly drowning in the water. Later, the same girl was pursued by ogres on land. Seeing this, Chipfalamfula sent a great wave to drown the ogres, and the girl got away.

Chapter 5: Trickster Tales

African trickster tales are very popular. Trickster tales are not purely African, of course; Native Americans tell tales about Coyote, Raven, and Nanabozho the Hare, and Japan has a trickster fox, Kitsune. The Vikings had the trickster god Loki, who tries to get Odin out of a fix by stealing the gold from the Rhine, and you may have read Br'er Rabbit tales when you were a child.

Why so many African trickster tales? Again, the answer is not necessarily that they make up an unusually high percentage of oral tradition (though it seems three out of every five Yoruba folk tales are trickster tales). Instead, it seems that they are highly appealing. Everyone likes a trickster tale, particularly when it tells of a tiny creature or a deprived individual getting ahead by using their wits and perhaps a little white lie or two. Sometimes, the tricksters are smart, small animals; sometimes, they're human. Tortoise, Hare, Jackal, Spider, and Gazelle are often trickster animals. Tricksters may be greedy, gluttonous, buffoonish, or even (like Legba) sexually insatiable.

In many Yoruba tales, Tortoise, Ijapa, is the trickster hero. He does some things that look pretty stupid. For instance, he once challenged the Hippopotamus to a game of tug of war. A tortoise is never going to win against such a huge animal! But, of course, Tortoise knew that. The fact is he had already got Elephant to agree to pull on the other end of the rope. Naturally, Tortoise won!

But Tortoise is greedy too. One tale tells how when his wife was trying to get pregnant, Tortoise visited an herbalist. The herbalist cooked up a fantastically tasty-smelling broth and put it in a calabash. "Give this to your wife," the herbalist said. "And don't be tempted to eat it yourself."

Tortoise started on his way with the calabash on his back, but that broth smelled so good. It was spicy, it was meaty, and he found he was going more and more slowly until, at long last, temptation got the better of him. Tortoise wolfed down the entire contents of the calabash without leaving any for his wife.

It tasted great. Of course, he had to tell a few little white lies to his wife, but Tortoise is a great liar, so that wasn't a problem.

Except that a few weeks later, he noticed his tummy was getting bigger and rounder day by day. You guessed it: Tortoise was pregnant. Even Tortoise would have difficulty explaining *that* to his wife.

Tortoise, like a lot of people who think they're smart, can also be really dumb at times. One day, he decided he wanted to collect all the knowledge in the world in a calabash and hang it up on a tree where no one else could get it. But he tied the calabash in front of him, and he couldn't manage to get up the tree.

Then, a little kid started laughing. "Just tie the calabash behind you, stupid!" he shouted. "Don't you know anything?"

Tortoise was so angry he threw the calabash down and smashed it. A good thing too; otherwise, none of us would know anything at all.

In a story from the Tsonga people, two tricksters go up against each other. Hare and Tortoise steal sweet potatoes from a farmer. They get a big pile of potatoes, but Hare starts to worry that the farmer will catch them.

"Why don't you go and check to make sure the farmer's not around?" he asks Tortoise.

Tortoise is immediately suspicious. Why does Hare want him out of the way? He thinks about it, and he tells Hare that there are two ways into the field. So, if he checks one, Hare needs to check the other, or else they could still get caught.

Hare thinks this is fine. He's faster than Tortoise, so he will be back to take all the potatoes for himself before Tortoise even reaches the gate. Off he goes, as fast as he can run.

Tortoise doesn't check the other gate. Tortoise climbs into Hare's bag and hides.

Hare checks the gate and comes back. Tortoise is nowhere to be seen. "Ha, ha! The potatoes are all mine!" he says. Hare starts chucking the potatoes into the bag. Then, he picks up the bag, and off he goes with all the potatoes. He won't have to share with Tortoise!

Meanwhile, Tortoise is inside the sack, methodically chomping his way through the tasty sweet potatoes. This story proves that the hare doesn't always beat the tortoise.

Perhaps the best-known African trickster is Anansi the spider from the Ashanti tradition. There's a lot of respect for *Kwaku Anansi*, Father Anansi, who is something of a cultural hero as well as a trickster. Sometimes, he works as a messenger for the supreme god Nyame, and he is also the creator of the sun, moon, stars, day, and night. Anansi brings rain and taught people how to sow grain. Although he can be too smart for his own good—like Tortoise, he tried to corral all the world's knowledge but couldn't climb up the tree—he's admired for his ingenuity and wisdom.

However, some Anansi tales are sheer slapstick. Once, he was hungry, but the farmer wouldn't give him any beans. He went to play with the farmer's children, but they wouldn't give him any beans either. So, he went away and covered himself in gum and then came back and rolled around on the ground with the children. He was soon covered in beans, which had stuck to the gum. Anansi went home to pick them off him and put them in a pot.

On another occasion, Anansi decided he wanted to own all the stories that have ever been told. Nyame owned the stories, but he was prepared to sell them to Anansi. The price was a high one: Anansi had to deliver Mmoboro (the hornets), Onini (the python), and Osebo (the leopard) to Nyame.

A spider against a swarm of hornets is not an even match. But Anansi was up for the challenge. He took a big gourd with a stopper. Then, he jumped in the water and got thoroughly wet. Next, he passed by the hornets' nest.

"What's up with you?" the hornets asked. "You're soaked!"

"A big storm's coming," Anansi answered. Then, he gave a start as if he'd just thought of something. "Hey, you should get in this gourd. It's much more waterproof than your nest."

Of course, once the hornets were in the gourd, he put the stopper in, and that was that.

Next was the python. Again, in a spider and python battle, the odds are that the spider will lose. But Anansi came equipped with a long bamboo stick. (What's this? Is he going to propose a pole-jump competition?)

Anansi stood there with the stick and looked at the snake. He looked back at the stick. Then, he told Onini, "My wife cut this stick, and she said, 'Hey, this pole is longer than the python!' And I think she's right!"

Onini was angry. The stick didn't look very long to him, and he told Anansi so. Anansi told him that no, he *still* thought the stick was longer. So, Onini stretched himself along the bamboo to show how long he was.

Anansi pointed out that snakes are wiggly, and bamboo grows straight, so he'd need to tie the python to the pole in a few places to make sure the measurement was right. Onini, suspecting nothing, said, "Okay, but make it quick."

So, that was that.

But a leopard? How could a spider manage to capture something like that?

Well, Anansi dug a pit and disguised it with branches. Then, it was just a matter of waiting for Osebo to fall in.

But how was Anansi going to get the leopard he'd trapped to Nyame? That was the deal, after all.

Anansi approached the edge of the pit and bent over. "Hello," he said in a friendly way. "What's all this? Has someone fallen in this hole?"

The leopard was furious, lashing his tail, but he calmed down when Anansi suggested a way to help him out. Anansi had a rope with him, and if Osebo could just tie the end to his tail, he could drag him out of the hole.

But Anansi had already tied the other end of the rope to a springy tree that he'd bent down. So, when the leopard got the rope around its tail, Anansi let go of the tree, and the leopard flew up into the air. He was trapped!

Even then, Nyame didn't want to give the tales away. Some people say he asked Anansi to catch a bush spirit. Anansi thought for a long time. It was impossible. Surely it was impossible? And then he had an idea.

Off Anansi went to the bush with a doll, a pot of sticky glue, and his breakfast. He found a tree where the bush spirits liked to hang out and set the doll under the tree. Anansi tipped the glue all over the doll, and then he put his breakfast in front of the doll and hid behind the tree. Soon enough, a bush spirit happened by.

"Hello," said Anansi from his hidey-hole. "Would you like some breakfast?"

"Thank you kindly," said the bush spirit, who sat down with the doll and began to eat. Soon, the bush spirit had finished its breakfast. Politely, it said, "Thank you." The doll said nothing.

"Good day to you," said the bush spirit. And still the doll said nothing.

"You might wish me a good day," grumbled the bush spirit. The doll still said nothing.

The bush spirit was getting pretty angry now. And the doll just kept looking at it with what was surely an insolent stare. So, the bush spirit slapped its face. Its hand stuck to the doll. It tried to pull away, but it couldn't, so it pushed the doll in the stomach with its foot—and its foot stuck to the doll too.

Once the bush spirit was tightly glued, Anansi took it back to Nyame. And so, all the stories ever told now belong to Anansi.

Once, there was a famine where Anansi lived. He could see an island offshore with a huge palm tree. But how could he reach it? His boat was broken and old. Still, Anansi decided to try. Six times the waves pushed him back to shore, but the seventh time, he made it through the breakers and got to the island, where he climbed up the tree and plucked the palm nuts.

Being lazy, he thought it would be easier to throw them down into the boat than carry all the nuts. However, every single nut fell in the water, not the boat! Anansi threw himself into the water in despair, but instead of sinking and drowning, he found himself in front of a house on the seabed. There, he met old man Thunder. After hearing Anansi's sad story, he gave him a pot.

"All you need to do," Thunder told Anansi, "is to tell the pot to do for you what it used to do for its master."

Anansi tried it out as soon as he got to shore. "Pot, pot," he said, "what you did for your master do for me." The pot instantly produced all kinds of good food and drink for him, and he ate it all up. And then Anansi thought of his hungry family. He could use the pot to feed them. But there were a lot of them, and the magic might run out. If he kept the pot for himself, he could eat well every single day. So, he hid the pot and only used it when he was alone.

Unfortunately, the family noticed that Anansi was getting fatter while the rest of them were starving. His son Kweku Tsin decided to follow Anansi to find out why. Kweku Tsin had a superpower. He could turn himself into a fly, so he was easily able to follow his father without Anansi suspecting anything. He saw Anansi take the pot from its hiding place and make a pig of himself, eating everything it could produce. Then, he buzzed off to let the whole family in on the secret.

Once Anansi had gone off for the day, Kweku Tsin fetched the pot. "Pot, pot," he said, as he'd heard Anansi say. "What you did for your master do for me." And the pot gave the family as much food as it could. But it overheated because there were so many mouths to feed, and it stopped working. Kweku Tsin hid it again. The next time Anansi used the pot, it had no magic.

Anansi went to Thunder's house again. This time, it was much easier to get past the breakers. Thunder listened carefully to Anansi's story, which was a slightly edited one, and then gave Anansi a stick.

"It works just the same way as the pot," Thunder said. "Just tell it to do for you what it does for me."

But a pot is a pot, and a stick is a stick. When Anansi said, "Stick, stick, what you did for your master, do for me," the stick started beating him. It beat him black and blue before he finally managed to get hold of it and throw it back into the sea.

Kweku Tsin was actually smarter than his father Anansi. He discovered all the best hunting places, but he wouldn't tell his father where they were. Anansi tracked him by making a little hole in his hunting bag and putting ashes in it. The next time Kweku Tsin went hunting, Anansi just followed the trail of ash. Knowing all the best hunting spots, Anansi got there first the next day and warned Kweku Tsin off. "This is my hunting land now," Anansi said.

Kweku Tsin worked out how he had been tricked and decided to get some revenge. Knowing that Anansi would go to sell the meat and animal skins at the market, Kweku Tsin got to the main crossroads and set up a tiny image with bells around its neck high in a tree. He attached a long string to this image and then hid in the bush. When Anansi arrived, Kweku Tsin made the little image jump and dance by pulling on the string.

"The gods are angry," Anansi thought. "I had better give this god some meat."

But the god was not happy. Anansi gave it some more meat.

The god was still not happy. It wasn't happy until Anansi had given it all the meat and run away. Kweku Tsin took the meat to sell. He got rich, and eventually, he held a big feast. He told the story of his cunning and how he had beaten Anansi. Anansi was so ashamed that he promised to give up his cheating and tricks. (Naturally, that didn't last long, but that's another story!)

Sometimes, tricksters are associated with the work of creation. Remember that Anansi helped Nyame. Another spider, Ture, helped people acquire water and fire, according to the stories of the Zande people in central Africa.

An old woman grew yams and built a dam to corral all the water in the world. When people passed her hut, she would offer them yams but nothing to drink, so they would choke on the dry yams. When they choked, she would kill them.

Ture went to find the water behind the dam and filled up his gourd with as much water as he could. Then, he cut a hollow reed to use as a straw so he could suck the water out secretly. And then he went past the old woman's hut.

She offered him a yam. He ate it, and when she wasn't looking, he took a quick sip of water so he didn't choke. He had another yam. His secret water supply prevented him from choking. He had another yam. And another. He ate all the yams, and then he ran to the dam and broke it down, letting the water out so that it could run across the fields. This is why there is water in the world.

The blacksmith clan used to be the only people who had fire. They wouldn't let anyone else have it. Ture decided this was not right, so he went to the blacksmiths for a visit. Before he went, he dressed himself in old bark cloth, which was very fragile and very dry. When he sat by the blacksmiths' fire, the bark cloth caught fire, and he ran away, taking the secret of fire with him.

But Ture, like other tricksters, could be foolish. He was supposed to be hunting termites for food but seduced his mother-in-law while he was out in the bush instead. His wife was furious when he came home with no termites. That wasn't a problem for Ture; he told her a tall tale about how things had gone wrong.

Unfortunately, at this point, Ture's penis decided to speak up for itself. When it told the truth about what Ture had done, his wife was even more furious.

Another animal trickster is Agemo, a chameleon who carries messages for the Yoruba god Olorun. Once, the sea goddess Olokun boasted that she could weave better than Olorun. The god decided to send Agemo to check out that claim.

Every time Olokun brought out a cloth, Agemo walked on the cloth and managed to change his color to match it. She started trying more and more complex patterns and designs, but when he managed to repeat the pattern exactly on even her most complicated weave, she gave up.

"If I can't even beat the messenger," she lamented, "how can I ever beat his master?"

Malian hunters tell a tale about Sirankomi the great hunter. He never came back from the bush without a kill. The animals were worried he would kill them all, so they sent the buffalo disguised as a woman to learn his secrets.

Sirankomi fell for it. The buffalo-woman seduced him, and he took her to his hut, where she learned all his tricks. Sirankomi could transform himself into a termite mound, a stump, or a tuft of grass so the animals couldn't see him. But as they were talking, Sirankomi's mother passed the hut and warned the hunter not to give his secrets away to a one-night woman.

The next day, the buffalo-woman asked Sirankomi to accompany her to her own compound. She had told the other animals the secrets, so when Sirankomi became a termite mound, the warthogs dug it up with their tusks. When he became a tree stump, the elephants ripped it up. When he became a tuft of grass, all the grass-eating animals started munching away on him.

But because he had heard his mother's warning, Sirankomi had one trick left. He turned himself into a dust devil and whirled away home.

Another hunter-trickster is the Khoi-Khoi (Bushman) hero Heitsi-eibib, who was both a trickster and a shape-changer. He was born from a cow and grew into a mighty bull. He ran away when he saw the butcher coming to kill him and turned himself into a man. When the butcher arrived, he found Heitsi-eibib carving gourds.

"Have you seen a bull?"

"What bull?"

Having escaped the pot himself didn't make him a vegetarian. When he found that a village was going to slaughter a cow, he turned himself into a huge pot. They cooked the meat, but Heitsi-eibib drank up all the fat so that the meat left in the pot was dry and tasteless.

On his travels, he met ogres who killed all their visitors. The first, Gama-Gorib, challenged Heitsi-eibib to wrestle. Gama-Gorib knocked his opponent into a great pit, where he would perish. However, Heitsi-eibib told the hole to lift him up so that he could carry on fighting. Eventually, he knocked Gama-Gorib into the hole, and the ogre died. The next, Han-Gai-Gaib (also known as Ga-Gorib in some versions), used to challenge visitors to throw a stone at him. However, the stone was magic and would rebound and kill the person who threw it. So, Heitsi-eibib told Han-Gai-Gaib to close his eyes while he threw the stone. Instead of throwing the stone, he bashed Han-Gai-Gaib on the head and killed him.

Many tricksters are child prodigies. The Zulus tell the story of Uhlakanyana, who cut his own umbilical cord with his father's spearhead and announced his own arrival. Like many tricksters, Uhlakanyana was greedy, and he often got caught.

For instance, one time, an ogre caught him stealing the birds from his hunting nets. The ogre was getting ready to eat Uhlakanyana raw, but he persuaded the ogre he would taste better cooked. The ogre took him home and gave him to his mother to cook.

"You have to get the water just right," said Uhlakanyana. "I don't think it's hot enough."

"No?"

"Why don't you test it?"

The ogress stuck one finger in.

"That's not enough," Uhlakanyana said. "You have to get in the pot to see if it's hot enough."

Foolishly, the ogress got in the pot, and Uhlakanyana slammed the lid down and ran away.

Another story shows how Uhlakanyana "traded up." Uhlakanyana found a tasty root and took it home to his mother to cook while he went to a wedding. However, she tasted it and liked it and then tasted it again until she ate it all.

Uhlakanyana complained, so she gave him a gourd.

He walked past some boys who were milking their cow, but they didn't have a pot. So, he lent them the gourd. But they broke it, and he complained. So, they gave him a little hunting spear. He went on his way.

Next, he walked past some boys who were trying to cut meat, but they didn't have a knife. So, he lent them the spear, but one of them broke it. He complained, so they gave him an ax, and off he went.

As he walked, he met some women collecting firewood, but they didn't have an ax. So, he lent them his, but one of the women broke the handle. He complained. They had a blanket, so they gave him that.

Later on, he met two hunters sleeping naked on the ground and offered to lend them the blanket. But they slept badly and, having nightmares, managed to tear the blanket. Uhlakanyana complained, and they gave him a big shield, and he walked on.

A little later, he saw some hunters who had cornered a leopard. But it was hissing and striking out with its claw, and they couldn't get close enough to kill it. So, he lent them the shield. They killed the leopard but broke the handle on the shield.

Now Uhlakanyana was really cross.

"You broke the handle of the shield that was given to me by the hunters who tore my blanket, which the women gave me when they broke my ax, which the boys gave me who broke my spear, which the boys gave me who broke my gourd, which my mother gave me after she ate my dinner while I was away at a wedding."

This story must have impressed the hunters because they gave him a huge war spear, and he took it home.

Not all trickster stories are fun. The Bakongo story of Moni Mambu is tough and unpalatable. First, he found two brothers who never quarreled; one was a fisherman, and the other tapped palm trees to make wine. Moni Mambu put the fish traps on the palm trees and the calabashes in the water, and the two brothers came to blows. Moni Mambu laughed to see them fighting.

Then, he visited a village and asked for hospitality. A woman said to him, "You can eat peanut stew with my children for lunch." He took her words literally; he roasted the children and ate the peanut stew with the meat.

Moni Mambu went hunting with the chief. The chief said, "Shoot everything that moves. I don't want anything left but the slugs and snails."

So, Moni Mambu shot the lizards, birds, snakes, antelopes, hunting dogs, children, and the chief's favorite wife.

The chief condemned Moni Mambu to death, but he said he could only be killed one way: by drowning. The people carried him to the river with a big fish trap to drown him in, but on the way, Moni Mambu managed to convince a stranger that he was a ritual priest and that he was waiting with the fish trap to anoint a king. The stranger, who thought being king would be great, got in the fish trap. Moni Mambu slammed the lid on him and escaped. The stranger was drowned instead.

Moni Mambu eventually came to a bad end. He found a talking skull, and he was so excited he told the elders of the village. They went to see the skull, but it wouldn't talk to the elders, so they accused Moni Mambu of lying to them and killed him.

Next, let's take a look at Eshu, a Yoruba god who is a bit more than a trickster but is definitely tricky. (Many of the tales told of Eshu are also told of his counterpart Legba.) For a start, Eshu is the god of chance, luck, accidents, and the unpredictability of life. He is also Olorun's messenger on earth, and he is the god of the crossroads and divination.

Once upon a time, there were two men who were the very best of friends. They were so happy that they said their friendship would last forever. But Eshu overheard them.

The next day, the two friends saw a man pass them as they worked on their farms. Later, when they were sitting under a tree and chatting, one of them mentioned the friendly greeting the man in the red hat gave them.

"Red?" the other man said. "It was black!"

"I'm not blind! It was red!"

They got more and more heated, and in the end, they came to blows over the issue.

Eshu actually had passed between the two of them while wearing a hat that was black on one side and red on the other. He tricked them into having that argument. Why? Because their idea of a forever friendship was boastful and proud, and he wanted to show them that life is all about change and chance.

A less well-known trickster comes from the Arabic stories of *One Thousand and One Nights* via Zanzibar, a trading post where Arabs not only traded but also settled and intermarried with the Swahili-speaking locals. Abu Nuwas got himself thoroughly naturalized as a trickster living in an urban environment and living by his wits.

For instance, when Abunuwasi (as he's known in Zanzibar) borrows a big saucepan from his neighbor, he returns it along with a much smaller pan.

"What's this?" his neighbor asks. "I only lent you one saucepan."

"Oh," says Abunuwasi. "I think the big saucepan must have been pregnant when you lent it to me. This is its baby."

Now, the neighbor thinks Abunuwasi is not the brightest cookie, but he's quite happy to have an extra saucepan. However, Abunuwasi isn't as dumb as he looks.

Next time he needs to borrow the big saucepan, he keeps it. After a few months, the neighbor is worried about where the saucepan is.

"Remember that big saucepan?" he asks Abunuwasi.

Abunuwasi bursts out crying. He sobs and sobs. He cries real tears.

"The saucepan died," he wails.

"Saucepans don't die," says the neighbor angrily. "Don't be so stupid."

Abunuwasi looks at his neighbor. "You believed me when I told you the saucepan had a baby, didn't you? And if they are born, they can die."

Abunuwasi even outsmarted the sultan. The sultan had given Abunuwasi a beautiful young wife along with a present of a thousand gold pieces. Abunuwasi and his wife were blissfully happy for a little while, but then the money ran out. It's difficult to be happy when you are hungry.

So Abunuwasi thought of a plan. He went to the sultan, weeping, and said his wife had died. What was worse, he had no money for the funeral. The sultan gave him his sympathy and, more to the point, twenty gold pieces.

At the same time, Abunuwasi's wife went to the sultan's wife and said that Abunuwasi had died and that he had been such a bad husband that there was no money left to bury him with. The sultana gave the girl her commiserations and twenty gold pieces.

When the sultan had dinner with his wife, he mentioned how Abunuwasi's wife had died and what a pity it was that Abunuwasi couldn't find any happiness in life.

"You've got it wrong," his wife said. "It's Abunuwasi who died. I saw his wife this morning."

So, they decided they had better find out who was right. They sent a servant to Abunuwasi's house. Abunuwasi made his wife hide under a sheet. "Don't breathe," he warned her. Then, he showed the servant his "dead" wife.

The sultana wasn't happy. She sent her own messenger to the house. Abunuwasi's wife recognized the girl who had been sent, so she got Abunuwasi to lie under the sheet. It was his turn to play dead.

The sultan and his wife were now thoroughly confused. They couldn't trust their own servants to tell them the truth, so they decided to set out to Abunuwasi's house together. Of course, the sultan was always preceded by his drummers and horsemen, so Abunuwasi had plenty of notice. Both Abunuwasi and his wife got under the sheet this time. When the sultan and his wife came into the house, they immediately saw the two "dead" bodies.

"This is a mystery," said the sultan. "It needs clearing up. I'll give a thousand gold pieces to anyone who can tell me what's going on."

The "dead" Abunuwasi sat up and shouted, "You're on! Give me the gold, and I'll explain!"

Chapter 6: Monsters and Mythical Beasts

If you look at a medieval map, you'll see Africa is full of monsters: unicorns, griffins, basilisks, and manticores, as well as elephants, crocodiles, and lions. There were men who had no heads and men with only one huge foot, which they used as an umbrella (though they were found in India too, according to the texts). For medieval Europeans, Africa was a fascinating but dangerous place. They knew about it mainly from texts written by the Greeks and Romans since very few Westerners had actually been there. Europeans let their imaginations run riot. However, as we know today, Africa is not like that.

Still, Africa has its own monsters, although they are very different from the ones that medieval monks drew so carefully. In fact, the monks were completely wrong about one thing: they missed the legendary vampires. And there are a *lot* of vampires in Africa.

For instance, there's the adze, which lives in Togo and Ghana. It looks like an innocent firefly, but it can transform into human shape. It can also possess people, making them into witches (*abasom*). The adze sucks blood from people as they sleep, and it's particularly dangerous since, in its firefly form, it can creep through cracks in walls or under doors. Its favorite victims are children with their sweet young blood.

If that makes you think of mosquitoes, you may be right; some scholars speculate that the adze might have been created as a metaphor for malaria. Make sure you sleep indoors in a well-protected place, and you'll be safe from both the adze and the bugs.

The Asanbosam, or Sasabonsam, is another vampire, which terrifies the Akan people of Ghana. It lives in trees and attacks from above. It has iron teeth, iron hooks instead of feet and hands, and bat wings, just like Count Dracula. The Asanbosam are spirits of the forest who defend the woods against humans. One should not go into the wild forest on Thursday, which is a day set aside for the forest to renew itself, or they will hunt you down. Basically, the Asanbosam is a moral guardian, ensuring that people keep the rules that allow the ecosystem to function properly. Nineteenth-century missionaries, of course, missed that point and instead interpreted the Asanbosam to be the Christian Devil.

The Ramanga of Madagascar blends a rather nasty reality with a scary myth. The myth says that the Ramanga is a vampire that eats nail clippings and drinks blood. However, the reality is that there was a class of ritual practitioners whose job was to ensure that witches could not get hold of the blood, nail clippings, or saliva of their chieftains to work evil magic on. There was only one way to do this, and that was to eat the nail clippings and suck up any blood that was spilled (for instance, in a hunting accident).

It's interesting how, now that most of the Betsileo tribe are Christian and no longer believe in such witchcraft, a monster more akin to the Western idea of a vampire has emerged.

In Ashanti folklore, the obayifo is both a vampire and a witch, which is quite a common pairing in African myth. It can inhabit any human body and is obsessed with food. You can recognize an obayifo by the light that shines from their armpits and anus. Obayifo can shapeshift and fly, and it can also possess animals; for instance, one could possess a bull and make it kill people in a blind rage.

Women who practice witchcraft often turn into obayifo. They like to suck children's blood and can travel great distances by night. But the obayifo can be deterred by putting a plate of raw meat at the entrance to the village; they will eat that and come no farther into the settlement. Ashanti people will also share a little food with others in case the person asking for food is an obayifo. If you give food to an obayifo, it will keep its teeth out of you.

There are also a number of cannibal stories. The Fulani tell how Debbo Engal had ten daughters and how each daughter took a lover so she could suck his blood. Bantus terrify their children with the story of

Tshikashi Tshikulu, the old woman of the forest who stalks women and children to eat them.

Apart from man-eaters and blood drinkers, Africa has various kinds of aquatic monsters. The Gbahali, for instance, is Liberia's version of Scotland's Loch Ness Monster; it's a huge crocodile-like creature that is said to live in rainforest rivers and ambush its prey. It can grow up to thirty feet long. Some people have suggested it bears a resemblance to the dinosaur *Postosuchus*, which died out two hundred million years ago. But no one appears to have seen one for a while; maybe it was just a big crocodile, after all.

Ninki Nanka is another legendary reptile that lives in the West African swamps. It comes out at night to hunt down and devour whatever it can find. Accounts of it vary; it is a dragon, it has a horse's head, it is thirty feet long, or it is as long as a palm tree is tall. It is unimaginably huge, or it looks like a python with a feathery crest and mirror-like scales. Maybe it was originally a pre-Islamic snake god, but nowadays, it's more often used as a bogeyman to scare children and keep them from wandering outside the village. Some Gambians, particularly in the towns, think it is a myth or has become extinct, while others are not so sure. At least one national park ranger claims to have seen it. The big problem in finding evidence is that when people see the Ninki Nanka, they usually die shortly afterward, so there are few living witnesses.

Another "Loch Ness Monster" is the Inkanyamba, a legendary snake, eel, or water monster said to live, among other places, at Howick Falls in KwaZulu-Natal Province, South Africa. According to the Xhosa, only sangomas (traditional healers) are able to approach the falls safely. The Inkanyamba is associated with rain and is said to be able to leave the water in the shape of a tornado or waterspout. The Inkanyamba is actually more of a god than a monster; remember, many other gods are associated with serpents (such as Lebe or Ala with her royal python).

The forests of central Africa are defended by the Biloko (plural; one of them is called an Eloko). These dwarf-like forest-dwellers are ancestor spirits that defend their hunting grounds ferociously. They live in hollow trees, dress in leaves, and ring little bells that cast a spell on anyone who hears them. (Fortunately, a talisman or fetish can be effective against this magic.) If this doesn't make them sound particularly vicious, you should know they will eat people if they can.

There is a tale about a woman who made her husband take her hunting. He had a hut in the forest that he used on his expeditions, and he left her there while he went to check his snares. He warned her about the Biloko and their little bells and told her to keep the door tightly shut and open to nobody but him.

However, when the woman heard the bells ringing, she forgot all about his warning and let an Eloko into the hut. When the hunter came back, he found only her bones.

Another animal of the Congo is something of a mystery. The Abada is similar to the West's unicorn since its horns are an antidote against poison and have other healing powers. The only difference is that, unlike the unicorn, the Abada has two horns and apparently is more the size of a donkey than a horse.

It is also known as the Nillekma, under which name it was noted in the Zoological Journal of 1829. However, there is not much information on the creature available, and it is possible that the Abada is not a monster at all and just an ordinary antelope. It is, according to one account, very tasty to eat.

Go to Ethiopia today, and you'll be lucky to find anyone who knows about the Ethiopian Pegasus. However, the Roman naturalist Pliny the Elder (who, incidentally, was a martyr to science, having decided to stay in Pompeii to observe the eruption of Mount Vesuvius up close) tells us all about this creature. According to him, they were winged horses with two horns, and they didn't actually come from Ethiopia; they bred on an island off the shore of Eritrea.

Although Pliny was, in some regards, a good scientist, he was too willing to believe travelers' tales and urban myths. This was exacerbated when medieval monks got hold of his works and used them as the basis for bestiaries, collections of what was known about the animal world. If you're looking for an Ethiopian Pegasus, your best bet is to find a library with a good collection of medieval illuminated manuscripts.

Another Congo inhabitant is perhaps more celebrated outside Africa. Kongamato, "breaker of boats," appears in the video game *Final Fantasy XIV*. The Kaonde people described this monster as a kind of pterosaur—a huge red-winged lizard—that enjoyed capsizing canoes and could cause a person to die by just looking at them. In the game, though, the Kongamato turns out to be a useful mount and can be summoned by using a special Kongamato whistle.

South Africa has two particularly interesting mythical animals. First is the impundulu, the lightning bird of the Zulu, which is often identified with the strange-looking hamerkop ("hammerhead"). It is a huge black and white bird that summons thunder and lightning.

While the impundulu is a natural phenomenon, its association with witches, who may pass the control of the bird down in their family, has helped to make it a bird of evil omen. It can be forced to become the servant of a witch, who can use it to attack her enemies, and it can also become a vampire that drinks human blood. It cannot be killed by any means except, oddly enough for a lightning bird, by fire.

Less noxious but still very annoying is the tikoloshe or tokoloshe, a mischievous spirit that has the power of invisibility. It's a common bogeyman that can be called on to scare children (he will bite off your toes when you're asleep, or so it is said). It can also cause severe illness or even the death of enemies. Unlike the impundulu, tokoloshe are easy to get rid of since any Christian pastor can banish them. They are also tiny little dwarves, so if you put your bed legs up on bricks, they can't do anything to you.

In urban South African culture, the tokoloshe has become a figure of fun like a gremlin or the Grinch; it appears in comic strips and is blamed for all kinds of common mishaps.

Let's finish this chapter with a story from the San people and their cultural hero Khaggen, "Mantis," who created the earth, the sky, and the animals. It shows how there is no distinction between the animal and human worlds to some African peoples, at least in myth.

Khaggen's daughter ran away to live with the snakes. His son, Cogaz, went to fetch her back, and she was willing to come but warned him that the snakes would try to bite them. So, they tied grass stalks around their legs to protect them, and that's how they got away from the snakes.

Khaggen was annoyed that the snakes had tried to bite his children, so he sent a flood to drown them. However, the chief of the snakes and his followers survived. Khaggen then struck them with his stick, and they became men.

Later, Khaggen heard about a group of giants that drank women's blood. He decided to send Cogaz to kill the giants, giving him one of his teeth to take with him. Cogaz found a woman being held prisoner by the giants and freed her, but the giants gave chase. To escape, Cogaz threw Khaggen's tooth on the ground, and it grew into a mountain. From the top of the mountain, Cogaz could shoot poisoned arrows. Realizing that Cogaz was in trouble, Khaggen decided to help. He cut his leather hunting bag into strips, which turned into dogs and chased away the giants.

When the baboons saw Cogaz collecting wood to make bows, they decided to kill him before he was able to use the bows. They hung his body up in a tree. Then, they sang songs that degraded Khaggen. However, when Khaggen arrived, they changed the words, hoping he hadn't heard what they had been singing. However, a baby baboon, which didn't know any better, carried on singing the old words. Khaggen was angry. He plugged up each baboon's backside with a wooden peg and banished them to the mountains, and that is why baboons have red backsides and live in the wilderness.

Khaggen secretly created an eland out of his son-in-law's discarded sandal by rubbing it with honey to make it grow. His son-in-law found out about it, and since the sandal was his, he reckoned the eland should be his too. So, he killed the eland for meat. Khaggen found the eland's gall, but it burst and covered him with foul-smelling mucus. Khaggen took an ostrich feather to clean himself, and when he had gotten rid of the gunk, he threw the feather up into the sky, where it became the moon.

Chapter 7: Heroes in African Myth

As well as gods and ancestors, Africa has an abundance of heroes. They quite often overlap with the other realms of myth, as well as with actual history. Some heroes have elements in their stories that are highly reminiscent of trickster stories, while Sunjata Keita is the archetypal hero of Mali but was also an actual historical figure.

The Kingdom of Luba in the southern Democratic Republic of Congo was founded in the 16th century and traces its origins back to Prince Kalala Ilunga.

The despot Nkongolo ruled in the Congo. He married his two daughters to a hunter from the east, Ilunga Mbidi Kiluwe, but after feeling threatened by the younger man, he chased Ilunga into exile. Ilunga's son, Kalala Ilunga, grew up in exile along with Mijubu wa Kalenga, the first diviner. Eventually, the young prince decided to go to take his place at his grandfather's court.

Nkongolo invited Kalala Ilunga to dance for him. However, Mijubu warned the boy that Nkongolo had dug a concealed pit and filled it with spears where Kalala Ilunga was supposed to dance. So, when Kalala Ilunga was called on, he uncovered the hidden pit with his own spear and then overthrew the tyrant Nkongolo.

Ever since then, the spear dance (*kutomboka*) has been performed at the end of every investiture of a new chief to commemorate the event.

Who is the hero of this story? Apparently, it depends on who is telling it; for some people, it's the young prince, but for others, it's the diviner, Mijubu wa Kalenga.

(By the way, Kalala Ilunga is said to have introduced advanced ironworking to the Luba. Finely made axes became symbols of power and prestige, though they are sometimes so ornate they might not have been usable as axes.)

In the bend of the Congo River, the Mongo have a hero who, like Kalala Ilunga, was on a mission for justice. Lianja's mother became pregnant and could not give birth for a long time. When she finally did, she bore a number of children, ants, birds, and whole tribes of men. Lianja refused to be born the normal way, saying that his mother's birth passage had already been used by too many people. Instead, he and his sister Nsongo were born from a wound made in their mother's thigh.

The wicked Sausau had killed Lianja's father, and even before Lianja's umbilical cord had been cut, Lianja started to make war on Sausau. First, he sent a swarm of flies and wasps, but Sausau protected himself with clouds of smoke. Then, he sent various clans of men, but Sausau killed their leaders, including Lianja's brother.

Finally, Lianja entered into single combat against Sausau. Sausau threw spears at Lianja. They went right through him but then flew back through the air toward Sausau. Lianja's wounds healed instantly, so Sausau hurled spear after spear without effect.

Eventually, Lianja grappled Sausau to the ground, asked Nsongo to give him his knife, and sawed Sausau's head off.

So far, this is a typical hero story, but now it takes an odd turn. Nsongo had fallen in love with Sausau. After being offered a reward by her brother for her part in the war, she asked him to bring Sausau back to life. So, Lianja did this and gave Sausau to his sister as a slave.

Lianja then brought all the dead soldiers on both sides back to life and, together with Nsongo, led them through the forest to the land that he had been promised.

Another tale tells how Lianja and Nsongo had to take refuge from an ogre in a baobab tree. The tree protected them, but the ogre called its friends to help. The ogres tore the tree's bark and branches before eventually giving up and going away. Before setting off again, Lianja healed the baobab tree. He is a hero who has both warlike and peaceful tendencies; in other words, he is a healer and a warrior.

Jeki la Njambe of the Duala in coastal Cameroon was a despised younger half-brother to eight other sons of his father, Njambe. His mother's only daughter had been stolen by a chimpanzee, and although she was heavily pregnant, she could not give birth. On one occasion, when she was made to stack firewood, Jeki jumped out of her womb to help her and then jumped back in again. Another time, all nine wives had been looking for shrimp in the coastal shallows, but the tide started coming in. Again, he jumped out of his mother's womb and rescued them all before jumping back inside.

Eventually, Jeki thought it was time to be born. Before he came out, his mother gave birth to woven cloths, metal ingots, musical instruments, amulets, a canoe, and finally Jeki himself, along with his own special amulet, Ngalo.

Jeki was hated by his father and brothers. His father tested him, showing him a big wooden chest and asking what was in it. Jeki would get a beating for each wrong answer. "Cloth," he said. No, it wasn't cloth, and all his half-brothers beat him. "Gold," he said next, but that was wrong too, so he was beaten again.

Finally, he gave the right answer, which he'd known all along: "A single louse from your head, father. Oh, and it's female." But now he knew just how much his brothers hated him.

A little later, Jeki was summoned by his father and told to wash a big wooden chest. When his father had come to power, he had summoned various magical animals and imprisoned them, and this became the secret of his power. In this chest was a ferocious leopard that he had imprisoned magically.

Jeki was about to open the chest, but his amulet Ngalo warned him not to, instead telling him to take the chest down to the river and wash the outside first. Jeki took the chest into the deep water and washed all around the outside. By the time he was ready to take it out of the river and clean the inside, the leopard had drowned.

Another of Njambe's magical defenses was a giant crocodile. He proposed a third test for Jeki. Jeki must bring the crocodile to him. Jeki took his canoe, which had been born just before he appeared from his mother's womb, and invited the crocodile politely to a council in the village. Then, he summoned up a great wave to wash the crocodile into the village, where it snapped up a few cows for breakfast before Njambe could get rid of it.

Finally, Njambe asked Jeki to climb the huge palm tree for nuts. Yet another magical creature, the vicious kambo bird, lived at the top of the palm tree. So, Jeki asked his half-brothers to climb the tree first, and they did. One after another was killed by the kambo bird. When they had all been killed, Jeki climbed the tree, protected by his amulet Ngalo, and collected the nuts. He caught the kambo bird and burned it to death.

Then, he found medicine and brought his brothers back to life.

Later, he went to the chimpanzee land to find his sister. The chimpanzees showed him dozens of lovely women, who all looked exactly the same, and told him to choose. Luckily, Ngalo had given Jeki good advice again. Jeki sent out a little bee, which was easily able to distinguish the real sister from the fakes.

Tragic heroes exist too. The story of Aruan is told in Benin. Aruan was one of two sons who were born to King Ozolua of the Kyama people on the same day. But Aruan did not cry out, whereas his half-brother Esigie did. Because of this, everyone thought Esigie had been born first, and he became the heir. Ozolua favored Aruan, though, and gave him a magical sword. Aruan was told to plant it in the ground where his capital would be. Ozolua wanted to be buried there when he died.

But Esigie tricked Aruan into planting the sword in a bad place. One of Aruan's servants dug a pit and filled it with his tears to create a huge lake. When Ozolua died, Esigie stole the body and buried it in Benin. Aruan went to war, wearing a bell on his breastplate. He told his servants that if they heard the bell, it meant he had lost, and they were to throw his entire household and all of his possessions into the lake.

Aruan won the war, but while he was celebrating his victory, the bell fell onto the ground and rang out. When he returned, he found his home devastated. Grieving, he threw himself into the lake and drowned.

The Fulani have a tale of another despised prince, Goroba-Dike, who was a younger son. He had no inheritance, so he disguised himself as a peasant and got a job working for a blacksmith.

Princess Kode Ardo declared she would only marry a man whose fingers were small enough for him to wear a tiny ring she had on her little finger. Many tried, but only Goroba-Dike could wear it. So, the princess had to marry the blacksmith's boy.

The king and all his warriors set off to make war with the Tuaregs, who had raided their cattle. Goroba-Dike went with them, riding on a donkey. However, when they left the city, he rode off in the wrong direction. Everyone laughed at him, particularly the king's other sons-in-law.

Secretly, Goroba-Dike transformed himself into a splendid horseman and rejoined the army. He told the king's sons-in-law that he would fight for them if they each gave him one of their ears, and they did so.

Goroba-Dike's wife, Kode Ardo, was kidnapped by the Tuaregs, and he rescued her, still wearing his splendid appearance. He had been wounded on the arm, and she used a piece of her dress to bandage the wound.

That night, he appeared back at court as a blacksmith's boy. Kode Ardo suddenly saw that her "peasant" husband had been wounded in exactly the same place as the splendid warrior and that his wound was tied up with the cloth she had given him. He told his story, but the sons-in-law were dismissive; they said he had invented it all.

So, he told the story of how the sons-in-law had each given him an ear. He showed the necklace of ears, and when the king looked at his sons-in-law, he saw that all of them except Goroba-Dike were missing one ear.

Kobe Ardo now knew she had a royal husband, and the king was so impressed that he handed over his entire kingdom to Goroba-Dike in gratitude.

Many of these heroes have an atypical birth and childhood. Aiwel Longar of the Dinka/Bor in Sudan is another enfant terrible. He was born when a river god heard an elderly widow weeping because she had no son. The god took pity on her and gave her a son. Aiwel Longar was born with a full set of teeth, which showed he would have great spiritual power. He was also already able to walk and talk. He instructed his mother to tell no one about his birth, or she would die, but she ignored his instruction. She died, so Aiwel went to live with his father, the river god, until he was grown.

When Aiwel returned to the village, he had an ox of every color and took over the cattle of his mother's dead husband. A drought came to the country, and while everyone else's cattle grew thin, Aiwel's cattle remained fat. When he touched the ground, water sprang up, and grass grew. Eventually, thanks to these gifts, he became the village headman. His spear was the sign of his divinity, and spearmaster priests still trace their origins from him and sacrifice oxen in his honor.

Unmarried women are often trouble in African stories. In many of these tales, women do not want to be single, and it's accepted that women are sexual creatures. But sometimes, they become heroes. Yennenga, the daughter of a king, was old enough to be married, but her father would not find her a husband. So, she found a partner for herself. However, the king was not pleased when she became pregnant, and he ordered her death. Her friends found out about his order and gave her a warning. Together, they stole horses from the royal stables and escaped. But Yennenga rode so hard that she had a miscarriage.

After many adventures and much riding, she came to the land of Rialle the elephant hunter. At first, Rialle believed Yennenga was a young man, as she was riding in men's clothes and her friends deferred to her as if she were a chieftain. But later, she told him the truth, and they were married. She called her son Stallion in memory of the horse whose speed saved her life. The royal house of the Mossi in Burkina Faso is thought to be descended from her.

A similar story is told by the Sereer people of Senegal about their aristocratic house of Guelowar. The Guelowar are matrilineal, with inheritance passing down the female line. How did that come about?

It happened when a Mande princess fell in love with a griot musician. Princesses and griots don't mix; they come from different classes. She knew her father would never let her marry the griot. But she was head over heels in love. When she became pregnant, she had to flee, and she ended up living in a cave by the edge of the ocean.

The king of that land heard of the beautiful woman in the cave and went to see for himself whether she was as beautiful as he'd heard. He fell in love immediately and asked her to marry him. She was pregnant and thought of her unborn child. She agreed to marry him if he made her child his heir. He agreed, and so she went with him.

When her child was born, it was a girl. The king immediately had it proclaimed that the infant's sons would rule the land after him, which is why the Guelowar still pass inheritance through the mother, not the father.

Finally, a different kind of hero is found in a delightful Shona story: a musician, one who played the mbira, or thumb piano as some people call it. He was the elder son of a poor father, and they had only saved enough for one son to marry. The younger son found himself a wife, so the elder son had to set off to find his fortune. He took his mbira with him to pass the time on his journey.

First, he came to the country of the hares, but they boxed his ears and would not let him pass. He couldn't go any farther, so he sat down and played his mbira. To his surprise, the hares started dancing to the music, and he was able to pass their country and go on his way.

Then, he had to pass through antelope country, but the antelopes threatened him with their twisty horns. Again, he sat down and played his mbira, and the antelopes began to dance. He moved on.

Then, he came upon a pride of lions, and they roared at him and showed their huge teeth. But now he had faith that his mbira would weave its magic, and so it did. The lions rolled about with their legs in the air and eventually went to sleep.

At last, the musician came to a lake, sat down to rest, and started playing just for his own pleasure.

But the water spirits that lived in the lake gathered around to listen and decided that the mbira player should play for their king. They took him down under the water to the king's palace, and he played in front of the royal court. The king loved the music and gave the young man a wife and a village in the underwater land.

The elder brother, still full of love for his family, went to tell them of the good fortune he had found, but his younger brother would not come. So, the mbira player went back under the lake, and no one has seen him since.

Chapter 8: Mythical and Legendary Kings and Queens

As the last chapter showed, there are varying degrees of "mythical," from outright invention to orally remembered history. Historians don't always agree on just how mythical these figures are. For instance, the Queen of Sheba might have been the queen of Yemen, which shared much of its culture with the Horn of Africa in early times and is not even in Africa. On the other hand, Akhenaten is definitely known from his own monuments, and you can see Ras Tafari's coronation on a newsreel from 1930.

Akhenaten was the tenth ruler of the Eighteenth Dynasty of Egypt. He came to the throne in 1353 BCE as Amenhotep IV but soon changed his name to Akhenaten, incorporating the name of the sun disk Aten. Aten became the patron god of his royal house, replacing Amun-Ra and all the other gods.

Akhenaten moved his capital to Amarna, where he patronized a new style of Egyptian art, which was more elongated and more realistic than the preceding styles. He made the royal family the unique link between Aten and the people, and reliefs show him, Nefertiti, and their daughters in intimate scenes of family life, not the hierarchical processions of earlier art.[103]

---

[103] Egyptian art rarely shows the male children of the king unless they have been given high office.

Akhenaten's reforms might have been intended to demonstrate the primacy of his particular god, weakening other priesthoods that were rival power sources to the pharaoh; however, many scholars believe his views came closer to monotheism.

His wife, **Nefertiti**, or Neferneferuaten Nefertiti in full, is well known for her majestic beauty. The bust of Nefertiti in the Berlin Museum is celebrated as one of the masterworks of Egyptian art, and her beauty contrasts strangely with the almost deformed depictions of her husband.

Nefertiti might not have been just a beautiful face. It's quite possible that she ruled in her own right. According to one interpretation of the evidence, five years before Akhenaten died, he made Nefertiti co-ruler of Egypt and renamed her Ankhkheperure Neferneferuaten. Upon his death, she took a new regnal name, reigning as Ankhkheperure Smenkhkare and acting as regent for her stepson, Tutankhamun.

Nefertiti must have been trying to keep her husband's dreams alive, but things began to fall apart. No one knows quite how, but the boy king Tutankhamun reintroduced the old gods, and when he died, Nefertiti's father Ay and then the general Horemheb ruled Egypt. Akhenaten's capital was lost under the sands, and his monuments were defaced. His name was erased from inscriptions, and king lists of later pharaohs make no mention of him.

Hatshepsut was another female pharaoh. She was the fifth pharaoh of the Eighteenth Dynasty. Egypt was then at the peak of its power, and Hatshepsut was at the top of the tree. She was the daughter of Thutmose I and the Great Royal Wife to her half-brother Thutmose II. Thutmose II died young in around 1479 BCE. On his death, her stepson became pharaoh as Thutmose III, and she took power first as regent (since he was only a child) and later as co-ruler. After Hatshepsut took power, she was depicted as a male pharaoh with a khat head cloth and a false beard.

Hatshepsut became a massive patron of building works in Thebes (Luxor) and elsewhere, particularly at Karnak and at Deir el-Bahari, where she built her own mortuary temple. She also funded a mission to the Land of Punt in the Horn of Africa; details of the expedition are shown in reliefs at Deir el-Bahari and show how the temple's forecourts were planted with rare frankincense trees from Punt.

Like Akhenaten, Hatshepsut suffered a campaign dedicated to wiping out her memory after her death. This might have been done by her step-grandson Amenhotep II, whose claim to the throne was not particularly secure. It also might have been motivated by the desire to wipe out the memory of female rulers (and worse, from the patriarchal point of view, a successful female ruler).

Queen Amina was a Hausa queen of Zazzau, with its capital in the city of Zaria in Nigeria. She is a controversial figure. Some historians believe she is only a mythical figure, and folk legends of her rule may not reflect reality. She was born in the mid-16th century and was the daughter of the king of Zazzau. When her brother became king, she led his cavalry. (Women warriors are well evidenced in historical times, as you will see later in this chapter.)

When the king died, Amina took the throne herself. She refused to marry and set Zazzau on an expansionist program. At the time, there were seven different Hausa states; she moved against the other six and created a larger empire. There are stories of her taking a new lover in every city she conquered but having him executed the morning after so that he couldn't challenge her rule. That's *probably* not true.

Whatever the truth of her history, Amina has provided powerful inspiration for Black culture in the 21st century. She appears in the video game *Age of Empires III*, and her story is read by the newly literate Kingsley Smith to his family in Steve McQueen's film *Education*.

Kandake or Candace was not a name but the title given to queens (or rather queen mothers) of Kush. The Kushite Empire was based in the city of Meroe in Sudan, which was a wealthy trading center on the Nile. Succession was matrilineal; the king's sister became Kandake, and her son became the next ruler. The first Kandake to rule in her own right appears to have been Narhiqo, ruling around 170 BCE, and at least seven ruling Kandakes followed her over the years.

Kandake Amanirenas was one of the most famous. Born around 40 BCE, she led Kushite armies against the invading Romans and is mentioned by the Greek geographer Strabo, a contemporary. She was apparently blind in one eye, but this didn't stop her from being a formidable warrior and negotiating an advantageous peace with Rome. It wasn't until the later emergence of Aksum that the Kushite Empire disintegrated.

In the medieval Alexander romances, which often have remarkably little to do with the historical facts of Alexander the Great's campaigns, Candace is shown as the queen of Ethiopia and even marries Alexander. This follows the mention in the Bible of "Candace, queen of the

Ethiopians," whose eunuch was converted to Christianity (Acts 8:27-39).

Makeda is known to us as the Queen of Sheba, and her story is told in the Ethiopian text *Kebra Nagast*, or the *Glory of the Kings*, which was written around 1321 CE. She is said to have reigned around 1000 BCE.

Makeda's father was a foreigner who arrived in Ethiopia to find the people were being oppressed by a wicked snake. He killed a goat and filled its guts with poison, then left it for the snake. The snake ate it and died, and in gratitude, the people made him king.

The king had a daughter, Makeda, who succeeded him as the ruler of Sheba. Having heard of the wealth of Solomon's kingdom from Ethiopian merchants who traded with Israel, she set off to Jerusalem. She toured the sights, studied with the wise King Solomon, and even accepted Solomon's Jewish faith.

The night before she returned to Sheba, Solomon offered her a heavily spiced and salty farewell banquet. Cunningly, he provided nothing for her to drink. He then persuaded her to sleep in the same room with him, but she made him swear to take nothing from her by force. He made her swear the same oath in return.

As part of his plan, Solomon had placed a bowl of clear water in the middle of the room between their beds. Makeda became more and more thirsty, but when she tiptoed to the bowl and started to drink, Solomon woke and accused her of taking the water by force, breaking her promise.

He told her that since she had broken her word, his was no longer valid, and they slept together as Solomon had planned. In the morning, Solomon gave Makeda a ring. He told her if she bore a male child, she must send the child to Jerusalem with the ring as a token. Despite her opposition, her son, Bayna Lekhem, eventually won her permission to go to Jerusalem. Solomon loved Bayna Lekhem and wanted him to succeed the throne of the Kingdom of Israel, but the youth insisted on returning to Ethiopia. Some say that Solomon gave him the Ark of the Covenant, while others say Bayna Lekhem stole it from the temple, putting a perfect duplicate in its place. Some believe Ethiopia still holds the Ark of the Covenant, or the Tabot, in the Church of St Mary of Zion at Aksum.

Bayna Lekhem, or in Arabic, Ibn al-Hakim, "son of the wise man," became the first emperor of Ethiopia. He took the regnal name Menelik I, which is simply a translation of Ibn al-Hakim and emphasizes the descent of the Ethiopian royal house from King Solomon. Menelik was the first emperor of the Solomonic dynasty that ruled Ethiopia all the way to the time of Haile Selassie, who was deposed in 1974.

The truth is more prosaic. Historians believe the Solomonic dynasty was founded in 1262 CE when the last Zagwe ruler of Ethiopia was deposed. Yekuno Amlak took power in Amharaland (the central province of Ethiopia) as Emperor Tesfa Iyasus. And as stated above, some scholars believe the Queen of Sheba ruled in Yemen, not Ethiopia, while others believe she never existed at all.

One African king who entered European mythology but was never found in Africa was Prester John. Originally thought to be a ruler of India, by 1250, Westerners were beginning to think that he ruled over Ethiopia, either as its king or as the head of the Ethiopian Church. In 1441, Emperor Zara Yaqob of Ethiopia sent delegates to the Council of Florence, an ecumenical council of the Catholic Church. Those delegates were flabbergasted to find they were representing "Prester John." To them, he was Kwestantinos I (Zara Yaqob) of the House of Solomon. Not for the last time, Europeans were showing themselves unable to distinguish between African fact and fiction.

Some African myths about the foundation of kingdoms include references to the Muslim and Arab world. Djenne in Mali is well known for its immense mudbrick mosque and other adobe architecture. It was an important town on the Saharan trade route, like Timbuktu. One man from the country near Djenne had gone to Arabia, where he fought on behalf of the Prophet Muhammad. Muhammad noticed how bravely the man fought, and after the battle, he asked who he was and where he had come from.

The warrior told him, and Muhammad said, "Go home to your country, and you will found a great city that will become a jewel of Islam."

The man went back to Djenne, where he secured a site for his new city. But every time he tried to build the city walls, they collapsed. Eventually, he asked the Bozo and Nono tribes that lived nearby to help him. They told him there was a spirit living there who was breaking down the walls. The spirit would have to be given a sacrifice.

Some people say that the head of the Bozo tribe gave his daughter to be buried alive on the site of the city. Others say that the warrior himself had to make that sacrifice. Whichever version you accept, the story seems a rather odd mix of African traditions and Islamic history.

Yaa Asantewaa, unlike the Queen of Sheba, is a verifiable historical figure. She was the war leader of the Ashanti Kingdom in Ghana.

Yaa Asantewaa was born in 1840. Her brother, Nana Akwasi Afrane Opese, was the ruler of Edwesu, and she became queen mother of Ejisu. During her brother's reign, the British were putting pressure on the Ashanti Empire, as they were on much of the rest of Africa. At the same time, recent civil wars had weakened the Ashanti. When Yaa Asantewaa's brother died, she nominated her grandson as ruler of Edwesu and became regent for him when he, together with the king of Ashanti, was exiled by the British.

The British demanded the Golden Stool of the Ashanti, the symbol of their sovereignty and royalty. A council meeting was held to discuss what action to take. Several Ashanti nobles proposed compliance. Yaa Asantewaa disagreed; the Ashanti had been humiliated, and it was time for them to fight. She seized a gun and fired it into the air to show her willingness to lead. She was chosen to lead the Ashanti army against the British.

This was the last hurrah of the Ashanti Empire. The British drafted new troops, and Yaa Asantewaa was exiled to the Seychelles, where she died in 1921. But she is much loved and respected in Ghana as an opponent of British colonialism and a foremother of Ghanaian independence, which was won at last in 1957.

Another much-respected queen was **Queen Tin Hinane of the Tuareg**. She fled from the rich lands of the Maghreb (modern Morocco and Algeria) when she became pregnant out of wedlock. Her servant Takamata accompanied her on her flight; Takamata was also pregnant.

But in the middle of the Sahara, they exhausted their food supply. Tin Hinane was exhausted and close to death. Takamata could see no trees, no plants, and no animals, but she found an anthill and broke it open. Inside the anthill, she found the grain that the ants had stored, which she brought back to her queen. The sparse meal restored Tin Hinane's energy, and they were able to continue.

When they got to Tamanrasset, the queen gave birth to a daughter, and Takamata had twins, both girls. They were the founding mothers of the Tuareg, and the Tuareg remain a matrilineal people to this day.

Shaka Zulu was the founder of the Zulu Empire and transformed the history of the Zulu people. He was born Shaka kaSenzangakhona around 1787 and was an illegitimate son of King Senzangakhona kaJama. Shaka fought as a unit leader and later as a general under Inkosi Dingiswayo, prince and later king of the Mthethwa Empire. Dingiswayo had consolidated power by assimilating nearby chiefdoms, which influenced Shaka's policies. Even though Shaka created a huge and fearsome army, he often preferred to take power through diplomacy.

In 1816, when Shaka's father died, Shaka decided to claim the chiefdom from his half-brother Sigujana. A year later, Dingiswayo was killed in battle by Zwide of the Nxumalo. Shaka welcomed what was left of the Mthethwa army into his own fighting force and set out for revenge. He had Zwide's mother shut up in a house full of hyenas, which killed and ate her, but he was unable to get his hands on Zwide until much later.

Shaka turned the Zulu people into a nation of warriors. He changed the way they fought, introducing a shorter stabbing spear instead of the thrown assegai and teaching his men how to use their shields to knock aside the enemy's shields, leaving them unprotected. It's said that he made his men march without sandals to toughen their feet, and his army could move fast when it needed to, marching up to fifty miles a day.

Shaka also appears to have invented the famous Zulu "bull horn" formation. The "chest" or center of his army would fight close with the enemy, and then the "horns" would enter the battle, outflanking the enemy on both sides. Just in case the enemy broke out, the bull's "loins" waited in the wings, giving Shaka's men confidence that they had a fresh reserve force.

Despite his success, Shaka made some serious enemies, particularly after the death of his mother, Nandi, in 1827. He seems to have gone slightly mad with grief; he executed thousands of people, ordered that no crops should be planted, and commanded that no milk was to be drunk. When he sent most of his forces north on a campaign the next year, his half-brothers assassinated him. Dingane took the chiefdom.

Oba Oduduwa was the Olofin (traditional ruler) of Ile-Ife and the Divine King of Yoruba. In Yoruba tradition, he is said to have been the first ruler of the state of Ife and the ancestor of the royal houses of Yorubaland. Many people say that every Yoruba is descended from Oba Oduduwa.

Before Oduduwa's time, the Ife area was divided into thirteen different states, each with its own Oba (divine king). As Olofin of the city of Ile-Ife, Oduduwa used his influence to bring the thirteen states together into a single kingdom, usurping his brother Obatala and creating a dynasty that included not only the first Ooni of Ile-Ife (spiritual leader of the Yoruba people) but also the ruling houses of Benin and the Oyo Empire.

However, some Muslims prefer to believe that Oduduwa was a prince of Mecca who was exiled to Africa.

Where things become slightly confusing is that Oduduwa and his brother Obatala are seen by the Yoruba as not just historical figures but also primordial gods or orishas. They were as old as time and sent by the creator Olodumare. So, whether they belong to the realm of myth or the real world or both is an intriguing question.

The same questions can be asked about the story of **Sunjata (Sundiata) Keita**, who founded the Mali Empire. The Sunjata epic has been sung by griots for centuries, and we know that Sunjata did exist since Arab traveler-historians ibn Battuta and ibn Khaldun both corroborate certain elements of his story. However, historians have suspected some of the details might have been added later.

According to the epic, two wives, the beautiful Sassouma Bereté and the ugly hunchback Sogolon Condé, of Chief Nare Famagan became pregnant at the same time. Sogolon gave birth to Sunjata and sent an old woman from her hut to tell her husband that his long-awaited heir had arrived. However, the old woman stopped to eat on the way to the king's hut, so the news of Sunjata's half-brother's birth arrived first. Dankaran Touman, Sunjata's half-brother, was accepted as the firstborn and made Nare Famagan's heir.

Sassouma Bereté suspected Sogolon Condé meant her no good, so she had spells cast to cripple Sunjata. The boy had to crawl on his hands and feet, and his mother was humiliated. When she asked Sassouma Bereté to give her some baobab leaves for a special meal, her rival told her nastily to ask Sunjata to climb a tree and pick them.

"Why can't you get up?" Sogolon Condé asked her son angrily.

"I will," he said and asked the blacksmiths to forge iron bars for him to use as crutches. However, when he tried to get up, he snapped them. He then asked for a stick made of the wood of the jonba tree, which his mother cut for him. Using this, Sunjata was able to get up and walk.

As he walked, he became stronger, and he made his way toward the baobab tree. By the time he got to it, he had become extremely strong. So, instead of picking the leaves, he picked up the entire tree and carried it back to his mother's compound.

Dankaran Touman eventually became king. Sunjata became a great hunter, but he never challenged his half-brother for the throne. However, Dankaran Touman still felt threatened, so he asked the nine witches of the Manden region to get rid of his rival. In return for this favor, Dankaran Touman gave them an ox to share between them. When Sunjata found this out, he gave the witches nine buffalo—one each—and they promised never to interfere with Sunjata.

Then, seeing he could never live with his brother, Sunjata went into exile to Mema, together with his mother and younger siblings.

Dankaran Touman was a weak ruler, and his realm was eventually invaded by Sumanguru, who took over the country and ruled as a tyrant. No one knew where Sunjata had gone, so a mission was sent out with spices from Manden country. In every town and village, they laid out their spices in the market. No one knew what they were. Then, in Mema, Sunjata's sister saw the spices and quickly bought them all, inviting the traders to come and eat with her. Sunjata was there, of course, and the members of the mission asked him to reconquer the Manden. Sunjata said his mother was too old to travel, and he had to stay with her. When his mother died quietly that night, he knew that he was fated to rule the Manden's thirty-three clans.

Sunjata invaded, but he couldn't defeat Sumanguru, who was defended by potent magic. Sunjata's sister, Sogolon Kulunkan, who was a great beauty, set out for Sumanguru's palace to seduce him. Sumanguru wanted to sleep with her, but she would not enter the bedchamber until he told her all his secrets.

Sumanguru's mother was passing by the tent and warned him, "Don't tell your secrets to a one-night stand!" Of course, this advice made Sumanguru mad, and he did exactly the opposite. He told Sogolon Kulunkan that the only thing that could kill him was an arrow tipped with a white cock's spur. Sogolon Kulunkan agreed to come into the bedchamber but said she needed to wash first. She took a long time. Sumanguru called her, and she answered, "Wait a bit!" He waited and called again. Again, she told him to wait. He got fed up with waiting and went to the privy and found she had run away, leaving two magical amulets to speak on her behalf and give her time to escape.

Now, Sunjata had the secret. He made a cock-spur-tipped arrow and set out to find Sumanguru during the next battle. Sumanguru fled, making his horse leap the wide Niger River, but Sunjata's arrow struck him just as he reached the other side.

After Sunjata had established his empire, he wanted horses. He sent to the king of Jolof to buy some. But the king refused to sell, instead sending scraps of leather with the insulting message, "He's a hunter, not a king. Let him make shoes. He can walk wherever he needs to go." Sunjata declared war on the Jolof Empire and made Tira Magan Traore his general. Every time Tira Magan won a battle, he said, "I serve a hunter; I'm only walking the dogs." Finally, he caught the king of Jolof and cut off his head, saying, "The dogs had a good walk. I'm going home."

Sunjata died in 1255 and was succeeded in turn by three of his sons. Eventually, his brother's side of the family took over the succession, and in 1312, the great-nephew of Sunjata, Mansa Musa, acceded to the throne.

Mansa Musa is often referred to as the world's richest man. By the time he inherited the empire, Mali had become immensely wealthy. It controlled the salt trade from the north through the Sahara and the gold trade from southern Africa. The whole area of the Niger Delta contained at least four hundred cities with a high standard of living. The Mali Empire had become a true urban civilization.

Musa incorporated the cities of Gao and Timbuktu into the Mali Empire, greatly increasing its size. He also extended friendly ties with the Muslim sultanates of the north and made Timbuktu a center of Muslim scholarship, creating the University of Sankore. Musa's worldview was highly cosmopolitan, and he attracted scholars and artists from all over the Muslim world. In addition, he sponsored building projects, including mosques and madrasas.

In 1324, Musa went on hajj to Mecca, taking a huge entourage (some sources say that sixty thousand servants accompanied him) and vast supplies of gold with him. In Cairo, his liberal handing out of gifts caused hyperinflation. He ensured Mali made a reputation abroad as a wealthy and civilized country, and this reputation traveled as far as the West. In the Catalan Atlas, produced around 1375, Mansa Musa is shown with a golden crown and orb, sitting in state in the middle of the map of Africa.

Ras Tafari was the last emperor of Ethiopia, and although his life spans the 19th and 20th centuries, he, too, blurs the lines between history and myth.

He was born Lij Tafari Makonnen and baptized as Haile Selassie. He is called Ras Tafari from the noble title "Ras" added to his secular name. Born in 1892, he was the son of Makonnen Wolde Mikael, the governor of Harar. He became influential in the court of Empress Zewditu and appears to have been involved in some form of coup against Lij Iyasu, the original heir to the throne who was rumored to have converted to Islam.

Zewditu made Ras Tafari crown prince in 1916, and he appears to have acted effectively as her prime minister. When she died in 1930, he became Negusa Nagast, "king of kings," of Ethiopia. Although he was not of the direct line, he had Solomonic lineage through his grandmother, which allowed him to take the throne.

As Emperor Haile Selassie, he embarked on the cautious modernization of what was still, at that point, a feudal state. He was responsible for Ethiopia's admission to the League of Nations, the predecessor of the United Nations, and he became a celebrity on his tours of Europe, Egypt, and the Middle East. In Jerusalem, he adopted forty Armenian orphans who had lost their parents in the Armenian genocide; they were taught music in Addis Ababa and became the imperial brass band. He also was instrumental in forming the Organisation of African Unity in 1963, the precursor of today's African Union.

Reforming Ethiopia was difficult. Haile Selassie gave the country a constitution, but it did not deliver full democracy due to the objections of the nobles. Even his tax reforms had to be diluted. The invasion of Ethiopia by the Italians in the 1930s forced him into exile in Britain, and when he liberated the country, it was with the help of the British Army. Unfortunately, he faced a dilemma; any reform was too much for the nobles but not enough for the younger generation.

In the early 1970s, Haile Selassie faced major problems. Eritrea had been included in Ethiopia after the Second World War, but it was fighting a war for independence, which it eventually won in 1991. This conflict stretched the country's resources. At the same time, there were famines in the northern areas: Wollo and Tigray. In 1974, Haile Selassie was deposed and imprisoned, and he died in 1975 under suspicious circumstances.

So far, you have been reading about the historical head of an African state. However, for a large number of people around the world, he is much more. The Rastafarian movement began in the 1930s in Jamaica as an offshoot of Marcus Garvey's pan-Africanist group. According to Rastafarians, Ras Tafari was the Messiah who would lead the African diaspora to freedom; in other words, he was God incarnate.

Haile Selassie visited Jamaica in 1966, where he was greeted by over 100,000 Rastafarians at the airport in Kingston. He never explicitly denied their belief in him as God and granted some Rastafarians land to live on in Ethiopia.

Right now, we're seeing the creation of new mythical "versions" of African rulers. For instance, Netflix has courted controversy by casting a Black actor as Cleopatra VII Philopator (*that* Cleopatra). She was descended from a Macedonian family and was probably, if not white, only mildly brown-skinned. Arguably, this matters more to us now than it did to Egyptians in Cleopatra's day, who were a remarkably cosmopolitan bunch and had already been ruled by Libyans, Persians, and Nubians.

African rulers figure in many video games and TV shows. Shaka Zulu features in *Civilization*, the Queen of Sheba appears as Bilquis in Neil Gaiman's *American Gods*, and Yaa Asantewaa has had a British radio series and a Ghanaian TV documentary dedicated to her. Mansa Musa appears in *Civilization* and faces off against Jeff Bezos in the YouTube series "Epic Rap Battles of History." (It's well worth watching!) Meanwhile, the Marvel universe includes the country Wakanda, which draws on African mythology and is represented as an African technological hub and superpower.

And, of course, modern African rulers are continuing to make history. Nelson Mandela achieved legendary status with his successful life-long campaign against apartheid and his term as the first-ever president of the "Rainbow Nation." Ellen Johnson Sirleaf became the first woman as an elected head of state in Africa when she became the twenty-fourth president of Liberia (2006–2016). Perhaps in the 22nd century, kids will be watching Mandela the superhero battling the forces of evil on their mobile phones.

Chapter 9: Shamanic Stories

Shamanism is a tradition in which practitioners use trance or drugs to achieve an altered state of consciousness and communicate with spirit beings. For instance, Siberian and Arctic shamans use drumming to create a trance state in which they can talk to animal spirits, such as the bear.

Possession allows people to communicate with the realm of gods and spirits (including, as always, ancestors) and is common in most African religious traditions, including those that have spread to the Americas and the Caribbean. However, it's not always called "shamanism." Masked dances, for instance, are a common way for individuals to communicate with gods or their ancestors, and in many African cultures, divination is the most important aspect of spiritual communication.

For instance, illness is seen as often being due to witchcraft or to magical or religious reasons, such as failing to observe rituals or taboos. This doesn't rule out scientific explanations; instead, it complements them. Someone may have a heart attack because he has a weak heart but also because a work colleague wished ill on him. Divination is used by healers to find the causes of illnesses or problems such as infertility, and then a second divination is often carried out to ascertain the right treatment.

In the Kongo religion, a nganga (plural banganga) can communicate with spirits and ancestors. The job of the nganga is to divine the causes of any illness and to heal. They often wear frightening costumes. Some wear white masks (white is the color of the dead), while others wear thick white eyeshadow and red and yellow stripes on their faces. They sometimes dress in wild animal skins and wear necklaces of animal teeth.

Banganga, like other shamans, are both religious and medical at the same time—a duality recognized in the pejorative name "witch doctor." In fact, Christian priests in Kongo areas were often referred to as banganga; like the shamans, they were seen as go-betweens, taking messages between the human and spiritual worlds.

While the Siberian shamans made their own drums as part of their initiation, the banganga would create a nkisi sculpture and charge it with spiritual power. A medicine pack would be placed in a hollow inside the nkisi, similar to the way in which Native American medicine men create their own medicine bag as a source of power and healing. The nkisi then had to be activated by driving nails or blades into it and by chanting.

In South Africa, two kinds of practitioners are found. There are inyanga, who are similar to the banganga, and sangomas, traditional healers. Their domains are different but not mutually exclusive.

Sangomas always have a "calling," sometimes in a dream or a vision. (This, again, is a common feature of almost all shamanic traditions.) If the person who has been called ignores their calling, they will find bad luck following them. They might experience severe illness until they accept the calling and seek out a teacher. The apprenticeship period involves living with a teacher, often in austere conditions and in relative isolation, for a period that can stretch from several months to years.

The training ends with a sacrifice and the final test of finding things that have been hidden. The other sangomas will hide the skin and gall bladder of a goat that has been sacrificed, as well as the apprentice's sacred divinatory bones. The apprentice sangoma has to find where they are.

Sangomas make their divination by throwing the bones. All illness is a form of disharmony, so the sangoma's task is to find out what will bring back balance, harmony, and health. That might be within an individual or within a family or community. The sangoma may then throw the bones again for specific advice, which can include reconciliation with estranged relatives, herbal medicines, or even Western medicine.

Muthi, or herbal medicines, which are usually psychoactive drugs, are often added to bathing water or steamed for inhalation. Some may be used as enemas or as emetics (to induce vomiting). Most sangomas collect their own herbs in accordance with advice from ancestors on the right time and right place to find them. Again, divination may be used as a way of finding where to get the herbs, or an ancestor may speak directly to the sangoma.

Every sangoma is possessed by ancestor spirits. But many now have to divide their lives between being a traditional sangoma and living a modern life, working in a university or in modern healthcare. There is a growing LGBTQ+ sangoma movement too, showing how the tradition is gradually evolving to accept different lifestyles. (In fact, a female sangoma can be possessed by the spirit of a male ancestor and the other way around, so despite the gender-inflexible nature of traditional Zulu society, this is not as big of a stretch as it may seem.)

There are even some white sangomas now. This has ruffled feathers among some, but other traditional healers explain that even though a white sangoma may have no African ancestors, they may be called on by "foreign spirits" that their ancestors had a significant relationship with. For instance, someone whose great-grandfather killed a Zulu may be called by that spirit.

Credo Mutwa, a Zulu shaman, traveled the path from indigenous traditional healer to New Age guru. He got involved with extraterrestrial encounters and ufologists. He also adapted elements of the Dogon creation myth. While for some, he gave a seal of authenticity to anything he touched as a traditionally trained sangoma, for others, he was simply a fraud and an opportunist or an oddball. He created what he called African cultural villages; seen as tourist traps at one time, people are now coming around to the view of Mutwa as an outsider artist, and the villages are being interpreted as art installations rather than museum-like institutions.

Zimbabwe has Shona spirit mediums who are similar to the sangomas. They are the svikiro and, like the sangomas, undergo possession by ancestral spirits who can give them advice. By helping keep balance and mediating between the spiritual and human worlds, the svikiro protect their society. Thus, they are given high status and respect. They are also often (though not always) healers.

Some of the spirits they channel are mhondoro, "lions," which are the spirits of kings and chieftains. It's interesting that while there's a perception that many traditional practices are dying out, after the civil war in Zimbabwe, there was a huge revival in spirit medium practices. People were looking for help with their experiences of violence, and the svikiro gave them a way of processing and dealing with their trauma.

Possession by gods and spirits is common in African ceremonies. It is often brought about by drumming, dancing, or both. The spirit possessing the person may make particular demands for food, drink, or clothing or may perform certain repetitive acts. The person possessed may not remember anything they have done while in a trance.

Ancestor worship and veneration are the basis of the majority of African cultures, and shamanic possession gives people a way to channel communications to and from their ancestors. It is also a potent way of unifying a group of people, such as a particular age group or a secret society.

The trance element is particularly important in African-origin religions that grew up in the New World, such as Candomblé and Voodoo (Vodou). In Brazilian Candomblé, for instance, a woman may dress up as Oshun (Oxúm) in yellow, holding the sacred fan in one hand, and dance Oshun's dance until she feels the imminent presence of the goddess. If someone in the congregation is possessed, the other members of the terreiro (temple) can communicate directly with the goddess through her (or sometimes him).

Divination is also common in many African societies and is usually performed by a practitioner who could be identified as a shaman. There are a number of stories about how divination was discovered. In Yoruba lore, the goddess Oshun wears a necklace of cowrie shells, symbolizing the sixteen shells that are used for Erindinlogun divination. She got them from her husband Orunmila, the god of divination. Other gods, like Eshu, use kola nuts. Whether cowries or nuts, the items are thrown on a cloth or a divination board, and the position in which they fall is then interpreted by the diviner.

Divination is so central to African thought that it is even used in worship, such as to determine whether a sacrifice has been acceptable to a god.

Not all shamans are good ones. A lot of today's sangomas are fed up with seeing classified ads in newspapers or on the internet for fake sangomas and mediums. Some sangoma trainers abuse their apprentices or use them as unpaid servants. Other sangomas make their clients dependent on them and demand more and more money and gifts from them while giving little in return.

Mali has a salutary tale of a shaman who ran a protection racket. He protected the cattle of one village from a ferocious lion; in return, he expected a nice fat cow to be given to him from time to time.

When a huntsman shot a huge lion nearby, the villagers breathed a sigh of relief. They thought they would no longer need to pay the shaman. Just as a precaution, they moved their herds to the other side of the river since a shaman can't cross running water. However, the shaman turned up, furious that he hadn't been paid, and found a ferryman to take him across. The villagers noticed the shaman's golden eyes, pointy teeth, and flowing mane of long hair. Suddenly, the shaman turned into a lion and sprang onto the fattest cow in the herd and ate her all up.

Fortunately, the ferryman was actually a local river god who decided the lion was fair game. He had a magic bow and arrow with him. The villagers never had any more problems with lions eating their cows.

Conclusion

African mythology infuses African cultures. While there are many different strands of African myth, you have probably noticed that many myths reflect similar concerns or have similar situations. Eshu and Legba are not by any means the same, but they are similar gods with similar positions in the pantheon. Many myths stress the enmity of half-brothers in a polygamous household against the solidarity of mothers and sisters.

But African myths aren't just for Africans. Many of the stories moved to the New World with African slaves and now make up a major part of Black American cultures. Anansi became Aunt Nancy in Jamaica, while the Yoruba and Fon pantheons were imported wholesale into Voodoo, Vodoun, Vodou, and Santeria. In the US, the trickster hare became Br'er Rabbit, who, through books and then through the Disney film *Song of the South* in 1949, became part of mainstream American culture.

It's interesting that African myths retain their fluidity on the other side of the Atlantic. For instance, in the Afro-Cuban religion, gods remain polysemous with multiple personalities. This is referred to as one *oricha* having several *caminos* or different paths. Sometimes, gods from different African traditions are blended together. Most of the American African-origin religions have blended to some extent with Catholicism. For instance, Oshun is often identified with the Virgin Mary and Ogum with Saint Anthony of Padua. (Some practitioners are now trying to "purify" or "re-Africanize" the religion by taking out the Catholic references.)

Most African traditional graphic and sculptural art relates to mythology. There are figures of gods and spirits, power fetishes, and ritual paraphernalia, such as the divination board. African art, having been dismissed during the 19th century as "primitive" and not worth preserving, was discovered by a generation of artists that included Picasso; it showed them new ways of seeing things. Appreciating how these artworks fit into the mythological and ritual pattern, though, stops us from simply appropriating them; we can see them in their context rather than just as "fine art."

And today, there's a whole lot of creative work going on that uses African myths, gods, and stories as a background. For instance, in contemporary science fiction and fantasy, Neil Gaiman's *American Gods* features Mr. Nancy, a tailor, drawing on Anansi's story. Other African gods also appear, including Mr. Ibis (the Egyptian god Thoth) and the goddess Yemoja.

Increasingly, people of color are writing fantasy and science fiction and using their own backgrounds as part of the setting. For instance, Paris-based Aliette de Bodard uses Vietnamese culture in her intricate space operas. African settings and stories have come to fantasy through such writers as Nigerian-American Nnedi Okorafor, whose characters include an albino witch, Legba, and a trickster spider. She espouses "Africanfuturism." Jordan Ifueko is another Nigerian-American speculative fiction writer. Her book *Raybearer* created a future world that is definitely African in background, though it is not in any way a pastiche of Yoruba myths.

Comics and now TV have accepted Africa as a full partner in their worlds. A breakthrough in this regard was the films *Black Panther* (2018) and *Wakanda Forever* (2022), which feature a black superhero and strong, authentic elements of African costume, such as the Zulu isicholo hat worn by the Queen Mother Ramonda. The films have gained a much greater audience than the comics and have even inspired African leaders in business and government to think about creating Wakanda-like technological cities.

For the last few hundred years, Greek and Roman mythology held pride of place. Look at the classical portico of the White House, and you can see how much the Greek ideal resonated with Americans at the time. Maybe in the next few hundred years, we'll see a lot more African mythology and influences across the world.

If you enjoyed this book, a review on Amazon would be greatly appreciated because it would mean a lot to hear from you.

To leave a review:
1. Open your camera app.
2. Point your mobile device at the QR code.
3. The review page will appear in your web browser.

Thanks for your support!

Here's another book by Enthralling History that you might like

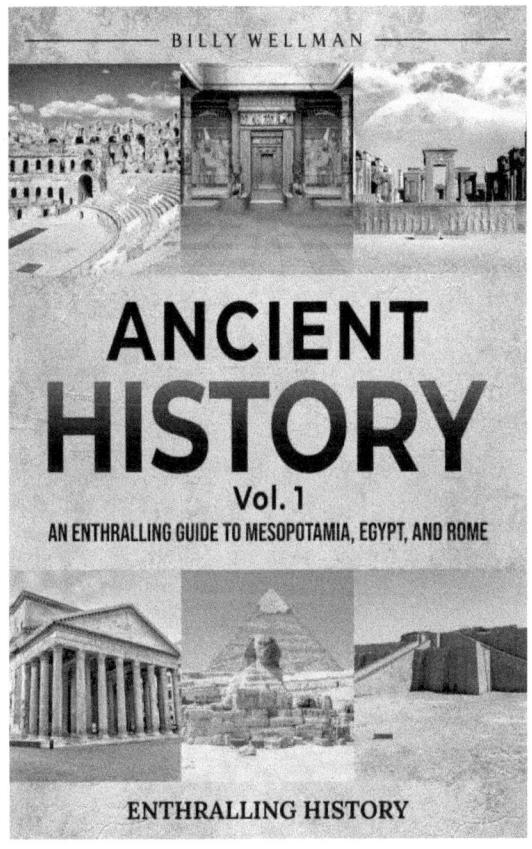

Free limited time bonus

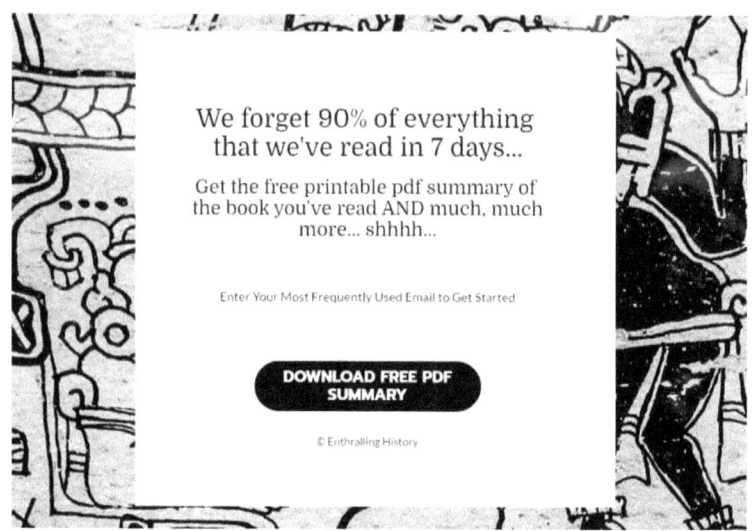

Stop for a moment. We have a free bonus set up for you. The problem is this: we forget 90% of everything that we read after 7 days. Crazy fact, right? Here's the solution: we've created a printable, 1-page pdf summary for this book that you're reading now. All you have to do to get your free pdf summary is to go to the following website: https://livetolearn.lpages.co/enthrallinghistory/

Or, Scan the QR code!

Once you do, it will be intuitive. Enjoy, and thank you!

Bibliography

Academic Accelerator. (2024, January 13). Archaeological Evidence for the Origins and Spread of Iron Production in Africa. Retrieved from Academic-accelerator.com: https://academic-accelerator.com/encyclopedia/iron-metallurgy-in-africa.

Afrikaiswoke.com. (2023, September 15). 10 African Contributions to Civilization. Retrieved from Afrikaiswoke.com: https://www.afrikaiswoke.com/african-contributions-to-civilization/.

Ancient Egypt Magazine. (2023, February 6). Neolithic Settlements of the Western Desert: Proto-villages of Stone Age Egypt. Retrieved from the-past.com: https://the-past.com/feature/neolithic-settlements-of-the-western-desert-proto-villages-of-stone-age-egypt/.

Ancientegptianfacts.com. (2024, January 19). Facts About Ancient Egyptians. Retrieved from Ancientegptianfacts.com: https://ancientegyptianfacts.com/ptolemaic-period-egypt.html.

Anplifyafrica.org. (2024, January 28). Africa Made Math: The Original Mathematicians. Retrieved from Anplifyafrica.org: https://www.amplifyafrica.org/africa-made-math-the-original-mathematicians/.

Bevan, E. (2024, January 19). Chapter IV: The People, the Cities, the Court. Retrieved from Penelope.uchicago.edu: https://penelope.uchicago.edu/Thayer/E/Gazetteer/Places/Africa/Egypt/_Texts/BEVHOP/4B*.html.

Blatch, S. (2013, February 1). Great Achievements in Science and Technology in Ancient Africa. Retrieved from Asbmb.org: https://www.asbmb.org/asbmb-today/science/020113/great-achievements-in-stem-in-ancient-africa.

Brewminate.com. (2019, April 17). The Art and Architecture of Middle Kingdom Egypt c. 2055-1650 BCE. Retrieved from brewminate.com: https://brewminate.com/the-art-and-architecture-of-middle-kingdom-egypt-c-2055-1650-bce/.

Brewminate.com. (2019, April 19). The Art and Architecture of New Kingdom Egypt c. 1570-1069.BCE. Retrieved from brewmintate.com: https://brewminate.com/the-art-and-architecture-of-new-kingdom-egypt-c-1570-1069-bce/.

Britannica, E. o. (2023, November 30). Mamluk. Retrieved from Britannica.com: https://www.britannica.com/topic/Mamluk.

Cartwright, M. (2016, June 16). Carthaginian Society. Retrieved from Worldhistory.org: https://www.worldhistory.org/article/908/carthaginian-society/.

Cartwright, M. (2016, June 17). Carthaginian Trade. Retrieved from Worldhistory.org: https://www.worldhistory.org/article/911/carthaginian-trade/.

Cartwright, M. (2016, May 26). First Punic War. Retrieved from Worldhistory.org: https://www.worldhistory.org/First_Punic_War/.

Cartwright, M. (2016, May 29). Second Punic War. Retrieved from Worldhistory.org: https://www.worldhistory.org/Second_Punic_War/.

Cartwright, M. (2016, May 31). Third Punic War. Retrieved from Worldhistory.org: https://www.worldhistory.org/Third_Punic_War/.

Cartwright, M. (2018, July 24). Lighthouse of Alexandria. Retrieved from Worldhistory.org: https://www.worldhistory.org/Lighthouse_of_Alexandria/.

Cartwright, M. (2019, March 5). Ghana Empire. Retrieved from World History Encyclopedia: https://www.worldhistory.org/Ghana_Empire/.

Cartwright, M. (2019, March 21). Kingdom of Axum. Retrieved from Worldhistory.org: https://www.worldhistory.org/Kingdom_of_Axum/.

Cartwright, M. (2019, May 13). The Gold Trade of Ancient & Medieval West Africa. Retrieved from Worldhistory.org: https://www.worldhistory.org/article/1383/the-gold-trade-of-ancient--medieval-west-africa/.

Cartwright, M. (2916, January 8). Carthaginian Army. Retrieved from Worldhistory.org: https://www.worldhistory.org/Carthaginian_Army/.

Cassar, C. (2023, August 25). Exploring the Egyptian Middle Kingdom—A Historical Overview. Retrieved from Anthropologureview.org: https://anthropologyreview.org/history/ancient-egypt/exploring-the-egyptian-middle-kingdom-a-historical-overview/?expand_article=1.

Cerise Myers, E. C. (2024, January 9). 5.2 Mesolithic Art. Retrieved from Libretexts.org: https://human.libretexts.org/Bookshelves/Art/Introduction_to_Art_History_I_%28Myers%29/05%3A_Art_of_the_Stone_Age/5.02%3A_Mesolithic_Art.

College Sidekick.com. (2024, January 13). The Bronze Age. Retrieved from Collegesidekick.com: https://www.collegesidekick.com/study-guides/boundless-arthistory/the-bronze-age.

DailyHistory.org. (2024, January 22). What Were the Causes of the Second Punic War? Retrieved from Dailyhistory.org: https://www.dailyhistory.org/What_were_the_causes_of_the_Second_Punic_War.

DeMola, P. (2013, March 14). Interrelations of Kerma and Pharaonic Egypt. Retrieved from World History Encyclopedia: https://www.worldhistory.org/article/487/interrelations-of-kerma-and-pharaonic-egypt/.

Dickinson College Commentaries. (2024, January 22). Carthage: Early History. Retrieved from dcc.dickoinson.edu: https://dcc.dickinson.edu/nepos-hannibal/carthage-early-history.

Editors, H. (2013, June 12). Punic Wars. Retrieved from Hisory.com: https://www.history.com/topics/ancient-rome/punic-wars#first-punic-war-264-241-b-c.

EDU, W. H. (2023, May 10). Aristotle's Analysis of the Carthaginian Constitution. Retrieved from Worldhistory.edu: https://worldhistoryedu.com/aristotles-analysis-of-the-carthaginian-constitution/.

Encyclopedia.com. (2024, January 27). Empire of Ghana. Retrieved from Encyclopedia.com: https://www.encyclopedia.com/history/encyclopedias-almanacs-transcripts-and-maps/empire-ghana.

EOTC. (2024, January 13). Beliefs and Teachings of Ethiopian Orthodox Tewahedo Church. Retrieved from keraneyo-medhanealem.com: https://www.keraneyo-medhanealem.com/beliefs-and-origins-7-sacraments-of.

Eries.org. (2024, January 13). Kingdom of Aksum. Retrieved from Eriesd.org: https://www.eriesd.org/cms/lib/PA01001942/Centricity/Domain/1041/6.2%20The%20Kingdom%20of%20Aksum-1.pdf.

Exponent, E. (2023, November 14). Ancient Africa's Contributions to Modern Science and Built Environment. Retrieved from The African Exponent: https://www.africanexponent.com/ancient-africas-contributions-to-modern-science-and-built-environment/.

Fitzgerald, S. (2023, November 21). Mummified Baboons in Egypt Point to a Long Lost Land. Retrieved from Atlas Obscura: https://www.atlasobscura.com/articles/mummified-baboons-punt.

Haughton, B. (2011, February 1). What Happened to the Great Library at Alexandria? Retrieved from Worldhistory.org: https://www.worldhistory.org/article/207/what-happened-to-the-great-library-at-alexandria/.

Hirst, K. (2019, May 12). The Kingdom of Kush: Sub-Saharan African Rulers of the Nile. Retrieved from Thoughtco.com: https://www.thoughtco.com/the-kingdom-of-kush-171464.

Historyskills.com. (2024, January 19). What Was the Middle Kingdom of Ancient Egypt? Retrieved from Historyskills.com: https://www.historyskills.com/classroom/ancient-history/anc-middle-kingdom-reading/.

Historyrise.com. (2023, December 24). Facts About Ancient Egypt Slaves: Historical Insights! Retrieved from Historyrise.com: https://historyrise.com/facts-about-ancient-egypt-slaves/.

Historyrise.com. (2023, December 25). What Advancements Did Ancient Egypt Make in Math and Science. Retrieved from Historyrise.com: https://historyrise.com/advancements-in-ancient-egyptian-math-science/.

Historyskills.com. (2024, January 19). How Egypt Became the Greatest Superpower of the Ancient World. Retrieved from Hisoryskills.com: https://www.historyskills.com/classroom/ancient-history/egypt-ancient-superpower/.

Hunt, P. (2024, January 22). Carthage. Retrieved from Britannica.com: https://www.britannica.com/place/Carthage-ancient-city-Tunisia.

Huysecom, E. (2024, January 9). Arguments for an Early Neolithic in Sub-Saharan Africa. Retrieved from Ounjougou.org: https://www.ounjougou.org/en/projects/mali/archaeology/arguments-for-an-early-neolithic-in-sub-saharan-africa/.

Iniguez, N. (2020, February 28). The Rise, Decline, and Collapse of the Aksum Empire. Retrieved from Storymaps.arcgis.com: https://storymaps.arcgis.com/stories/9b7b377398724be99a0d94dfa9f55550.

Jones, M. (2024, January 3). The Second Punic War (218-201 BC): Hannibal Marches Against Rome. Retrieved from Historyooperative.org: https://historycooperative.org/second-punic-war-hannibals-war-in-italy/.

K. Krois. Hirst. (2019, May 12). The Kingdom of Kush: Sub-Saharan African Rulers of the Nile. Retrieved from Thoughtco.com: https://www.thoughtco.com/the-kingdom-of-kush-171464.

Kemezis, K. (2009, November 22). Ancient Kush (2nd Millennium B.C. - 4th Century A.D.). Retrieved from Blackpast.org: https://www.blackpast.org/global-african-history/ancient-kush-2nd-millennium-b-c-4th-century-d/.

Kessing, F. M. (2024, January 9). Stone Age-African Tools, Artifacts, Culture. Retrieved from Britannca.com: https://www.britannica.com/event/Stone-Age/Africa.

King, A. (2018, July 25). The Economy of Ptolemaic Egypt. Retrieved from Worldhistory.org: https://www.worldhistory.org/article/1256/the-economy-of-ptolemaic-egypt/.

Kipling, Rudyard (1899). The White Man's Burden. https://historymatters.gmu.edu/d/5478/.

Koutonin, M. (2016, August 18). Lost Cities: Racism and Ruins—The Plundering of Great Zimbabwe. Retrieved from Theguardian.com: https://www.theguardian.com/cities/2016/aug/18/great-zimbabwe-medieval-lost-city-racism-ruins-plundering.

Lane, M. (2024, January 21). How Did Muslims and Non-Muslims Interact in Ghana. Retrieved from Ncesc.com: https://www.ncesc.com/geographic-faq/how-did-muslims-and-non-muslims-interact-in-ghana/.

LibreTexts. (2024, January 27). 12.6 The Ghana Empire. Retrieved from LibreTexts.org: https://human.libretexts.org/Courses/Lumen_Learning/Book%3A_Early_World_Civilizations_(Lumen)/Ch._11_African_Civilizations/12.6%3A_The_Ghana_Empire#:~:text=Ghana%E2%80%99s%20economic%20development%20and%20eventual%20wealth%20was%20linked,expansion%20to%20.

LibreTexts. (2024, January 22). 4.2 Ancient Carthage. Retrieved from Libretexts.org: https://human.libretexts.org/Courses/Lumen_Learning/Book%3A_Early_World_Civilizations_(Lumen)/Ch._03_Early_Civilizations_of_Africa_and_the_Andes/04.2%3A_Ancient_Carthage.

Lifepersona.com. (2024, January 19). The 9 Most Important Contributions of Egypt to Humanity. Retrieved from Lifepersona.com: https://www.lifepersona.com/the-9-most-important-contributions-of-egypt-to-humanity.

Lynch, P. (201, May 5). A Brutal and Bloody Affair: 6 Key Battles That Decided the First Punic War. Retrieved from Historycollection.com: https://historycollection.com/roman-military-might-6-key-battles-decided-first-punic-war/.

Marc. (2022, October 14). The Kush Kingdom: A Major Power in the Ancient World. Retrieved from Ilovelanguages.com: https://www.ilovelanguages.com/the-kush-kingdom-a-major-power-in-the-ancient-world/.

Mark, J. J. (2016, November 9). Ancient Egyptian Science & Technology. Retrieved from World History Encyclopedia: https://www.worldhistory.org/article/967/ancient-egyptian-science--technology/.

Mark, J. J. (2017, September 21). Social Structure in Ancient Egypt. Retrieved from History World Encyclopedia: https://www.worldhistory.org/article/1123/social-structure-in-ancient-egypt/.

Mark, J. J. (2023, July 25). Library of Alexandria. Retrieved from Worldhistory.org: https://www.worldhistory.org/Library_of_Alexandria/.

Mummified Baboons Point to the Direction of the Fabled Land of Punt. (2023, November 11). Retrieved from Ars Technica: https://arstechnica.com/science/2023/11/mummified-baboons-point-to-the-direction-of-the-fabled-land-of-punt/.

Museum, T. B. (2024, January 9). Rock art and the origins of art in Africa. Retrieved from Khanacademy.org: https://www.khanacademy.org/humanities/ap-art-history/global-prehistory-ap/paleolithic-mesolithic-neolithic-apah/a/apollo-11-stones.

New World Encyclopedia. (2024, January 19). Ptolemaic Dynasty. Retrieved from New World Encyclopedia: https://www.newworldencyclopedia.org/entry/Ptolemaic_dynasty.

New World Encyclopedia. (2024, January 25). Aksumite Empire. Retrieved from NewWorldEncuclopedia.org: https://www.newworldencyclopedia.org/entry/Aksumite_Empire.

New World Encyclopedia. (2024, January 27). Ghana Empire. Retrieved from New World Encyclopedia: https://www.newworldencyclopedia.org/entry/Ghana_Empire.

Openstax.org. (2024, January 13). 9.2 The Emergence of Farming and the Bantu Migrations. Retrieved from Openstax.org: https://openstax.org/books/world-history-volume-1/pages/9-2-the-emergence-of-farming-and-the-bantu-migrations.

Pbs.org. (2024, January 19). Art & Architecture. Retrieved from Pbs.org: https://www.pbs.org/empires/egypt/newkingdom/architecture.html.

Peter F. Dorman, M. S. (2024, January 19). Thutmose III. Retrieved from Britannica.com: https://www.britannica.com/biography/Thutmose-III/Adornment-of-Egypt.

Pressbooks.bccampus.ca. (2024, January 19). Middle Kingdom Art. Retrieved from Art and Visual Culture: Prehistory to Renaissance: https://pressbooks.bccampus.ca/cavestocathedrals/chapter/middle-kingdom/.

Pressbooks.bccampus.ca. (2024, January 19). New Kingdom Art. Retrieved from pressbooks.bccampus.ca: https://pressbooks.bccampus.ca/cavestocathedrals/chapter/new-kingdom/.

Robert Maddin, T. S. (1977). Tin in the Ancient Near East: Old Questions and New Finds. Retrieved from Penn Museum: https://www.penn.museum/sites/expedition/tin-in-the-ancient-near-east/.

Ross, E. G. (2002, October). The Age of Iron in West Africa. Retrieved from Metmuseum.org: https://www.metmuseum.org/toah/hd/iron/hd_iron.htm.

S., A. (2015, December 21). Mesolithic Social Life and Art. Retrieved from Shorthistory.org: https://www.shorthistory.org/prehistory/mesolithic-social-life-and-art/.

Scoville, P. (2015, November 6). Amarna Letters. Retrieved from Worldhistory.org: https://www.worldhistory.org/Amarna_Letters/.

Shuttleworth, M. (2024, January 28). Egyptian Astronomy. Retrieved from Explorable.com: https://explorable.com/egyptian-astronomy.

Smith, P. (2015, September 16). Nabta Playa: The Oldest Man-Made Structure in the World. Retrieved from Historic Cornwell: https://www.historic-cornwall.org.uk/nabta-playa-the-oldest-man-made-structure-in-the-world/.

Smithsonian Institute. (2024, January 3). Climate Effects on Human Evolution. Retrieved from Humanorigons.si.edu: https://humanorigins.si.edu/research/climate-and-human-evolution/climate-effects-human-evolution.

Soto, N. (2024, January 16). Who Destroyed the Ghana Empire. Retrieved from Ncesc.com: https://www.ncesc.com/geographic-faq/who-destroyed-the-ghana-empire/.

Staff, E. (2021, October 31). Carthaginian Trade: Trade Routes of Ancient Carthage. Retrieved from Carthagemagazine.com: https://carthagemagazine.com/carthaginian-trade-routes-of-ancient-carthage/.

Taronas, L. (2024, January 19). Akhenaten: The Mysteries of Religious Revolution. Retrieved from Arce.org: https://arce.org/resource/akhenaten-mysteries-religious-revolution/.

Team, E. (2018, October 21). Kingdom of Punt: When Ancient Egypt Envied Somalia. Retrieved from Thinkafrica.net: https://thinkafrica.net/land-of-punt/.

Team, E. (2018, November 3). The Kingdom of Kerma (2500-1500 BC). Retrieved from Thinkafrica.net: https://thinkafrica.net/the-kingdom-of-kerma-2500-1500-bc/.

Thomas Garnet, H. J. (2024, January 13). Egyptian Art and Architecture. Retrieved from Britannca.com: https://www.britannica.com/topic/Martin-Luther-King-Jr-1929-68-2229053

Tyson, P. (2009, December 1). Where is Punt? Retrieved from PBS.org: https://www.pbs.org/wgbh/nova/article/egypt-punt/.

Wasson, D. L. (2016, September 29). Ptolemaic Dynasty. Retrieved from Worldhistory.org: https://www.worldhistory.org/Ptolemaic_Dynasty/.

Wendorg, M. (2023, April 23). Ancient Egyptian Technology and Inventions. Retrieved from Interesting Engineering.com: https://interestingengineering.com/lists/ancient-egyptian-technology-and-inventions.

Battle of Ticinus, November 218 BC, 31 March 2002, http://www.historyofwar.org/articles/battles_ticinus.html. Accessed 22 November 2022.

Battle of Cannae, https://www.cs.mcgill.ca/~rwest/wikispeedia/wpcd/wp/b/Battle_of_Cannae.htm. Accessed 23 November 2022.

"Ancient Carthage | World Civilization." *Lumen Learning,* https://courses.lumenlearning.com/suny-hccc-worldcivilization/chapter/ancient-carthage/. Accessed 13 November 2022.

"Ancient Tyre." *World Monuments Fund,* https://www.wmf.org/project/ancient-tyre. Accessed 4 November 2022.

Cartwright, Mark. "Carthaginian Society." *World History Encyclopedia,* 16 June 2016, https://www.worldhistory.org/article/908/carthaginian-society/. Accessed 25 November 2022.

Cartwright, Mark, and Alexander van Loon. "Carthaginian Army." *World History Encyclopedia,* 8 June 2016, https://www.worldhistory.org/Carthaginian_Army/. Accessed 25 November 2022.

Corinne, Bonnet. "Religion, Phoenician and Punic." *Oxford Classical Dictionary,* Oxford University, 30 05 2020, oxfordre.com/classics. Accessed 3 11 2022.

Cremin, Aedeen, editor. *The World Encyclopedia of Archaeology: The World's Most Significant Sites and Cultural Treasures.* Firefly Books, 2007.

"The First Punic War." *Dickinson College Commentaries,* https://dcc.dickinson.edu/nepos-hannibal/first-punic-war. Accessed 18 November 2022.

Herodotus. *The Landmark Herodotus: The Histories.* Edited by Robert B. Strassler, translated by Andrea L. Purvis, Knopf Doubleday Publishing Group, 2009.

Hunt, Patrick, and E. Badian. "Battle of the Trebbia River | Roman-Carthaginian history." *Encyclopedia Britannica,* https://www.britannica.com/event/Battle-of-the-Trebbia-River. Accessed 22 November 2022.

Justinus, Marcus Junianus, and Justin. *Epitome of the Philippic History of Pompeius Trogus.* Edited by R. Develin, translated by J. C. Yardley, Scholars Press, 1994.

Liver, J. "The Chronology of Tyre at the Beginning of the First Millennium B.C." *Israel Exploration Journal,* vol. 3, no. 2, 1953, pp. 113-120. *JSTOR,* http://www.jstor.org/stable/27924517. Accessed 4 11 2022.

Merideth, C. "Northwestern Iberian Tin Mining from Bronze Age to Modern Times: an overview." *Archive ouverte HAL*, 21 March 2019, https://hal.archives-ouvertes.fr/hal-02024038/document. Accessed 13 November 2022.

Miles, Richard. *Carthage Must Be Destroyed: The Rise and Fall of an Ancient Civilization*. Penguin Publishing Group, 2012.

Paton, W. R., translator. *The Complete Histories of Polybius*. Digireads.com, 2009.

"Phoenix | Facts, Information, and Mythology." *Encyclopedia Mythica*, 3 March 1997, https://pantheon.org/articles/p/phoenix2.html. Accessed 3 November 2022.

"Punic." *U-M Library Digital Collections*, https://quod.lib.umich.edu/d/did/did2222.0003.974/--punic?rgn=main;view=fulltext;q1=Paul+Henri+Dietrich%2C+baron+d++Holbach. Accessed 8 November 2022.

Quinn, Josephine. *In Search of the Phoenicians*. Princeton University Press, 2019.

Sasson, Jack M. "The Phoenicians (1500–300 B.C.) | Essay | The Metropolitan Museum of Art | Heilbrunn Timeline of Art History." *Metropolitan Museum of Art*, https://www.metmuseum.org/toah/hd/phoe/hd_phoe.htm. Accessed 2 November 2022.

Sullivan, Richard E. "Hieron II | tyrant and king of Syracuse." *Encyclopedia Britannica*, https://www.britannica.com/biography/Hieron-II. Accessed 18 November 2022.

Thucydides. *The Landmark Thucydides: A Comprehensive Guide to the Peloponnesian War*. Edited by Richard Crawley and Robert B. Strassler, translated by Victor Davis Hanson and Richard Crawley, Free Press, 1998.

Torr, Cecil. "The Harbours of Carthage." *The Classical Review*, vol. 5, no. 6, 1891, pp. 280-284. *JSTOR*, http://www.jstor.org/stable/693421. Accessed 11 11 2022.

Urbanus, Jason. "Masters of the Ancient Mediterranean." *Archaeology*, vol. 69, no. 3, 2016, pp. 38-43. *JSTOR*, http://www.jstor.org/stable/43825141. Accessed 07 11 2022.

Wolters, Edward J. "Carthage and Its People." *The Classical Journal*, vol. 47, no. 5, 1952, pp. 191-204. *JSTOR*, http://www.jstor.org/stable/3293326. Accessed 7 11 2022.

Barker, William H. West African Folk-Tales. CMS Bookshop, Lagos, 1917.

Barnes, Sandra T & Ben-Amos, Paula. "Benin, Oyo, and Dahomey: Warfare, State Building, and the Sacralization of Iron in West African History." *Expedition Magazine* 25.2 (1983). Penn Museum, 1983.

Burstein, Stanley, ed. Ancient African Civilizations: Kush and Axum. Princeton, N.J., 1998.

Chidester, David. Credo Mutwa, Zulu Shaman: The Invention and Appropriation of Indigenous Authenticity in African Folk Religion. Journal for the Study of Religion, Vol 15, No 2 (2002) pp/ 65-85.

Diop, Cheikh Anta. The African Origin of Civilization: Myth or Reality. New York, 1974.

Diop, Ismahan Soukeyna. African Mythology, Femininity, and Maternity. Springer Nature Switzerland. Cham, 2019.

Griaule, Marcel. Conversations with Ogotemmeli: An Introduction to Dogon Religious Ideas. Oxford University Press, Oxford. 1965.

Jonker, Ingrid. A study of how a sangoma makes sense of her 'sangomahood' through narrative. University of Pretoria, MA dissertation, 2006.

LaGamma, Alisa. Art and Oracle: African Art and Rituals of Divination. Metropolitan Museum of Art, New York, 2000.

Lugira, Aloysius M. African Traditional Religion. Chelsea House, New York. 2009.

Murphy, Joseph M and Sandford, Mei-Mei. Osun Across the Waters: A Yoruba Goddess in Africa and the Americas. Indiana University Press, Bloomington Indiana, 2001.

Nkabinde, Nkunzi Zandile. Black Bull, Ancestors and Me: My Life as a Lesbian Sangoma. Fanele, Auckland Park SA. 2008.

Ogundipe, Ayodele. Eshu Elegbara: Chance, Uncertainly in Yoruba Mythology. Kwara State University Press, Ilorin, 2012.

Peek, Philip M and Yankah, Kwesi. African Folklore: An Encyclopedia. Routledge, New York and London, Shakarov, Avner, and Senatorova, Lyubov. Traditional African Art: An Illustrated Study. McFarland & Company, Jefferson NC. 2015.

Skertchly, J. A. Dahomey As It Is: Being A Narrative of Eight Months' Residence in That Country, With a Full Account of the Notorious Annual Customs. Chapman & Hall, London, 1874.

Passé, Présent et Futur des Palais et Sites Royaux d'Abomey. Getty Conservation Institute, Los Angeles. 1999.

Wallis Budge, Ernest Alfred. Legends of the Gods. London, 1912.

Žabkar, Louis V. Hymns to Isis in Her Temple at Philae. Brandeis University Press. 1988.

www.ingramcontent.com/pod-product-compliance
Lightning Source LLC
Chambersburg PA
CBHW070326010526
44107CB00004B/427